for Mom, with love

Publisher's Cataloging-In-Publication Data
(Prepared by The Donohue Group, Inc.)

Names: Newmark, Amy, compiler.
Title: Chicken soup for the soul : for Mom, with love : 101 stories about
    why we love our mothers / [compiled by] Amy Newmark.
Other Titles: For Mom, with love : 101 stories about why we love our
    mothers
Description: [Cos Cob, Connecticut] : Chicken Soup for the Soul
    Publishing, [2016]
Identifiers: LCCN 2015960925 | ISBN 978-1-61159-962-6 (print) |
    ISBN 978-1-61159-261-0 (ebook)
Subjects: LCSH: Mothers--Literary collections. | Mothers--Anecdotes. | Mother and
    child--Literary collections. | Mother and child--Anecdotes. | Grandmothers--
    Literary collections. | Grandmothers--Anecdotes. | Anecdotes.
Classification: LCC HQ759 .C45 2016 | LCC HQ759 (ebook) | DDC 306.8743/02-
    -dc23

PRINTED IN THE UNITED STATES OF AMERICA
on acid∞free paper

25 24 23 22 21 20 19 18 17 16   01 02 03 04 05 06 07 08 09 10 11

Chicken Soup for the Soul

for Mom, with love

101 Stories about Why We Love Our Mothers

Amy Newmark

Chicken Soup for the Soul Publishing, LLC
Cos Cob, CT

Chicken Soup for the Soul

Changing your life one story at a time®

www.chickensoup.com

Contents

Introduction, *Amy Newmark* 1

❶

~Thanks for Being My Teacher~

1. The Good Parts, *Victoria Fedden* 7
2. Mom's Christmas Stocking, *Daryl Wendy Strauss* 9
3. Everything I Would Need to Know, *Barbara Ann Burris* 11
4. Staying Sharp at 95, *Jacqueline Seewald* 15
5. It Doesn't Hurt to Smile, *Katrina Anne Willis.* 19
6. How Running Helped Me Heal, *Kristin Julie Viola* 22
7. A Strike at the Ballpark, *Amy Newmark* 25
8. Standing Out, *Patricia Gordon* 29
9. The Girl with the Golden Curls, *April Knight* 32
10. The Next New Step, *Jennifer Harrington* 36
11. Grandmother's Gift, *Elizabeth Rose Reardon Farella* 39

❷

~Thanks for Always Being Right~

12. Cheer Leader, *Victoria LaFave* 47
13. Mom's Tour de Force, *Aimee Lorge* 50
14. The Fertility Specialist, *Mary Ellen Flaherty Langbein* 54
15. Sleepless Nights, *Melissa Face* 56
16. Product Design, *Hank Musolf* 58
17. Party Invitation, *Barbara LoMonaco* 62
18. A Positive Step, *Beth M. Wood* 64
19. Ugly, *Ali Lauro* 67
20. The Most Important Day of My Life, *Patrick B. Coomer* 71
21. The Last Night Home, *Michelle Vanderwist.* 75
22. Celebrating the Tears, *Kim Stokely* 78
23. The Tiny Waist of the Fifties, *Carole A. Bell* 80

3

~Thanks for Being There~

24. A Child Like Me? *Lisa J. Schlitt* 87
25. My Mother, My Father, My Everything, *Natalie Scott* 89
26. Coming Home, *Logan Eliasen* 91
27. Always a Mother, *Kelle Z. Riley* 94
28. Happy Birthday, My Sunshine, *Monica A. Andermann* 97
29. Pizza Night, *William Mark Baldwin* 101
30. A True Mother, *Sonja Herbert* 104
31. Mom to the Rescue, *Mimi Greenwood Knight* 106
32. A Pink Dress and a Promise, *Gail MacMillan* 108
33. The Matriarch, *Rhonda Brunea* 111
34. Motherhood: Not Quite a Stroll in the Park,
    Maizura Abas 115
35. Wreath Rivalry, *Winter Prosapio* 119

4

~Thanks for Your Strength~

36. Worth More than Money, *Chris Mikalson* 125
37. Return to Heart Mountain, *Jessie Miyeko Santala* 128
38. To My Other Mother, *Penny Smith* 132
39. The Girls on the Bus, *Nancy Julien Kopp* 135
40. Her Turn, *Kara Johnson* 138
41. Urban Cowgirl, *Isabel Harris* 141
42. Racing with Heart, *Carrie Monroe* 145
43. Finding Christmas, *Annette McDermott* 148
44. Hair Is Overrated, *Janet H. Taylor* 152
45. Wonder Mom, *Susan Blakeney* 154
46. Tea in the Afternoon, *Nancy Bravo Creager* 158
47. Dance Lessons, *Judith Fitzsimmons* 161

5
~Thanks for the Memories~

48. A Glorious Ride, *Tracy Crump*..................................167
49. Momma's Christmas Cookies, *Kevin J. Kraemer*..................169
50. Just the Way I Like It, *April Knight*..........................172
51. The Healing Power of Toilet Paper, *Toni Becker* 175
52. Mom Didn't Play Fair, *John M. Scanlan*.........................179
53. Joy in an Unexpected Friendship, *Julie Hornok* 181
54. House of Sunshine and Tears, *J.D. Chaney*.....................183
55. Gifts to Keep, *Susan R. Ray* 187
56. Love You Forever, *A.B. Chesler*...............................190
57. Early Mornings with God and Mom, *Ronda Armstrong*.......193
58. Tables Turn, *Winter Prosapio* 196
59. Lillian's Daughter, *Sally Schwartz Friedman* 199

6
~Thanks for Being My Role Model~

60. The Lady in the Mirror, *Terri Lacher* 205
61. Father's Day, *Denise Reich*...................................207
62. Midnight Grace, *Shawnelle Eliasen* 210
63. No Complaints, *Donna F. Savage*...............................214
64. Burned, *Lisa Wright-Dixon* 216
65. Hope for the Future, *Tricia Downing* 220
66. The Locket, *Donna Brothers* 223
67. Forgiving the Unforgivable, *Sheridan Kee*.....................227
68. Focusing on What We Have, *Lisa Hutchison*.....................230
69. Adventures in Staying, *Ann Kronwald*..........................233
70. A Life Lesson in Courage, *Donia Moore* 236
71. Turning Into My Mother, *Karen Kullgren* 240

❼

~Thanks for the Laughter~

72. Granny's Bible, *Robin Rylee Harderson* 247
73. Sense of Humor Needed, *Lucille Engro DiPaolo* 251
74. A Fist Full of Dollars, *Gail Eynon* 254
75. The Cooking Lesson, *Ava Pennington* 257
76. The Little Woman, *Jill Burns* 261
77. Answer the Phone, *Cindy D'Ambroso-Argiento* 264
78. The Cursed Jersey, *Michelle McKague-Radic* 266
79. Serious Business, *Beth Morrissey* 269
80. A Simple Wedding Dress, *Debra Mayhew* 271
81. Cotton Balls, *Lava Mueller* 274

❽

~Thanks for Being My Rock~

82. Nighttime Mothering, *Jennifer Knickerbocker* 281
83. There All Along, *D'ette Corona* 284
84. Unconditional Love, *Angel Therese Dionne* 286
85. From Despair to Peace, *Kimberly Ross* 288
86. Granny's Cedar Chest, *Lee Ann Sontheimer Murphy* 290
87. Finding Strength in Love, *Holly Wilkinson* 293
88. She Never Stopped Loving Me, *Leigh Ann Bryant* 296
89. The Spelling Bee, *Mary Elizabeth Laufer* 300
90. Independence Day, *Ellarry Prentice* 303
91. Grandma's Trade Secret, *Courtney Conover* 307

❾

~And Now I Take Care of You~

92. Clothed in Love, *Pam Giordano* 313
93. In Her Hands, *Judy Brown* 317
94. The Missing Stocking, *Teresa Ann Maxwell* 320

95. Talking Potato, *Linda Rose Etter* 322
96. A Turkey of a Thanksgiving, *A.J. Cattapan* 324
97. A Little Child Shall Lead Them, *Candace Schuler* 328
98. Accidental Destiny, *Cecile Proctor* 330
99. Like Mother, Like Daughter, *Anna Fitzgerald* 333
100. Daffodil Month, *Jennie Ivey* 336
101. Rewind, *Kala Cota* 339

Meet Our Contributors 345
Meet Amy Newmark 361
About the Boys & Girls Clubs of America 363
Thank You 365
About Chicken Soup for the Soul 366

Chicken Soup for the Soul

Introduction

he inspirational author Marion C. Garretty said, "Mother love is the fuel that enables a normal human being to do the impossible." Mothers do achieve the impossible, finding time to raise their children, run their households, work, volunteer, and care for spouses, pets and elderly parents. You don't understand how hard it is until you become a mother yourself.

My fellow editors and I are all mothers, so we get it. It was with that understanding that we lovingly compiled this collection of stories from our library, to show our fellow moms of all ages how much they are appreciated and loved.

We don't just honor mothers in this book. We include stories about grandmothers, stepmothers, mothers-in-law, and the other moms in our lives. These touching stories will sometimes make you laugh, occasionally make you tear up a little, and most importantly, they'll make every mother feel great about the impact she has on her children.

There's a special twist to this book, too. We're donating the author royalties to the Boys & Girls Clubs of America. Boys & Girls Clubs are an integral part of many communities, providing a safe place for kids to learn and grow, to have ongoing relationships with caring, adult professionals, and to engage in sports and other life-enhancing programs and character development experiences. The clubs are often used for after-school care by busy moms, and they provide youth with hope, opportunity, and — best of all — a great time!

I'm sure you'll enjoy the stories in Chapter 1 — Thanks for Being My Teacher — because that's such an important part of what we mothers do. In "Everything I Would Need to Know" Barbara Ann Burris describes watching her mother run her own deli and catering business. Barbara resented the business when she was a teenager but she now realizes how many lessons she learned "about faith and determination, hard work, responsibility and most of all, about caring."

In Chapter 2 — Thanks for Always Being Right — you'll read stories that validate what we moms already know: we ARE always right! In "Party Invitation," our own senior editor Barbara LoMonaco tells us about the time she had to turn down a day at Disneyland with her best friend because she had already accepted an invitation to another girl's birthday party. Barbara's mom wouldn't let her renege on the first acceptance. Doing the right thing, however reluctantly, Barbara went to the birthday party and had a great time after all, explaining, "My mom was right… as usual."

Prolific Chicken Soup for the Soul contributor Mimi Greenwood Knight shares her story, "Mom to the Rescue," in Chapter 3 — Thanks for Being There. In Mimi's case, her mother quickly cooked a special dinner at home after Mimi's date had car trouble that caused them to miss their pre-prom dinner at a restaurant. Her mom even washed, dried, and ironed her date's oil-stained shirt while they ate, "remedying yet another mini trauma in my life," according to Mimi.

Have you ever wondered how you do some of the things that you do as a mother? Chapter 4 — Thanks for Your Strength — is about those superhuman feats that moms manage to perform. In "Wonder Mom," Canadian Susan Blakeney tells us about the time her mother kept the children calm and happy during a big snowstorm that stranded them at home for a week. Their father couldn't get home for days and the storm was so bad that soldiers ended up being deployed to clear their road. Susan's mother was terrified the whole time but never let on to the kids, even though "she had never been so overwhelmed as a mother, or so alone."

Chapter 5 — Thanks for the Memories — is about those special moments that become part of family lore, like Toni Becker's story, "The Healing Power of Toilet Paper." Toni and her ninety-two-year-old mother, who was in the final stage of cancer, decided to have one last adventure together, toilet papering the yards of Toni's brother and sister. Toni says, "In the coming weeks, Mom and I shared many more laughs after each of us received calls from puzzled family members wondering who had done those strange things."

There's no doubt that we moms are role models, and our lessons persist long after we're gone. In Chapter 6 — Thanks for Being My Role Model — Lisa Hutchison writes in "Focusing on What We Have" about how her mom's "positive attitude" after a stroke that paralyzed her "helped me to keep going, to have faith and to remain connected to her, especially after her death." Lisa says her mother's example "certainly changed my life."

Good parenting should include a lot of humor, right? And that goes for grandparenting too. Robin Rylee Harderson had me laughing out loud in "Granny's Bible," which is one of the many funny stories in Chapter 7 — Thanks for the Laughter. Robin's grandmother was a font of wisdom, often "quoting" the Bible. One day when someone called Robin a brat, Granny said, "You just go right back home and tell him that the Bible says it takes one to know one." Robin concedes that Granny's "Bible," suspect as it was, "always solved whatever problems had been thrown in my path."

In Chapter 8 — Thanks for Being My Rock — you'll meet some moms who were steadfast in their unequivocal support for their children. I've always been amazed by Leigh Ann Bryant's story, "She Never Stopped Loving Me." Leigh Ann's mother was her rock during her trial for killing the husband her mom had warned her not to marry. Leigh Ann says, "She stayed by my side and loved me through it all. When my jurors spared me from prison, she gave me a thumbs-up and mouthed, 'I love you.' A smile crossed my face — I believed her. My mother loves me, no matter what."

Our moms love us unconditionally and we love them back, in all 101 stories in this inspiring collection. We offer you these stories in the spirit of "mom solidarity." I'm already smiling as I imagine you reading them.

~Amy Newmark
Author, Editor-in-Chief, and Publisher, Chicken Soup for the Soul

Chapter 1

for Mom, with love

Thanks for Being My Teacher

Whenever I am in trouble I ask my heart "What should I do?" Every single time it replies "Do what your mother would tell you to." Mom, thanks for being my guiding light.
~Author Unknown

The Good Parts

A mother is a person who seeing there are only four pieces of pie for five people, promptly announces she never did care for pie.

~Tenneva Jordan

When I was growing up my mother ate the most disgusting things. Dry crusts from my sandwiches, burnt toast, the soggy last few inches of pizza slices that I always left behind. She ate the dark meat, gizzards even, broccoli stems and the dust of crushed chips left in the bottom of the bag. Hers were the broken crackers, the baked potatoes with the black spots in the middle. She'd peel an apple for me and eat the skins, which was horrifying, and then when I was done, she'd eat the fruit I'd left around the core. I thought something was wrong with her.

My mother dressed ugly too. She never got herself a decent looking pair of sneakers and her sweatpants were all faded. I never understood why she dressed so badly because she always bought me really cute, trendy outfits. She still had some awful velour sweatshirts from the 1970s and I'd pray she'd never show up at my school wearing one. If she did, God forbid, she'd probably be eating a burnt pizza crust and a peach pit.

My mother was so embarrassing.

Then one morning, recently, I finally got it. After eating my daughter's unwanted toast crusts and a plum skin for breakfast, we went shopping. I needed new shoes for a wedding we were attending that weekend. Except, once we got to the mall I realized that my feet weren't growing. It was just a party. No one was going to be looking at my feet. But the baby? She'd nearly outgrown all of her shoes and would be in a new size soon. She needed new shoes more than I did.

I considered a new sundress, but did I really need one? No. My little one was going to be in a size 2T soon and I wouldn't have a thing that would fit her. I decided to wait and spend the money on her.

When we got home, we had lunch. She ate the fluffy tops of the broccoli and I realized I'd learned to love the tough stems. I peeled her a peach and sucked all the flesh from the pit while she ate the good parts. I wanted a graham cracker but there were only two left, so I decided that I didn't really like graham crackers as much as I did when I was little anyway. Neither did my mom and that's why she always let me have the last ones in the package too.

When you're a parent, you don't mind giving up the good parts. I don't need a bunch of new stuff because I have all I need. I have my daughter and her happiness and I have a mother that I finally appreciate — a mother who once gave me all the good parts in hope that one day I'd grow up to be that kind of parent too.

~Victoria Fedden

Mom's Christmas Stocking

*Open your heart — open it wide; someone is
standing outside.*
*~Quoted in Believe: A Christmas Treasury
by Mary Engelbreit*

Our mother, June Parker, was a spiritual researcher, historian, student of life, journalist and writer. She did none of these as a profession, but as her passion. After she died, I found myself in her sunny, well-organized office looking through the files of her many newspaper articles, letters to the editor and genealogy notes, each neatly typed on her IBM Selectric typewriter.

One sheet of paper caught my eye. It was entitled "Mom's Christmas Stocking" and here's what it said: "Every Christmas you have always filled a stocking for Mom. I want you to continue doing so. Choose the very things I would love. Find someone to give this filled stocking to — a woman in prison, or in a rehab, or a homeless center. This is the most precious Christmas gift I could receive or you could give — sharing the love we know with someone who really needs a shot of love. And, in this way I will continue to share your Christmases and continue to be a part of my wonderful family."

I gave copies to my sisters and brother and tucked a copy away for myself.

As our first Christmas season without Mom approached, I purchased some fun and useful items for her Christmas stocking. I bought a beautiful white stocking and wrapped each item, filling that stocking with care. I found an organization in New York City, where I live, called Women In Need (WIN) — this would be the perfect place to donate Mom's stocking! I felt the presence of my mother with me as I walked to the center on my lunch hour. I told her how happy I was to be sharing our love in this way, knowing she was right there with me.

The women at the office of WIN were grateful and touched by my mom's request and promised to find a special woman to receive the stocking.

The loving feeling carried me through the day and when I saw my friends that evening at my gym I shared with them what I had experienced. The following Christmas season we had a Girls' Night and played board games, had refreshments and filled eight stockings for Women In Need.

Their enthusiasm helped me create our annual Mom's Stocking event where we collect donations of needed items and fill upwards of 150 Christmas stockings for women living in homeless shelters in New York City. The event has grown to include filling stockings for babies and young children and gift cards for teens. Friends and their children are invited to our open house Christmas event to fill stockings, enjoy refreshments and participate in giving and sharing shots of love.

My sisters and brother live in other states, and they and their families fill Christmas stockings and deliver them to their places of choice. Our mother's extended family also donates to our Mom's Stocking event in various ways. All donations are welcome and all are used for this loving cause.

Each year I thank my mother for giving me the most precious Christmas gift, the opportunity to share love where truly needed.

~Daryl Wendy Strauss

Everything I Would Need to Know

There are some things you learn best in calm,
and some in storm.
~Willa Cather

My mother was the "different" mom. Rarely home, she more closely emulated the dynamic career women who would not become commonplace for another decade. The year I turned ten, Mom bought a deli and started her catering business in the back room. My friends arrived home from school to mothers in the midst of cooking dinner, eager to hear about their day. I often came home to an empty house and a dinner made by my grandmother or heated up in the oven by my sister or me.

I never liked school, but by high school I absolutely hated it. I used to fake all sorts of illnesses to get out of going. Mom had little energy left from her seven-day workweeks to argue with me. Her reputation as a caterer had grown. And impossible as it seemed, her work hours increased too, something I highly resented. Between designing wedding cakes, making entire meals and expanding deli hours to attract early commuters and last-minute evening shoppers, she was often on her feet a grueling seventeen hours a day. She simply had nothing left to deal with her willful fourteen-year-old. So she punished me the only way she could.

"I don't know what you're trying to avoid," she said. "But you're not going to stay here in bed all day if that's what you're thinking."

Impatiently, she sipped a cup of coffee while I showered and dressed.

Our first stop was Temmler's Bakery. At five-thirty in the morning, when the business district was empty and dark, the kitchen at Temmler's was brightly lit. We arrived at the back door as the men, all dressed in white, were just winding down from hours of mixing, baking and decorating. Business was about to shift to the front end of the building where the salespeople, including Mrs. Temmler, were sliding huge silver trays filled with sweets onto shelves in preparation for the arrival of hungry business people on their way to catch the train to Chicago.

Slouched atop a stool and holding a mug of steaming coffee, Mr. Temmler brusquely directed my mother to her orders through the ocean of sugary treats and racks of aromatic bread loaves. With his thick German accent, he sounded severe. But I noticed he always pointed her toward the best assortments. We lugged the heavy trays jammed with sweet rolls, cream horns, jelly doughnuts and coffee cakes out to her station wagon. Loaves of warm, unsliced bread were carefully placed into large brown bags and gently tucked into available nooks and crannies. A few miles away at her store, Mom parked the car on the empty street. We hauled everything inside to the deli's bakery section just beyond the front door where the appealing aromas would waken another set of early risers headed for the train.

I hated the deli business, with its unpredictable ebb and flow of demanding customers. I preferred the kitchen. At the back of the old narrow wooden building, the kitchen occupied an enormous space with twenty-foot ceilings that hoarded heat in winter but suffocated us with a thick blanket of warmth in summer. Rows of fluorescent lights suspended above the workspace cast a warm glow on the worn wooden floors and bounced light off metal prep tables. I was fascinated by the old Hobart mixer that stood nearly as tall as me. It was twice my age but its low-pitched motor whirred along reliably, mixing enormous bowls of ingredients into silken smooth cake batters. The big black pizza oven in the far corner looked like no oven I'd ever seen with its six-foot wide, one-foot high ovens stacked atop tall legs. But it effortlessly baked pies and cakes by the dozen.

My first job of the day was usually to make the doughnuts. Mom didn't trust me with the mix, so she prepared it herself. She poured it into the conical dispenser that hung suspended over the gurgling grease pit. I glided the dispenser over the sizzling pool, pressing the lever that dropped doughnuts one by one. The smell of fresh, hot doughnuts was at first inviting but eventually disgusting as the greasy fragrance permeated my clothes and hair. I swirled blistering hot doughnuts in pans of chocolate and vanilla glaze, then dropped them into huge tubs of brightly colored jimmies or fluffy coconut before settling them onto large silver trays like those from the bakery. I handled so many scorching hot doughnuts by the time I was fourteen, I swore my fingerprints had been permanently removed.

Mom might've been good at talking to me about my problems and the reasons I didn't want to go to school, but I wasn't listening. If we talked at all, it was usually a blazing verbal battle that got nowhere fast and ended abruptly with a slap across my face for some impertinent remark.

Ultimately, she gave up talking and just worked. And I worked alongside her. I learned to clean and prepare huge shrimp and make an attractive sandwich loaf layered with crabmeat or tuna and iced like a wedding cake with cream cheese and savory decorations of olives and chives. I stood for hours carefully cutting canapés from loaves of bread and learning to decorate them neatly. I noticed her attention to detail and the way she smiled and her posture straightened when customers praised her lovely presentations and the delicious flavors of her food. I listened to her conversations with the deliverymen. She knew everyone's name and all their stories. They looked forward to seeing her and sharing their lives with her. I saw how everyone respected and admired her. And I was proud she was my mother.

I scrubbed floors with a heavy rag mop and wiped down the equipment. I washed piles of pots and pans, and kitchen utensils. There was no electric dishwasher, only me. My back ached from standing over the old porcelain sink but I soon realized that if I hadn't been washing dishes, the person doing all the washing up would've been my mother. That was why she was always late for dinner or not home in time to eat at all.

In time, I understood her tenacity and determination to fulfill this dream. I loved how she brightened when we met the deadlines that constantly loomed over her, both from a production standpoint and a financial one. And I learned what price a dream can extract when, at the end of the day, she collapsed into bed knowing the routine would begin again within a few hours. But I saw how much she valued her dream and believed it worth that price.

Before I finished high school, I understood overhead costs and marketing, scheduling and payroll. But more importantly, I learned about faith and determination, hard work, responsibility and most of all, about caring. Mom and I never really had any of the conventional mother/daughter conversations you read about. But wordlessly, over pies and cakes, canapés and sandwich loaves, she explained everything I would need to know.

~Barbara Ann Burris

Staying Sharp at 95

*Aging is not lost youth but a new stage of
opportunity and strength.*

~Betty Friedan

I've been interested in ways to boost brain power for quite some time. I'm not getting any younger and I am finding it harder to remember names — something I did effortlessly in my youth.

The people I know who continue to have sharp minds into old age have certain characteristics in common. They are all active physically as well as mentally. Case in point, my mother-in-law. My husband and I regularly talk to and visit his mother, Lillian, a woman of ninety-five. Up to the time she broke her hip six months ago, she was physically active. However, she has managed to adapt.

"Don't you want live-in help?" my husband asked on our last visit.

"I had help when I couldn't get around. Now I manage quite well with my walker. I need to do as many things for myself as possible," she said.

Lillian hired a cleaning lady, has food delivered much of the time, and remains living independently in the family home, a large Victorian house. Her mind is as active as ever and she is on the mend from her injury.

"Okay," she said, "let me see if I can stump you." She looked down at a sheet of paper on which she'd written questions. Then she asked us questions she'd collected from her favorite quiz shows on television.

Over lunch, which we shared in her kitchen, I decided to interview her. "I know you never forget a phone number, anniversary or birthday. How do you manage it?"

"Simple," she responded. "I write everything down and study it. If I see it, then I can remember it." She then rattled off our phone number to prove her point.

"What keeps you young in spirit and sharp in mind and memory?" I asked her.

"For me, it's contact with family and friends. Since I can't get around the way I used to do, I talk on the telephone. It keeps me connected. I also sit out on the front porch and observe what's going on in the neighborhood. I particularly like to watch and listen to children playing. Sometimes neighbors drop by and visit."

My mother-in-law, besides being feisty and strong-willed, is very interested in people. It keeps her going. Talking to her children, grandchildren and great-grandchildren also keeps her mind active and agile, as does watching game and talk shows on TV. She feels connected to what's happening socially and politically in the world. Human interaction is a crucial element in keeping her mind sharp and boosting her memory.

She frowned at me because I was serving the lunch we brought to her house. She stated she wanted to order in from a restaurant and treat us as guests. We would not hear of it. We like to pamper her when we visit. We shop for her. My husband does minor house repairs. We bring pictures of her great-grandchildren.

"Do you do anything special to keep your memory sharp?" I asked her.

"Every night before I go to sleep I recite the alphabet backwards."

On a number of occasions, I've taken my mother-in-law to her doctor for a checkup. Lillian's doctor has observed that genetics and lifestyle both enter into whether or not a person will eventually suffer from dementia or Alzheimer's disease.

People suffering from high cholesterol, high blood pressure and diabetes are particularly vulnerable. Scientists have found associations among Alzheimer's disease and high blood pressure, which can damage blood vessels in the brain. So controlling high blood pressure is also important. My mother-in-law does, in fact, take medication to control this problem. And she watches her dietary salt intake as well. Seniors also have to be careful of drug interactions, which can affect their memory and thinking.

Lillian stimulates her mind with activities such as reading books and completing crossword puzzles. She's kept her mind active and curious in past years with such activities as reading, writing, attending lectures, and even gardening.

For those of us who are in good physical condition, walking, swimming and dancing are some of the activities that can help keep our minds sharp. My in-laws were active swimmers and square dancers for many years. They also enjoyed traveling to new places and meeting new people. All of these activities build cognitive reserve. A variety of leisure and physical activity has kept Lillian's mind sharp over the years.

I have observed that those who are active physically, mentally and socially show the least signs of cognitive decline. This was confirmed by Lillian's doctor, Barbara Paris, who encourages socialization and staying mentally active to keep your mind sharp. "If you don't use it, you lose it," Dr. Paris emphasizes, and she also says that committing to a sense of community and socialization are important. These are the very things my mother-in-law does each day.

"So why do you think you've lived such a long and relatively healthy life?" I asked Lillian.

She was thoughtful, running her fingers through her white hair. "Well, I believe in eating healthy foods, lots of fruits and vegetables, but not overeating. I try to be optimistic. I appreciate each day, and I keep myself as busy and active as possible. I try to find solutions for my problems as much as I can."

This is all true. Essentially, Lillian sees the glass as half-full. She doesn't harp on negative things. She also sees the best in other people. Her positive outlook on life, strength of character and determination to live life to its fullest and overcome all obstacles, keeps her mind sharp and sound. When there are problems, she looks for solutions. She doesn't throw pity parties. We can all learn a great deal from people like Lillian about how to boost our brain power.

~Jacqueline Seewald

It Doesn't Hurt to Smile

*Before you put on a frown, make absolutely sure there
are no smiles available.*

~Jim Beggs

The last time my eighty-three-year-old mother-in-law visited, I asked how she was feeling. It's a valid question. She has, after all, had two knee replacements, a metal rod inserted in her femur, and a liver transplant. Pins hold her wrist together, and arthritis is settling into her bones so thoroughly she can no longer roll the dough to make her famous cinnamon crisps. She moves slowly and with precision to avoid another fall.

But she hasn't stopped moving. In fact, she and my father-in-law attended their first Jimmy Buffet concert this summer... where they sat on the lawn. Here's the thing about my in-laws: They never say no to an invitation or a new adventure. If they can make it work, they're willing to try just about anything. When we need them to come stay with the kids, we have to get on their calendars far in advance.

They inspire us daily.

When asked how she was feeling, my mother-in-law responded without an ounce of self-pity: "Well, most everything hurts every day. Some days are better than others. But you know what I've discovered? It doesn't hurt one bit to smile. So that's what I've decided to do... smile at everyone I see. I may not be able to do all the things I used to do, but I can at least brighten someone's day."

It is such simple wisdom, and such a profound shift.

Moving the focus from what we don't have, from what we've lost, from how we've been burdened, to what we can offer others is the difference between living in the dark and radiating light. And illumination, of course, makes traveling so much easier for us and for others.

The key to a life worth living, I think, is to change perspective...

From inward to outward
From giving up to giving back
From self-consciousness to global awareness
From closing our minds to opening our hearts
From "No, thanks" to "Yes, let's!"
From judgment to acceptance
From self-importance to humility
From things to people
From indifference to love

You don't have to cuddle babies in a faraway orphanage or underwrite the expense of a much-needed surgery. It's not necessary to start a foundation that supports victims of domestic abuse or to ride your bike across the country while raising money for undernourished children. Of course, if you have the time and the means and are able-bodied to do those things, then by all means... Go! Do them! Ride like the wind! Start something important! Write giant checks!

But my point is this: Sometimes change arrives in a brown-papered package much smaller and less dramatic than the one with the glitter and the shiny pink bow. Sometimes change looks uncannily similar to everyday kindness and empathy. Sometimes change begins with letting a driver merge in front of you, with holding the door for a mother juggling an armful of groceries, with graciously acknowledging the curmudgeonly store cashier (even though he's much more comfortable mumbling and frowning than accepting a word of encouragement), with tipping your server extravagantly, with giving a hungry stranger something to soothe the rumble in his belly.

In chaos theory, the butterfly effect maintains that the smallest breeze from a butterfly's wing can change the path of a hurricane halfway across the world.

Imagine, then, the possibilities that exist within a single smile. Mamaw knows.

~Katrina Anne Willis

How Running Helped Me Heal

I've learned that finishing a marathon isn't just an athletic achievement. It's a state of mind; a state of mind that says anything is possible.

~John Hanc

I t was a week after my mom had died, and I didn't know how to go on with life. Instead of going to work or the grocery store, I covered myself with blankets, wishing that I, too, could disappear. I was twenty-eight years old, and my mom had been fifty-four. It felt like I had been robbed.

So when I received an e-mail from a friend about a 5K benefiting pancreatic cancer research, I ignored it. It seemed too close to the heart, as pancreatic cancer was the disease that had taken my mother away from me. But something about my friend's words — "I can help organize the whole thing" — stuck with me. I felt obliged to agree, if only to accept her support.

Together, my friends and I walked in honor of my mom. I tried to ignore the shirts of other participants, many bearing pictures of the loved ones they had lost. They were a painful reminder that my mom was no longer there for me to vent about life's everyday annoyances, or to see me get married or have kids.

My friends and I grabbed lunch after, and I actually enjoyed myself. But I immediately felt guilty.

In the weeks to come, I managed to reenter the world of the living. I knew my mom would have wanted it that way. She was the type who never got defeated. In fact, when she was pregnant with me, the doctors had warned her that as a diabetic she'd be risking her life to have me. "But I was going to have you, no matter what," Mom told me. It was this very spirit that helped me get by.

Besides, keeping myself busy was preferable to driving myself crazy with things like wondering what would have happened if I had had the chance to say goodbye. It haunted me that I had gone to work on her last day instead of taking time off to see her, although I knew she wasn't feeling well. But Mom had instilled a serious work ethic in me, discouraging me from ever taking a day off.

A year later, to my surprise, I signed up for the same 5K. It seemed like the right thing to do. I checked our team's website daily, feeling a twinge of pride each time a donation ticked up our total.

The majority of our team walked the 5K, but several members ran the 10K. When the race ended, I noticed the runners all had one thing in common: They were beaming. They made it look so rewarding — and effortless. I wanted in.

So I enrolled in a 10K two months later. Considering I could barely run a mile, it was ambitious. But my boyfriend and I devised a training plan so I wouldn't come in last. I followed it religiously and didn't let anything get in my way — not even a trip to San Francisco.

Running up and down the city's hills, I was flooded with memories. I had lived there after college and my mother had visited often. I passed Bloomingdale's, recalling the time she and I had gotten into a screaming brawl there, much to other shoppers' dismay. It had all started because my sister and I had a spat over the fact that I had been thirty minutes late meeting her somewhere. "Why can't you guys just get along?" Mom had asked. I turned on her, too.

I was about to beat myself up when I remembered what Mom had once said after her diagnosis. "I don't want you to feel guilty about anything." Her paper-thin hands had held me tightly. She knew I could be my own worst enemy, always eager to blame myself. A weight lifted from my shoulders. I ran with a surge of energy.

In the following months, I found myself laughing with friends again without feeling the remnants of guilt. And I was able to sleep without having nightmares about my mom's final moments. Life felt lighter.

When race day arrived, I gave it my all — not for myself, but for my mom — and for all she had taught me and continued to teach me. As I ran, whenever I felt like slowing down, I pictured her cheering me on, as she had done at all of my soccer games and recitals as a kid.

Crossing the finish line, I was filled with her love and a sense of peace. So much so that shortly thereafter I signed up for a half marathon.

~Kristin Julie Viola

A Strike at the Ballpark

The human spirit is stronger than anything that
can happen to it.

~C.C. Scott

I entered the kitchen to find my mother looking quizzically at our Nespresso machine. "What is that, an onion?"

"No Mom, it's a coffeemaker."

"And what are those — little onions?" she said, pointing to the little pods that went in the machine.

My mother doesn't like technology or coffee, so it wasn't surprising that she didn't "get" our coffee apparatus. I thought she was just fooling around when she started calling other things in our kitchen "onions."

It was the Fourth of July and we were going to the Mets game for my mother's eighty-first birthday. My mother and sister had met at our house so that we could all drive together to the game.

As we drove down the highway my mother continued to act a little weird. When my husband executed a rather smooth move to exit the highway and avoid a traffic jam, she was overly effusive about his driving skills. We got to the stadium twenty minutes later, and my mother was still chatting away, saying strange things.

I didn't know much about strokes but it occurred to me that she might be having one. I asked for directions to the medical station and started to walk my mother there without telling her where we were going.

As we took the elevator, Mom was exclaiming that we needed

to see the "emperor"—which I came to realize was her word for the new Citi Field stadium. Apparently she was making the jump from baseball "stadium" to "Coliseum" to Roman "emperor," all words with common Latin and historical roots. She kept trying to veer off course to show us the emperor while I steered her toward the paramedics.

The paramedics did their normal stroke assessment, my mother duly identified the pen they held up as a "key," and we were rushed off in an ambulance to the stroke unit at a hospital in Queens. My mother's language skills were rapidly deteriorating by then.

We were fortunate that we caught my mother's stroke within the window of time allowed to administer the drug TPA. This drug, in layman's terms, stops the stroke in its tracks, like turning off a hard drive that is starting to erase itself. But TPA is a strong anti-clotting drug and it can kill the patient too. There were some tense moments when I had to make the decision, but I knew that my mother would rather risk death than let the stroke continue doing its damage. My mother received TPA at the first hospital, survived it, and we got back in an ambulance to go to a more sophisticated stroke unit at a hospital in Manhattan.

After a stroke the brain swells from the injury and the symptoms get worse and worse. My mother went from calling things "onions" to not even knowing her own name. But despite the fact that she didn't know her name, she said that she didn't want to cancel the sixtieth anniversary party that she and my father had scheduled for the following week. When I pointed out that she was missing a lot of words and she wouldn't know anyone's name, she said, "They'll just think I'm a little peculiar... but then they've always thought I was a little peculiar."

Even at the depths of her loss, Mom retained her self-deprecating sense of humor!

When she figured out her first name and her maiden name a couple of days later, but she couldn't recall her married name, she waved it off, saying, "That doesn't really matter," which seemed a bit like a commentary on her well-worn marriage. Stroke damage is a paradox. When I matter-of-factly gave my mother a form to sign in the hospital, she did it perfectly, inscribing her first, middle, and last name. I showed it to her and suggested she sign her name and then read it back to herself when she couldn't remember it.

After a few days my mother was sent home with a diagnosis of receptive and expressive aphasia. That meant she had trouble understanding spoken and written language and also finding the right words to express herself. I made a big poster with photos of family members and their names inscribed underneath. It hadn't been helping my relationship with my brother and sister that Mom was calling them both by my name. Everyone in the family was "Amy" for the first few days.

We got my mother into a language therapy rehab program that she would attend several days a week. When they were testing her capabilities, and discovered that she couldn't pronounce R's, I intervened and explained that she was from Boston, where they "pahked cahs" instead of parking cars. God forbid they wasted precious insurance-paid visits on trying to reinstate an "R" sound that my mother never had!

My sister signed on to drive my mother to therapy and help her with her nightly homework. For the next few months, my mother diligently went to speech therapy and spent hours on her homework each night, relearning words, especially those tricky pronouns and units of time. She still has trouble with masculine and feminine pronouns, units of time, and understanding spoken letters and numbers but she regained almost all her other words or found substitutes.

Aphasia lasts forever, and even now, three years later, my mother cycles through a few pronouns before she lights on the right one, especially when she is tired. She still attends an aphasia support group. This is her new life, but she feels fortunate. She knows how lucky she was to have the stroke in front of us, so that we could get her medical help right away. If she had been home alone or asleep while having the stroke, there's no telling how bad the damage would have been.

Right from the start, my mother bravely informed store clerks and other people she met that she had a "strike" and thus had trouble finding her words. She called it a strike instead of a stroke, which seemed appropriate, since it was like her brain was on strike when it came to language.

I've been so impressed with the way my mother has handled

this dramatic change in her senior years. Her fortitude, her lack of embarrassment, and her can-do attitude have been inspiring. In fact, just two weeks after the stroke, my mother and sister were back at Citi Field for another Mets game. Mom was a little anxious about going to the same place where she had the stroke but she decided to face her fear head-on.

That first day back at the stadium, or "emperor," my mother discovered the cure for her anxiety — the gigantic margaritas they sell at Citi Field. She bought one and sipped it for the entire game. And she has had a margarita at every Mets game since. Mom has found workarounds for the words that she has permanently lost and she has found a workaround for watching the Mets without having a stroke, or strike as it were, despite the Mets' ups and downs!

~Amy Newmark

Standing Out

Courage is being afraid but going on anyhow.
~Dan Rather

I always knew my mom was different from other moms. It wasn't just her appearance — her petite frame, black hair, and dark almond eyes contrasted sharply with the statuesque blondes who accompanied the other kids to school. Her speech was peppered with extra syllables, and sometimes words would come out in the wrong order. It didn't bother me that she was different — after all, I looked different from my friends, too!

On the outside, our house looked like every other house in the neighborhood. But inside, beautiful dolls dressed in colorful kimonos posed in their glass cases. Our refrigerator and cupboards held foods other kids had never seen. I never thought about the significance of these items. They were just a part of my life.

At lunchtime, other kids asked to trade the cookies and candies in their lunches for the rice crackers I brought. And they asked me to show them how to fold squares of paper into little toys like cats, baskets, and birds the way my mom had taught me. If there was any malice directed toward us, my siblings and I were sheltered from it by our wonderful teachers and the other adults in our lives.

The only thing that bothered me was not having relatives nearby. Other kids went to visit their cousins, and talked about their aunts and uncles. My relatives lived on the other side of the world. I knew I had cousins, but I saw them only in pictures. When Mom talked to her sisters on the phone, she used a language that sounded mysterious and fun. At Christmastime, we got beautiful cards embellished with strange looking characters.

It wasn't until I enrolled in a Japanese language class in college that I realized how great an adjustment my mother had made when she followed her husband to his homeland. Until then, Japan was an exotic faraway place, where people spoke differently and ate food that we couldn't find in most Midwest restaurants. Thanks to the international students on campus, I learned more about the customs and culture. In the class I managed to learn several words and phrases, but there were few opportunities to use them once I began my teaching career.

Later on, I became a mom myself. My children inherited my dark hair and eyes, but they were not the only children of Asian descent. By now there were others — children adopted by Caucasian couples, as well as children of immigrants. They, too, were taught to celebrate their differences. When my older daughter was a toddler, my mother and I took her to visit our relatives in Japan. I loved visiting my relatives, but it was frustrating not being able to communicate with them. On shopping trips, my cousins, even though they were younger, watched over me as they would a small child, knowing I couldn't read the street signs or make purchases on my own. Again, I was different. Now I looked like everyone else, but I stood out because I couldn't understand. Was this how Mom felt when she first came to America?

Now that I'm retired from full-time teaching, I have more time to pursue some of my earlier goals. One goal is to learn to speak Japanese fluently. The single year of instruction during my undergraduate years was not enough to carry on a conversation with my aunts and cousins when they came to visit. I want to get to know these relatives. I want to learn about their likes and dislikes, to know about their daily lives, and share stories about our families.

They say it's more difficult to learn a new language after you become an adult, and since I've been an adult for many years, I'd say it's true. But I'm enjoying this new venture. Four days a week, I sit in a classroom with people less than half my age. Four nights a week, I pore over the exercises and diligently complete the worksheets. It may be more difficult for me to retain the new vocabulary, but I have the time now to do the work and practice. I'm doing this for me, not for a grade. But even more, I'm enjoying the connection to my culture. Every night when I finish my homework, I call my "personal tutor" to check my grammar. She's glad I took on this task. It must have been difficult for her, having to be the interpreter for every visit to Japan, and for each time a relative came to visit. If I become fluent, I can share the burden. But even more, we're building a precious connection to the land she loved and left.

I still think my mom is different. She is different in that she had the courage to leave behind everything she knew and go to a new place and build a new life. She had the intelligence to learn how to assimilate into this unknown society and raise three children, teaching them by example the importance of hard work, perseverance, and respect for others.

I hope I'm different too, and that my kids and grandkids appreciate the difference.

~Patricia Gordon

The Girl with the Golden Curls

Just like the butterfly, I too will awaken in my own time.
~Deborah Chaskin

"But I don't want to take care of Grandma!" I said. I was seventeen, and it was the first day of summer vacation. I was looking forward to the best summer I'd ever have. In September, I'd start my senior year, and after graduation I'd have to get a job. This was the last summer I'd ever be completely free, and now my mother was trying to steal my last summer by forcing me to take care of my grandmother. My grandmother lived two hundred miles away. If I went to stay with her, I'd be cut off from all my friends.

My grandmother was eighty years old and had diabetes. She was in bad condition, and it was only a matter of time before her foot would be amputated. She also needed an insulin shot every morning. I would have to learn to give her a shot, cook all her meals, do all the housework and laundry, and take her to her weekly doctor appointment. It wasn't fair!

Although we had a large family, no one else could or would take care of Grandma. I was told that if I didn't take care of her, she'd have to go to a nursing home. A heavy burden of guilt was heaped on my shoulders. If I didn't agree to take care of her, I was a selfish, terrible, spoiled teenager who only cared about myself.

I'd spent very little time with Grandma while I was growing up, and I barely knew her. This was going to be the worst summer of my life.

I practiced giving injections on an orange, but the first time I had to give her an insulin shot, I nearly got sick. Her diet was very strict, and her food had to be measured and cooked a certain way. She blamed me for what she considered "tasteless" meals.

I missed my friends and knew they were having fun going to the mall and on dates. I wasn't going to have a single date all summer. My life was over.

The only things in her house to read were *National Geographic* magazines from the 1970s. I asked her if there was anything else to read, and she said she thought there was a dictionary in the desk. I had the feeling that before the summer was over, I'd be reading the dictionary and be glad I had it.

Twice a day, I had to change the bandages on her right foot. Two of her toes were black. It was only a matter of time until they fell off in the bandage or had to be amputated. Every time I changed the bandage, I prayed when I removed the gauze that her toes would still be attached to her foot.

She was confined to a wheelchair, and one day I pushed her out into the yard under a shade tree and sat on a lawn chair next to her. A butterfly fluttered past us, and she smiled for the first time since I'd arrived.

"When I was a little girl, I loved butterflies. I would chase them, but I never caught them, because if you catch them, they die," she said.

I tried to imagine Grandma as a young girl who liked butterflies, but I couldn't. She was just a sick, old woman, and I was stuck with her.

"When I was a young girl, I had beautiful, long, golden curls that hung past my waist. In fact, when I sat down, I had to pull them aside or I'd sit on my hair. Everyone was jealous of my long curls. My mother would wrap my hair around her fingers at night and tie little strips of rags around my hair to make curls," she said. "My mother died when I was eleven. I had to take care of my two younger sisters and my three younger brothers. From then on, I did all the cooking and cleaning. My father was a quiet man; he hardly ever talked. I had to stop going to school in the fourth grade. I cried because I couldn't go to school anymore."

I realized I'd never known anything about my grandmother.

"My father said he'd lost our farm, and we had to move from Kentucky to Kansas. I hated leaving the green hills of Kentucky for the flat, dry plains of Kansas. I had friends in Kentucky. I never got to make friends in Kansas because I was too busy taking care of my father and my five brothers and sisters. When I was sixteen, a neighbor boy asked me to marry him, and I said yes. We'd never even had a date or kissed, but I was so tired of cooking and cleaning and taking care of five kids that I wanted to get away. He had pretty blue eyes, and so I married him. My two sisters were old enough to take over the cooking and cleaning," she said as her eyes looked far into the past.

Every afternoon after lunch, I'd push her wheelchair into the yard, and she'd tell me more stories about her life. I don't think anyone had ever heard the stories before.

She'd always lived on a farm, and it had barely provided enough food for the family. When she was still in her teens, she had two daughters who were stillborn. She had nine more children.

I'd been upset about not going to the mall and having dates. When she was my age, she'd lost her mother, left school, helped raise five siblings, gotten married, and had two stillborn babies.

Every day, we sat in the yard and drank iced tea while she told me about her life. The days flew past. It was hard to believe that I'd ever dreaded spending time with her.

By the middle of July, her diabetes had become so bad that her foot had to be amputated, and the family decided to put her into a nursing home. She needed more care than I could give her, and I'd have to leave and return to school soon.

I went home. I still had half of a summer ahead of me, but I wasn't the same person I'd been when I left six weeks earlier.

I never saw Grandma again.

The summer I'd thought was going to be my worst turned out to be one of my most memorable. I was always grateful for the opportunity to know and love my grandmother.

When I think of her, I don't think of the white-haired, old woman in a wheelchair. I think of her as a beautiful, young girl with long, golden curls who loved butterflies.

~April Knight

10

The Next New Step

What is a mom but the sunshine of our days and the
north star of our nights.
~Robert Brault, www.robertbrault.com

I barely pulled off the road before the tears spilled onto my steering wheel. I turned off the engine and finally sobbed the long, panting, private sobs of despair that I had been holding deep inside me. I had just left my mother at her new home in an Alzheimer's care facility.

I found myself talking with my mother in my imagination: "Oh Mom, you held me when I broke up with my boyfriend and cried through the night. You took me from store to store to store to find the perfect prom dress. You went to all of my concerts, helped me fill out college applications into the night, and gave me advice on the curtains for my first house. I helped you find a new apartment after the divorce, and later had lunch with you at the new office you were so proud of. Together, we got lost driving, worried about whether Thanksgiving dinner would come out right, created homemade Christmas cards, and cried through my wedding. You cared for me when my first baby wouldn't stop crying. And now, today, we cry separately. And that is what hurts most."

After a while, the sobs quieter, I realized that I couldn't sit forever in a car full of tears by the side of the road. So I slowly put the car into gear and drove home.

The next day I went to visit Mom in her new place and found her happily folding napkins. I sat down to join in, privately thinking how sad it was that we were reduced to napkin folding. But, fold-by-fold, we watched a neat pile of smoothed napkins growing between us. She seemed okay with it all, and I found some of my own tension lifted when I left that day.

"Thanks for a good day, Mom," I thought, as I punched the numbers into the security lock to go outside.

A few weeks later, I thought it worth a try to go ice skating. Someone had said that activities from childhood were good for those with dementia, and she had loved to ice skate. I was not hopeful, thinking of the balance involved, the cold, the new-ness, and the frustration of wrestling into tightly laced skates. Leaving for the rink, I noticed she had mismatched shoes and I groaned inside. This was probably a mistake.

Later, after lacing up the skates and hiding her shoes under a bench, I helped Mom gingerly step onto the rink, and then she was in front of me skating and laughing. I couldn't help a few familiar tears as I watched her remember her way across the ice. She turned and caught me crying, then skated on.

"Thanks for the wonderful day," I said when we were done skating.

Slowly, I learned what worked and what didn't. A trip to the store made a lovely afternoon, especially if we stopped for ice cream. I began to notice that the pressure of trying to think of new and interesting things to do was going away. Nothing earth shaking was required; it was good to simply sit and eat ice cream or walk through a garden. Each day Mom stopped at more or less the same place and noticed the flowers in bloom and the birds flying by. Soon I did, too.

Later, when Mom was unable to leave her room, I found it best to just sit by her side, without trying to talk. We listened together to the pleasant sounds around us and when it was time to leave, it was a simple "Bye, Mom, thanks" that completed the day.

And so it was that the world I had mourned so deeply that day in my car was replaced with a new world — a world that Mom owned, controlled, and embraced, once I gave her the chance. And then, magically, it was a world she allowed me to enter with her after I let go of my own tangled expectations and let her show me how it was done.

It was a world with lovely flowers to smell and smooth, graceful napkins piling up into a beautiful stack. It was a world of quiet, gentle walks, delight in the adventure of a trip to the grocery store, a world where mismatched shoes do not matter, and an afternoon on ice skates was all we needed on our agenda. In her world, she showed me the beauty of the quiet and the completeness of two chairs side by side.

Oh Mom, you held me and helped me when I was small and when you were the grown-up. Now, just when I thought it was my turn to be the grown-up, you have showed me yet again how it is done. It should be no surprise that one thing has not changed at all — it was you who took my hand to show me how to take the next, new step.

Thanks, Mom, for all the wonderful days, then and now.

~Jennifer Harrington

11

Grandmother's Gift

Books are the quietest and most constant of friends;
they are the most accessible and wisest of counselors,
and the most patient of teachers.
~Charles W. Eliot

My grandmother has been gone for many years now and while she was alive, we were not particularly close. We saw each other infrequently and each conversation was strained. How is it possible that a woman whose life only briefly intersected with mine would influence me in such a profound way? This is a story of a grandmother who loved a little girl and bestowed upon her a gift. She did not know if she would ever receive a thank you. This grandmother knew that what she had to give was one of the greatest gifts a child could receive.

My grandmother lived alone, far away in an apartment in a big imposing building my brother, sister and I called "the castle." She was well educated, spoke several languages, traveled through Europe alone, collected antiques, and listened to opera. Her apartment was decorated with antiques and filled with hundreds of books she read and spoke of often.

I lived in suburban Long Island and only saw her once each year or so. My father would call her on Sunday nights and ask me to speak on the phone with her. I would wail at the thought. My father would always make eyes at me, which told me I didn't have a choice. He would always insist that she missed me and loved me but I didn't really ever believe him. I knew she would ask me about school, about what I was reading and what I was learning about. I was a horrible student who could never pay attention and squirmed in my classroom seat. I wanted to be outside playing and talking with my friends.

I would begrudgingly take the phone and speak to her for a few long moments. "I wish this lady would get a clue to what life is really about," I would think as I hung up the phone. Her inability to know what was important was never more evident than at gift-giving time.

Each year, on Christmas morning, my brother, sister and I would run down the stairs and see a beautiful tree surrounded by brightly wrapped packages. We would dive into the pile with great delight, ripping the paper and revealing all the latest toys. Eventually, I would see an odd-looking package deep under the tree that I knew could only be from Grandmother. She never used traditional Christmas paper and her presents always had brightly colored ribbons in yellows, oranges or lavender. Each year I would take that package, feel the weight of it in my hand, knock on it with my fist and hear a sharp tap. "Another book, just like every year!" I would think and then promptly toss it aside without even opening it. I would gleefully play with my toys on Christmas morning and for days and even weeks after. Eventually, I would open Grandmother's gift and glance through the pages of the book she had chosen. My grandmother, in her distinctive, beautiful handwriting, would inscribe each book: "To Elizabeth Rose, with love, from Grandmother." I would read the book and sometimes memorize the text. I still didn't count this as playing, or having fun. I certainly knew in my heart that reading a book or talking about school was no fun for a child.

As the years passed, my interest in school remained minimal. It was all too boring and formal for me. I was more resistant than ever to speaking to Grandmother on Sunday evenings. School, books and what "interesting things I had learned lately" were boring topics for old people to discuss. Didn't Grandmother know that all I cared about was friends, clothes and boys? Each Christmas, more books were under the tree, reinforcing my belief that she really didn't care.

Although I was not interested in school, I had enormous patience with younger children. Our neighbor across the street asked me to help her daughter with her homework after school. I was able to teach her in the way I wish I were able to learn. I made up songs and stories to help her memorize facts and we played games to test what she had learned. Her mom remarked, "You should become a teacher when you grow up Liz; you are so good at helping children." At first, the idea seemed ridiculous to me. I was a terrible student. How could it ever happen?

Slowly the idea took root and I decided to give college a try. Having a goal made things easier for me and I began to apply myself. Selecting courses and having different teachers suited me as well. My second semester, I sat in my first required education class — Children's Literature. The professor spoke about making children's books come alive, filling children's worlds with rich vocabulary, and the characteristics of a classic children's book. It was my favorite class and I was always eager to get there and participate in each discussion. About midway into the class our teacher discussed the differences between a children's book that is here for the moment and those that are enduring classics. She flashed a list of books on her overhead projector that included titles that had been awarded a Newbery Medal or were Caldecott winners. It was then a lump began to form in my throat.

Armed with a handwritten copy of my teacher's list of classics, I raced home, dropped my schoolbooks and ran to the basement. There in the corner on a dusty shelf sat the most amazing collection of children's books any teacher could hope to have. As I ran my fingers across the bindings of *Frederick*, *Tales from the Ballet*, *The Trumpet of the Swan* and *Stuart Little* memories came flooding back. Memories of receiving these books, staring at those pages late at night curled up in my bed and gazing at beautiful pictures. I remembered my grandmother reading Leo Lionni's *Frederick* to me when she came to visit one spring. I was so sure I had figured out the ending, and finding out I was wrong delighted me.

It was then I realized I didn't remember most of the toys I had gotten all those Christmases and with the exception of one old doll, all of the mounds of presents did not make it to my adulthood. Most, in fact, were discarded soon after they were played with or were broken or sold at garage sales. Now I stood before a treasure that I would not trade for anything. As I bent back the cover of *Make Way for Ducklings*, I saw my grandmother's familiar and stylish handwriting that read, "To Elizabeth Rose, with love, from Grandmother." Love was exactly what my grandmother had been giving me all of my years. She resisted the happiness of a beaming child opening an expensive toy and replaced it with a gift that was a part of her. She didn't give me what I wanted in my little girl mind, but what she knew I needed — a gift for the soul that would last a lifetime. Now I saw how wise she had been and how each book was so carefully selected at different times of my life.

I sat down that day and wrote my grandmother a letter. I expressed as well as I could how much I was enjoying school and how my collection of children's books was a treasure. I wrote about my happy memories reading them and about how much I knew I was loved. I placed my letter in a box with a pillow that had a mallard duck on the front. It looks like the duck in the book, *Make Way for Ducklings*, I wrote. This letter was as much for me as it was for her and I planned on telling her more about school and hearing more about her favorite books each time we spoke. Sometimes, what we plan never happens. Shortly after she received my letter, my grandmother died. My aunt who lives nearby told me how much my words had meant to her in her final days.

I continued to water the seed she planted so long ago. I graduated college with honors and received my master's degree in remedial reading. I became a teacher and I try my best to plant those tiny seeds in all my students. Sometimes I can see the world of words opening up right before their eyes. Some students squirm and do not pay attention, but I do not lose faith or feel as if all my efforts won't someday change their lives and that seed won't take root. I know now that I don't have to see the finished product to believe that a work I have started may take many years to reach completion.

I find that I am most happy now only when I am stealing moments in my busy day to read a good book. Although my own children can now read independently, I still take delight in reading aloud to them.

This summer I read them *Island of the Blue Dolphins* and they would groan when I called them over to listen. Undaunted, I would read, and by the close of each session they would always ask for more. Now, I consider my time reading peaceful, a world of possibilities, second only to church. As I open the cover to a new book, I feel the shadow of my grandmother beside me and it is almost as if the inside cover of every book reads, "To Elizabeth Rose, with love, from Grandmother."

~Elizabeth Rose Reardon Farella

Chapter 2

for Mom, with love

Thanks for Always Being Right

Kids don't stay with you if you do it right. It's the one job where, the better you are, the more surely you won't be needed in the long run.
~Barbara Kingsolver

12

Cheer Leader

Cookies are made of butter and love.
~Norwegian Proverb

As I stepped off the school bus and looked up at the house, I suspected she knew. She was peering around the curtain through the kitchen window as I made my way up the driveway. My five siblings raced past me, but I slowly sauntered along, kicking the gravel as I approached the back door. The buttery smell of freshly baked cookies filled the air as I opened the door and slipped off my shoes. As my brothers madly reached for cookies, my sister slapped their hands away.

Mom was oblivious to the chaos as she dried her hands on her apron and looked at me, examining my eyes. Donning her oven mitt, she pulled out a cookie sheet with a fresh batch of chocolate chip cookies, all the while keeping one eye on my ravenous brothers and one on me going through my backpack. I threw down my backpack, and headed straight to my room with my head down. I shut my door, only to hear a light knock.

"Vicki, can I come in?" her quiet voice asked as I watched the doorknob turn. She untied her flour-stained apron, and held her arms out to me. "I called the office at school to find out. I know you didn't make it."

"You what?" I couldn't believe that she would be so nosy as to call the office to find out who made the cheerleading squad. But when I felt her arms embrace me, I immediately felt her empathy and started crying, while rehashing all the horrible details. Through my sobs, I somehow relayed the entire scene.

"Mom, they posted the girls who made the squad on a big white poster board taped right on the wall of the main office! I could see from down the hall that my name wasn't on it!

"Megan and Sara's names were on it! Can you believe they made the team but not me? They can't do aerials or back handsprings!"

She just listened and nodded, as I relayed the painful details of how my friends' names were on the list, but not mine. I cried profusely, retelling her all the earth-shattering minutiae and she just sat and listened, stroking my hair.

"Mom, I even forgot an entire verse of the Eskymos' Fight Song! Can you believe that?"

She looked away at that one, and I realized she was fighting giggles as she covered her mouth. "How can you laugh at that, Mom? It's not funny!"

"I'm sorry, Vick. It just reminds me of my own sophomore year when I tried out for the flag corps and I kept dropping my flag in tryouts!" Her blue eyes twinkled, as she looked straight into mine, then tipped her head back in laughter.

I couldn't help but giggle through my tear-filled eyes. "Did you make the team?" I asked, half-laughing and half-crying.

"Of course not. I was shaking so much that I was surprised I could flip the flag even once!" ENdEd UP TiGHT HERE

We laughed together, and she wiped my eyes, holding my chin in her rough hands. "Vicki, I know you're devastated now, and I was disappointed too, but pretty soon, you'll find something else you love to do, and you'll look back and laugh at this."

I had to admit, I no longer felt like throwing up.

"Oh, don't start," I laughed, hitting her playfully on the arm. "I'm getting sick of everyone telling me it'll be okay, and that I can always try out for basketball."

Still holding my chin in her hands, she said, "Vicki, we're all just trying to encourage you." Of course, she was right. I hugged her, and as I looked over her shoulder, I realized my two little brothers had cracked open the door and were peeking through, watching us. She didn't budge though, and kept wiping my eyes until I smiled up at her.

Ever since I can remember, my mom always seemed to say just the right words, and has always given each of us the attention we needed. Even though she had five other people's problems to attend to, Mom made me feel like my problem was her only concern. Each one of us at different times was her only concern.

After wiping my tears and listening to my tale of woe, she said something that I'll never forget. Though I was devastated at the time, my mom knew exactly how to soothe my pain. From that day on, she ended our many talks with two simple sentences: "Vicki, keep your chin up. That way, you can always see what's coming next."

And she was right — through all the disappointments of high school, she somehow made me feel that the crisis at hand would pass and there would soon be something new to look forward to. Just one month after consoling me, she was the first to congratulate me with another plate of cookies when I made the gymnastics team.

I'll never forget that day, because my mom gave me the most simple, yet most important gift a mother can give her daughter. She didn't get me the Guess jeans or the new stereo I had been begging for. She taught me compassion. She taught me that a mother puts her children's needs ahead of her own. And I have used her gift in helping my own two children through their most troubling times. Whenever I hug and encourage my kids with their grandmother's words, it always helps to dry their tears.✓

My mom raised my five siblings and me to "keep our chins up" and always look to the next challenge — and in true mom style, she never asked for anything in return — well, maybe just a little bite of a chocolate chip cookie.

~Victoria LaFave

Mom's Tour de Force

A mother understands what a child does not say.
~Jewish Proverb

I've never been a fan of arranged marriages, not that I've found the right person on my own, but I certainly can't imagine my parents being able to find that person. However, it dawned on me recently that I did something quite similar — I let my mother make one of the most important decisions of my life, one that led to a marriage of sorts... I let her pick my college. How we got there is interesting, and how it all turned out proves that despite all the stress, work, and sometimes strife involved, the college admissions process does work out in the end.✓

A high school overachiever and the first child leaving the nest, my college decision process was more dramatic than a night at the opera... and on a few occasions we wondered if the fat lady ever would sing. It all started in my sophomore year of high school when my (equally overachieving) parents decided we should get a leg up on the admissions process. I remember leafing through the large college guide I was given one cold winter weekend and highlighting those schools that interested me. It should come as no surprise then that most of them fell below the Mason-Dixon Line, and I ultimately ended up in North Carolina. But to get there my mother and I embarked on a journey that took us from the mountains of Tennessee to the banks of Lake Michigan and proved just how blessed I was. You see, decisiveness is not my gift. And my mother indulged what I now realize was an absolutely erratic college visitation spree spurred on by my inability to make a decision.

It began slowly with visits tacked onto family vacations. I toured Tulane when my father had business meetings in New Orleans, and William and Mary over a holiday trip to Williamsburg. But as I edged closer to senior year, with nary an idea of where I would end up, there was an increased urgency.

Soon my mom was leading our team of two. She created a hand-written spreadsheet to record information and my feedback on all of the twelve schools to which I applied. Our dining room table became College Central, as mom rewrote my college applications in her neat and steady print, kept us on deadline, and charted a series of road trips. My path to college consumed both of us. Mom was my partner, someone just as vested as me, someone who understood the trepidation, the work, and exasperation involved in getting into college.

Mom tracked down a former admissions counselor to answer our questions; she scheduled campus interviews, tours, and our accommodations around her work and my school. And we were off! We visited so many schools: big schools, small schools, urban and rural schools, from the blue hens to the spiders, and many schools in between. Sometimes my father came with us, sometimes my best friend, or grandmother. But often we were on our own. And that's the way I liked it best.✓

Despite my initial yearning for someplace warm, the idea of attending Northwestern University, in Evanston, Illinois, lodged itself in my head like a pesky sinus infection. I toured the school and interviewed with a college representative, and then I was promptly rejected. Unfortunately, I had so obsessed over Northwestern that nowhere else seemed suitable. I baked and devoured an entire apple pie out of self-pity and then announced that I was no longer interested in any other schools. Looking at me across the dining room table, it's a miracle that Mom didn't throttle me with our heavy college guidebook; instead (thankfully) she did what she does best; she turned the situation positive, planned an impromptu trip and we were off... again!

In Nashville, we got our first taste of country music; in Virginia, we saw the northernmost palm tree; and in Delaware, my parents offered me a new car if I chose the state university. But yet, I was paralyzed: nervous and frightened, stubborn and unable to make a decision.

The last school we visited was Wake Forest University in Winston-Salem, North Carolina. We almost didn't get there, as midway through the eight-hour drive I announced in dramatic fashion that I still believed Northwestern was the only place for me. Mom pulled to the side of the road and said, "If you're not going to give this place a chance, I am going to turn around right now instead of wasting our time." She wasn't messing around. And she was right. I shut up, and we continued.

Arriving in Winston-Salem, we drove up a tree-lined hill that opened on a vast expanse of green. "It's beautiful," my mother said. But I scowled, reluctant to make a fast judgment, or even worse, be pushed to like it. After the campus tour, Mom was obviously excited: "So what do you think?" she asked. I mumbled something about the sports arena being too far from campus, an amusing complaint from a girl who had no interest in sports. I was still stuck and my mom could see it.

The deposit would be due soon, and my parents had already spent untold amounts of time and money trying to help me. It was time to draw a line in the campus dirt. My mother made it clear that they would not be paying two deposits.

"Aimee," she said, "Wake has a great reputation; it's small, but not too small. Look around you — it's beautiful, the people are kind and it feels like a family. What's not to like?" I didn't answer. She continued, "I think I am going to go buy a sticker for our car, what do you say?" I agreed, not feeling compelled to argue about a sticker, able to accept it mentally by telling myself "it's just a sticker after all." But we both knew it was more.

That night on the phone in our hotel room, I heard my mom tell my dad, as if in code, "Well, we bought a sticker for the car, Dan." And I think they both breathed a sigh of relief. The sticker was the type of commitment that I could handle. My mother knew me and it seems she knew her psychology as well. The sticker turned into the deposit, and the deposit turned into enrollment. And at the end of my freshman year, my mother and I again looked over that vast green expanse of campus together.

This time things were different. This time it was my home. We were swinging on swings that had been installed as a student art project. They were engraved with words like "dream" and "trust" and "hope" and "love" and I was crying because I did indeed love this place. That I had fallen in love so quickly and completely, after so much hesitancy and doubt, made it all the sweeter, and leaving it, even just for the summer, was one of the hardest things I had to do. My mother knew this. That was why we were on the swings. Just as I had to take baby steps to get to this place, I too had to take baby steps to leave it. So we swung for a while, and then Mom said, "Aimee… time to go." And though I didn't want to, I felt compelled to trust her. And as we walked up the hill to our car, where a streetlight illuminated the sticker that started it all, I knew why.

~Aimee Lorge

14

The Fertility Specialist

Mother love is the fuel that enables a normal human
being to do the impossible.
~Marion C. Garretty

y mother was a special woman. It's hard to put into words, but somehow we all believed she possessed a rare gift, like she always knew a bit more than she let on. Her premonitions were always spot-on. Deep down I knew I had inherited this ability, but I spoke of it infrequently or only when one of my predictions was proved accurate.

I was living in California in the 1990's, married with a five-year-old daughter. We had tried unsuccessfully for the past four years to have another child. I called my mom and she asked the usual question: "So, when are you having another child?"

I was one of nine, so having an only child was inconceivable to her. I explained that I had made an appointment with a fertility specialist. She responded as expected: "You don't need a fertility specialist. You just don't pray enough." I assured her that I prayed, but unfortunately I needed more than prayers at this point. My thirty-second birthday was around the corner and I really wanted answers.

A few days later, my beloved mom, who was barely seventy and in good health, unexpectedly died in her sleep. I went back to New Jersey for the funeral. It was surreal walking through the door and seeing her petite body in a casket; and then something even more surreal happened. I was halfway to her when I felt a force hitting me in the gut. It was like an air gun had hit me. I felt my body pushed back. I continued to make my way to her, but now with a smile. I knelt before her and shook my head. "I know what you just did. I know what just happened there. You never cease to amaze me, Helen."

The following day, which was my thirty-third birthday, my mom was laid to rest. I returned home to California exhausted and drained. I missed my little Lauren and needed to be home. I lugged my suitcase out of the car and began walking up the path to the front steps. The first thing I noticed was a box on my front porch. I put down my suitcase and with trembling hands I opened it. The first thing I saw was her handwriting on the outside of the birthday card. Inside the box was a beautiful white statue of a mom holding a baby boy. Today it remains in a hutch in my living room.

Logan was born on August 13, 1996, exactly nine months to the day after my mother was laid to rest.

~Mary Ellen Flaherty Langbein

15

Sleepless Nights

If you have a mom, there is nowhere you are likely to
go where a prayer has not already been.
~Robert Brault, www.robertbrault.com

Mom wasted no time returning my phone call. "Don't put the baby on eBay," she urged. "I'll be over in an hour to give you a break." She showed up in a few minutes and removed my screaming newborn from my arms. She proceeded to rock her grandchild and sing to him while I went upstairs for a nap.

It was a well-deserved rest. I had gone without a good night's sleep for the first four weeks of my child's life. While everyone else in the world counted sheep, I counted down the minutes until the baby's next feeding. That was when the room would finally be peaceful again. Then, in the early morning hours, I burped, changed, and rocked my baby as the sun rose on a new day.

There were times when my fatigue caused me to be a bit short tempered with my mom — a very silly thing to do when someone is offering you help. "You are not the only new mother who has ever felt stressed and overwhelmed," she reminded me. "We've all been there."

My mom told me about spending late nights and early mornings in the rocking chair. "There were times when I tried everything to get you to stop fussing. I was at the end of my rope. But those days passed quickly for me. They will for you too."

I knew she was right. It would pass quickly — too quickly — and then there would be other reasons for staying up all hours of the night: driver's licenses, proms, dates, etc.

I remember coming home a bit late from a date when I was a teenager. I slid my key in the lock, quietly turned the door handle and closed the door behind me. I tiptoed past the squeaky floorboards in the dining room and headed toward my room. Then, a light flicked on and there sat my mother, waiting for me in the living room.

"Where have you been?" she demanded. "You were supposed to be home at eleven o'clock."

"It's only midnight," I argued. "What difference does an hour make?"

My mom grounded me for arguing with her and for breaking my curfew. She tried to make me understand that she was only angry with me because she was worried. I thought she was mean and unfair. It would take me years to realize otherwise.

There were several other occasions when my mom went without sleep because of me. She tossed and turned when I moved two states away and she undoubtedly paced the halls when I announced that I had withdrawn from college. I kept her awake with the kind of worry that only a mother can feel.

It's four o'clock on a Wednesday morning and my baby and I are wide awake. He has eaten and has been changed but he will not stop fussing unless I hold him. So together we sway in the rocking chair, his tiny head against my chest and my head drooping from exhaustion.

Years from now, I will be awake for other reasons. He will be late for curfew, driving for the first time, or going away to college. I will wonder where he is and whether or not he is okay. I will long for the late nights and early mornings that we spent together in the rocking chair. Then, when the sun rises and the rest of the world is awake again, I will call my mother. She will understand.

~Melissa Face

16

Product Design

Children require guidance and sympathy far
more than instruction.
~Annie Sullivan

It seems like the day I started high school, every single teacher I had said that it was important to get good grades because then we'd have high GPAs, and then we'd be able to go to college. None of the teachers actually came right out and said it, but the unspoken message was that if you messed up even ONE SINGLE TIME, your entire life would be ruined. The pressure to look ahead to the future seemed to start the first day of high school.

I did okay in the first half of ninth grade. I took all the classes I was supposed to take and got mainly B's with a few A's tossed in. For electives, I had classes that I liked, a few I didn't, and some I couldn't wait to get through. But I passed them and that was all that mattered. I was always thinking about that stupid GPA and the fact that I had to keep at least a B average if I ever wanted to do something with my life other than collect aluminum cans from the side of the road.

Then came the second semester and an elective I took called Product Design. For some reason, I thought that this would be a class about designing things like labels or cereal box covers. I like to draw and I figured Product Design would be an easy A. How hard could it be to come up with a new design for a pop can?

It took about three seconds into the first hour of Product Design to figure out that I should have read the course description a whole lot more carefully. Product Design had nothing to do with logos or pop cans or cereal boxes. It was about using things like drills and lathes and welders. It was basically a metal shop class that I belonged in about as much as a candy bar belongs on the dashboard of a car on a ninety-degree day.

To make everything even worse, the teacher was one of those I'm-telling-you-this-for-your-own-good types. Only he wasn't only just telling us things for our own good — he liked being nasty when he told us we stunk at welding or drilling or whatever he had us do.

Looking back, I should have dropped Product Design after the first week. But I didn't. I kept waiting, thinking it would get better or I'd somehow miraculously get better at doing things I'd never done before. I also didn't drop because of my GPA. I wanted to keep it high and I was sure I could at least score a B in Product Design.

That was the longest semester of my life. Every single project I did was a nightmare. And everything took me two times longer to do than it did for the rest of the class. From January to May, my grade hovered around a C, and that was only with staying after school four days out of five to work on whatever the latest project was.

The stress was getting to me. At night I dreamed about welding. I woke up positive that I was going to weld my fingers together or go blind from the flame on the arc welder. I felt like I was going to throw up every time I stepped into the Product Design room. All I wanted was for the year to end.

But I didn't want to flunk. What would an F do to my GPA? I'd already decided that I wanted to go to college someday and I was pretty sure that I'd need a scholarship. So how could I get a scholarship if I got an F in Product Design?

And what about my parents? I'd never flunked anything before. They'd freak out if I brought home an F on my report card. I stopped having nightmares about welding because I stopped sleeping. All I could think about was why I didn't drop that stupid class when I had the chance.

Finally, after I messed up the last assignment and knew that I'd never be able to pull my grade up above a D, I told my mom. I figured that it would be better for her to know what was coming instead of being blindsided when report cards arrived.

She listened, nodded her head, and shrugged her shoulders. "Don't worry about it," she said.

I stared at her. She must not have been listening as closely as I thought she was. "I'm getting a D or an F in Product Design," I repeated.

"That happens," she said. "It's not the end of the world."

"But I might not be able to get into college!"

Mom looked at me. "Who told you that?"

"Everyone tells me that. The teachers, the guidance counselor—they all say you have to get all A's and B's if you want to go to college."

Mom hugged me. "Honey, you're a freshman in high school. Why are you worrying about college now? I didn't even think about college until I was a junior."

"It's different now."

"Not in this house," she told me. "You have plenty of time to get your GPA up. Tell me one thing: did you learn anything in Product Design?"

"Yeah. The teacher was a jerk."

"Did you learn anything about welding and metal work and all that other stuff?"

"Yes," I admitted. "But I suck at all of them."

"The point is, you know more now than you did going in. Isn't that what really counts?"

"I guess so."

"Then don't sweat it. And next year when you sign up for electives, you might want to know what you're taking first."

"Believe me, I will."

Mom hugged me again. I felt better. Not great, but better. And the more I thought about it, the more I decided she was probably right. I had three more years to take classes and get decent grades. I wasn't going to sweat it.

And I was definitely going to know what I was taking in every single class for the rest of my life.

~Hank Musolf

17

Party Invitation

A man has to live with himself, and he should see to it
that he always has good company.
~Charles Evans Hughes

I was excited. I had been invited to go to my friend's birthday party. Tori was not my best friend, but she was in my class and we did stuff together. And I liked to go to parties. I asked my mom and she said I could go, so I told Tori that I'd be there.

And then, two days later, my very, very best friend called. She and her family were going to Disneyland for the whole day. She invited me to go with them. Disneyland! I loved Disneyland so much. I really wanted to go... more than anything. I ran to ask my mom if it was okay. That's when my mom reminded me that Tori's party was on the same day. She said I couldn't change my mind just because something better came along.

I was mad. So mad. Disneyland was my most favorite place in the whole world and I loved to go there... and I especially liked going with my best friend. My excitement about going to the birthday party was gone. Tori's party would be okay but not as fun as a whole day at Disneyland, and besides that, Tori wasn't even my best friend. I begged my mom. She said no. I cried. I sulked. I pouted. My mom still said no. What I wanted to do wasn't nice. It wasn't right.

I couldn't get her to change her mind. I tried every excuse I could think of. My mom explained to me again — once you accept an invitation to something, you can't change your mind and go to something else just because you want to do the other thing more. That isn't nice. She asked me to think about how I would feel if someone did that to me. If someone had said they'd come to my party and then, because something better came along, they changed their minds and didn't come, how would I feel? I thought about it. Although I didn't want to admit it, my mom was right. It would hurt my feelings if someone did that to me. Although I didn't want to, I told my best friend that I wouldn't be able to go to Disneyland with her.

So my friend and her family went to Disneyland and my mom dropped me off at Tori's party. I did not want to be there. But something interesting happened after I got there. In spite of the fact that I had not wanted to go, I had a great time! We did stuff that was fun and different. We watched a movie that hadn't come out in theaters yet; we were the first people to see it and that was pretty amazing. There was a make-your-own pizza contest. We each got a piece of dough and then there were all of these toppings to choose from. We all got covered in pizza dough, cheese and toppings. You're supposed to take a present to the birthday person and we all did. But Tori's mom and dad had a special present to give to each of us too! That was so cool.

When my mom came to pick me up I didn't want to leave. After we got home I told my mom all about the fun things we had done. She was so glad that I'd had a good time and she told me that she was proud of me for understanding why you can't just dump someone because something better comes along. Not only did I love the party and have a great time, but I learned an important lesson. My mom was right… as usual.

~Barbara LoMonaco

18

A Positive Step

The first step binds one to the second.
~French Proverb

"I don't want her to come," I whispered conspiratorially to my brother. At fourteen, he was three years older and, from my eleven-year-old perspective, much braver than me. Not only did I look up to him, but I trusted him to stand up for me, and to speak for me when I was too afraid. And he did.

"Dad," he said to our father from across the tiny apartment. "We really just want it to be the three of us."

It was Fourth of July weekend, and we were heading downtown to watch the fireworks. Me, my brother, my dad, a blanket to sit on, a cooler filled with soda pop, and fireworks to light up the sky were on my agenda. My dad's girlfriend was not part of my plan.

My father was angry. And hurt. He had been dating Mary for several months and he wanted us to accept her. We saw her as competition. What little time we had with him, we didn't want to share. Not only was I protective of my time with my dad, but I worried about my mom, too. In my own mind I thought that if I let myself like Mary, I'd be hurting my mom. My dad had already decided that he liked her better than my mom. What if my mom thought we liked her better, too?

Dad remarried a few years later, but it took me much longer than that to even give Mary a fair chance. She was always kind to my brother and me. But, I think I held back from a false sense of loyalty to Mom.

Twenty years later, while my husband and I were in the midst of our own divorce, my boys, nine and seven, came home from a visit with their dad in tears. They confided in me that their dad had sat them down earlier in the day and told them he had a girlfriend. Patty, he told them, would be spending quite a bit of time with them. I knew the boys thought she was nice. I knew that if they decided not to like her, it might be because they somehow felt that they needed to, out of loyalty to me. I didn't want my kids to make the same mistake I did.

You see Mary has been like a second mother to me. She takes nothing away from my mom, who is wonderful in her own right, but Mary has been another person in my life who I can lean on. Technically, I am Mary's stepdaughter. But when she looks at me, she sees no "step" — she sees someone she loves, someone she'd do anything for — and she has. She has been there for me through thick and thin. And she loves my kids the same way their biological grandparents do.

So when my boys looked at me that night and told me about Patty, I thought about all the years I'd wasted being angry with Mary. I could finally see some good coming out of that difficult time.

"Guys, listen," I said to my boys. "I know exactly what you're going through." They both rolled their eyes. "No, really." I tucked a foot under me and leaned forward. "After my mom and dad got divorced, my dad got a girlfriend."

"Papa had a girlfriend?" asked seven-year-old Jack. Now they were both interested.

"Yep. And I didn't like her at all. I was afraid that she would try to be my new mom. And I already had a mom I loved very much. I was scared. And I thought if I liked her it would make my mom sad. And she was already sad."

They both nodded, completely familiar with the emotions that I had gone through all those years ago when I was eleven.

"Well, I guess I just wish my mom would have told me it was okay to like my dad's girlfriend, because it turns out she was a really neat person and I wasn't nice to her for a very long time, because no one ever told me it was okay."

The room was quiet. My boys looked at each other and then at me.

"Guys? Do you know who that girlfriend was?" They both shook their heads.

"Your Grandma Mary." Nine-year-old Connor looked at me with big, round eyes.

"Grandma Mary?" exclaimed Jack. "Wow!"

"Yep. Can you even imagine your life without Grandma Mary in it?"

"No," they said in unison.

"So," I said, taking each of their little hands in mine. "I want to tell you right now that it's absolutely okay for you to like Patty. You are not going to hurt my feelings. And you are not going to make me sad if you enjoy your time with her and your dad. She's a nice person, and as long as she's nice to the two of you and your little sister, then that's all I care about. Okay?"

I got big hugs that night. As a child going through the pain and sadness of my own parents' divorce, I couldn't possibly have imagined that one day I would actually be grateful for that experience. But, all these years later, it turned out to be a wonderful gift that I was able to give my own children. Everything happens for a reason, and now I finally understood that what I had gone through as a child had given me the tools to help my own children when they needed it most.

~Beth M. Wood

19

Ugly

Everything has beauty, but not everyone sees it.
~Confucius

*I*t was the last day of school before winter vacation. Gray clouds drifted across the darkening sky; icy winds whipped outside my sixth grade math class, and despite the fact that I normally paid very close attention in class, I found myself slipping into a reverie. After all, how could one focus when Christmas and all its joy were just a few days away?

The bell rang and students darted out of classrooms. I joined the crowds, in a daze as backpack after backpack thumped against my body and voices roared over my head.

I made my way out of the school, and smiled as I saw my twin sister Meli and our good friend Peter chatting near a frozen tree. I raced toward them, and I found Meli wearing an odd, almost breezy smile. Peter's eyes glowed with the promise of juicy gossip.

"Hey," I said, glancing toward our temporarily immobile school bus waiting a good distance away. I didn't want to miss my ride home, after all.

"Aaron called us ugly," my sister said. "Peter sits with them in math class and he told me. Sam said you did a weird licking thing with your tongue whenever you talk, too," she added.

For a moment I was stunned, confused, and sad. In an instant, those emotions melted together into humiliation and shame.

Meli seemed oblivious to my hurt feelings. "I don't even know who

Aaron is," she admitted and Peter laughed. I thought for a moment. It was our first few months in the new middle school. Both boys were from the elementary school on the other side of town, and I knew Sam from numerous classes we had together. I only vaguely recalled Aaron. He was a jock with a petite girlfriend.

My eyes began to tear up. "Thanks a lot, Peter," I managed to spit out before racing away from the people who I couldn't wait to talk to moments before.

I rushed toward the bus, burrowing into the corner of a two-seater. My breath fogged up the cold window I leaned my cheek against. I fought the lump in my throat, the tears behind my eyes. As if things couldn't get any worse, a girl I was slightly friendly with sat next to me. We had played softball together for the last few years on the recreational team and lived near one another. I turned my face away from her as the first hot tear rolled down my cheek. She said a few things to me, nothing I can remember. It took her a moment to realize I was crying, I believe, and she stopped talking. I silently thanked her.

All my insecurities had transformed into sharp knives, and each one was stabbing me over and over again, a relentless force.

My hair was too frizzy. My eyes too brown. I had uncool clothes. I was fat. I was ugly.

Ugly.

After what seemed like a million years, the bus rolled to a stop in front of my house. Hunching forward, I stepped out, my sister walking quickly several feet in front of me.

I was eager to tell my mom about my horrible day, but my sister sprinted upstairs first, and I couldn't bear to face both of them at once.

I took a few minutes to wash my puffy face, trying to hide the tears I'd shed. My mother would make it better, I knew. Well, I hoped. At this point, it was the only thing I had left to hold onto.

When I heard my sister heading into the kitchen, I trudged upstairs. My mom was typing away on her laptop, her glasses propped on the straight bone of her nose. She looked up when I entered.

"A boy at school called me ugly," I said, my voice drained of any pride, my pulled-together demeanor crumbling.

Mom nodded. "He called Meli ugly, also."

My eyes stung as that awful lump swelled again in my throat. "Well, a different boy said I did a weird thing with my tongue, too!"

My mother switched gears from college professor to concerned mother. "Come here," she soothed, and I fell onto her bed, as my repressed tears sprang forward.

"Meli said she didn't care. She didn't know the boy," Mom said matter-of-factly.

"He's in my advisory!" I spit out. This wasn't working out as I'd planned; my mother simply didn't understand the pain I was feeling.

She looked at me with wide green eyes. "Do you care?"

I jumped off the bed, wiped away my tears and yelled, "You don't get it!" I slammed her door and stormed to our bottom floor, past my older brother Matt and into our overheated laundry room, where my sister and I shared a computer.

My heart ached and anger surged through every one of my limbs.

How dare they destroy my vacation, I thought bitterly, cursing Sam and especially Aaron.

The fury was overwhelming and it took up so much space in my body it cast away everything else: my good grades, my loyal friends, any confidence I had in myself. I was a mess, and all because of one little word. A few minutes later, my mom quietly entered the room and sat next to me. "Al," she said and I looked at her. "I don't want you to be upset. He's just a boy. One boy might think licking your lips or whatever is weird; another might think it's beautiful." She went on. "And so what if one person thinks you're ugly? You're not ugly. Not everyone will think you're great looking, but no one will think you're ugly, because you're not. Even Matt said he's just some stupid boy."

I looked at her and nodded. My anger toward her melted away easily, as it always did. We embraced and I felt slightly better. Everything she said made sense. Considering she was my mother, her compliments weren't the biggest confidence booster, but I could feel my spirits lift a little bit.

Two and a half years later, my life has moved on from the words of two boys I had barely ever spoken to. Still, there have been days when

I've gone back to that horrible moment in time, and felt myself shrink back to sixth grade. I've used it as an excuse to cry, to pity myself. But, I've realized over the years that if I render those two boys and their words powerless, then I am the one in power, and I choose when and why I don't feel good about myself. I am superior.

No one, I think, ever forgets the first person who calls them ugly. But, I'm lucky enough to realize that I don't need to forget what happened to understand that other people's words — no matter how cruel — are as important as I make them. In this case, they're meaningless.

~Ali Lauro

20

The Most Important Day of My Life

You are never given a wish, without also being given
the power to make it come true.
~Richard Bach

"He has suffered brain damage," the doctor gravely told my mother after I was born. "We're not sure about the extent, but he will never walk or speak. He's probably severely retarded, and I suggest you find a suitable institution in which to place him."

That's what people did with their developmentally disabled children in 1960. They called them "retarded" and they put them in institutions. Mom's response was a stubborn determination to prove him wrong.

Due to a prenatal injury, I was born with a subdural hematoma on the top right side of my head. It was the size of an orange, and the blood put pressure on my brain. Doctors assumed the injury was severe enough to significantly limit my muscular and cognitive functions. They had not, however, met a mother so fiercely devoted to her children.

My mischievous four-year-old brother had played a role in this saga. He had asked why the baby hadn't arrived as scheduled. Mom had shrugged and told him I just wasn't ready.

"What would make him ready, Mommy?" he asked.

"I don't know," she replied. "Perhaps if I slipped and fell…"

You can guess what happened next. Billy spread magazines all over the tile floor. Then he yelled "Mommy, Mommy, come quick!"

Mom flew through the door, slipped on the magazines, and fell. I was born the next day.

The next year should have been one of firsts, but mine came slower than average. I lacked any muscle tone. The lump gradually melted away, and portraits show a healthy child. What you can't see are Mom's hands supporting me from behind because I couldn't sit up. Although my motor skills were lacking, my cognitive abilities convinced her I was normal.

Mom began to exercise my flaccid limbs. She cross-patterned left arm to right leg, reversed, and repeated after each diaper change. Challenging me to push and pull against her pressure, she coaxed my muscles to work. Progress was slow, but she persevered.

Several trips to "crippled children" hospitals didn't convince specialists of any progress. At eighteen months, I refused to speak to doctors. This convinced them I was also mentally disabled. During one visit, *after* the doctor left the room, I asked, "Go home now?"

Accelerating the "workouts" earned dividends. At age two I could sit up and scoot around on my behind, yet I didn't crawl. A torturous device was added: the "standing box." Locked into an upright position, I screamed for freedom. Mom had to reassure the neighbors I wasn't being abused. Gradually, my leg muscles strengthened. My brain learned balance. After each session, she would hold me close, reassuring me I would someday walk. She was gentle but firm in her resolve.

For six months this device was my daily nightmare, but it worked. One day, as I was mimicking TV cartoon characters, I jumped up and started running around the room. Laughing and jumping around, I called out to Mom. She watched silently from the kitchen doorway, nodding through a veil of tears. Finally, her little Patrick had defied the "experts."

Although I don't remember this specific moment, I'm told this bright March day became the most important of my life.

Mom took me back to the hospital, where I walked for the stunned specialists. Her dedication had trumped their expertise. They remained convinced I was mentally deficient because I still refused to speak to them. Mom's disdain had evidently rubbed off on me; it would be a while before I spoke to a doctor.

Although the doctors stubbornly disagreed, my parents enrolled me in preschool. Already able to read and write, I excelled. Therapy improved my slurred speech. I grew into a happy and healthy little boy.

When I reached third grade, I did not get along with my teacher. I decided she was a worm-faced monster. She was mean and insulting. I lost interest in school.

"He's retarded, Mrs. Coomer," Mrs. Battle-Axe said. "He doesn't belong in my class."

My mother responded fiercely, in front of the school principal and psychologist. "No, he's not," she exclaimed. "You're the one who's retarded. Patrick just doesn't like you, and I don't either. He's plenty smart enough to succeed, but he needs someone who inspires him. You are right about one thing: he doesn't belong in your class."

I was transferred into a class taught by a young lady who was sweet and patient. My grades soared.

As I grew into adolescence, my legs grew stronger. I played basketball, but my upper body remained weak. I ran twenty miles daily on my high school cross-country team, which won two state championships. An honor roll student, I wrote for the school newspaper and participated in several clubs.

During my first year of college, I was editor of our award-winning student newspaper. Mom urged me to keep writing when I left journalism. She encouraged boldness, refused to accept excuses, and cheered every success.

Ornery yet fun, Mom was intelligent and opinionated. Her love of history and literature inspired me to read the classics. She respected diversity and resented bigotry. As our political beliefs diverged, our debates were spirited but respectful. Her grasp of history demanded I argue with facts, not rhetoric. We became close friends, even during some rough stretches. Although she could make me angry, I knew her love for me was steadfast. Many who were diagnosed as I was were indeed forgotten. Because of her, I've challenged my own children to never say, "I can't."

Mom passed away nine years ago, but not before I provided my parents with plenty of grandchildren, including my first child, Anna, who even gave them a great-grandson.

Knowing Mom would be angry if I melted with grief at her passing, I coached my son's basketball team that evening. Later, on my nightly walk, each step was a memorial to her devotion. Tears of gratitude mixed with the cold Oregon rain, and I lost track of my lap count. It seemed fitting to walk for hours. It was the best memorial I could give her.

At her service, I recited Robert Frost's poem, "The Road Less Traveled."

Thanks, Mom… the road you chose has made all the difference.

~Patrick B. Coomer

21

The Last Night Home

How lucky I am to have something that makes saying goodbye so hard.
~Carol Sobieski and Thomas Meehan, Annie

I have many photographs tacked to the corkboard above my college desk. One of my family, one of my cats, a few of favorite musicians and concerts, and one giant picture of twelve kids piled on a couch, several caught unaware and mid-laugh as others pulled goofy faces with arms draped over shoulders and limbs tangled in a teenage heap.

That moment, captured on my last night in my hometown with my high school friends, occurred only a few short hours before the night ended and I retreated to my room in tears. After an entire summer of excitement and dorm-shopping, a summer spent anticipating college freedom, I suddenly looked at my packed belongings and reality hit me like an eighteen-wheel semi — I was leaving.

I was one of those sheltered kids, the first-born and only girl, who never went to sleep-away camp, had never traveled alone, and had never spent more than two or three nights away from her parents at a time. Born and raised in suburban Ohio, I had convinced myself that what I desperately wanted was an escape from the Midwest cornfields. So why, on the brink of leaving for our nation's capital, was I terrified out of my wits?

In all my excitement over college and everything it stood for (freedom, novelty, adulthood, independence), I had forgotten the sacrifice

I made when I chose Georgetown over universities closer to home—I had chosen to leave my friends and family behind. Too shortsighted to remember that I'd be home soon enough for Thanksgiving break, I bid my friends farewell that night as if I were on my deathbed, and began to sob uncontrollably when I shut the front door behind the last of them. Withdrawing to my room, I cried until there was nothing wet left inside me, and then wandered aimlessly and zombie-like under the pretense of packing my last few possessions.

Soon enough, I heard my mom's soft knock at my door. I sat still and waited for her to leave, reasoning that hugging my mother and seeing her sympathy would only make it harder to say goodbye to her later. Predictably, she didn't go away, and I turned away in a (poor) attempt to hide my tear-streaked face as she let herself into my room and sat down on my bed.

"What's wrong?" she asked gently.

Rather than attempt an intelligible and thought-out response, I simply began to sob again and buried my head in her shoulder. Somewhere in between my blubbering, I managed to choke out, "I'm... not... r-ready...."

My mom stroked my hair until I calmed down enough to listen, and then held me by the shoulders and looked me in the eyes. "I know you're not ready, Michelle... none of us is until it actually happens. I'm not ready to say goodbye to you either. But, you know what? I've seen how capable you are. I know how smart you are. And I'm absolutely positive that you'll be fine. You know why?"

I shook my head slowly, squinting as hard as I could to keep fresh tears from burning their way down my cheeks.

"Because I've seen how far you've already come. I know you can do this. It's hard, I won't deny that, but you know that I'm here for you, and that I'll be right there with you every step of the way." She brushed the tears from my face and stood, darting into the hallway and calling, "Stay right there... I'll be right back...."

I waited on my bed, looking at the boxes and bags surrounding me in an empty room I barely recognized as mine. Finally she returned with a bag, handing it to me and explaining, "I had been waiting to give this to you when we got there, but you look like you could use this right now instead."

I opened the bag, and inside I found an old and tattered stuffed rabbit that I had clung to throughout my childhood. He was always my favorite and my most battered, and I had thought he was lost for the last several years. Alongside it was a DVD of a *My Little Pony* movie I had almost forgotten existed. We had rented that movie so many times in my younger years that it surprises me we didn't simply buy it — we must have paid rental fees at least ten times what the movie was actually worth.

I stared at these gifts, two simple yet central parts of my childhood, and couldn't find words. Instead, I let new tears escape as my mother wrapped her arms around me once again, rocking me like she would when I was younger.

"I just wanted to give you these to let you know that, no matter how old you get, it's always okay to still be a little girl."

In that moment I knew that she understood and I realized that the world was not going to end when I moved into my dorm. With a mix of sadness and excitement, I prepared myself to enter this new world, knowing that I was finally ready to leave.

~Michelle Vanderwist

22

Celebrating the Tears

Today I close the door to the past, open the door to
future, take a deep breath, step on through and start a
new chapter in my life.
~Author Unknown

I stared with dread at the square on the calendar. The words "Moving Day" seemed to gleam on the page as if printed in neon lights, not black ink. A lump rose in my throat every time I thought of leaving our apartment in Virginia. I'd known when I'd married my husband John, an officer in the Navy, that we'd have to move often. I just hadn't known how hard it would be. I hadn't grown up in a military family. In fact, I'd lived in the same house for twenty-two years before I'd become a wife. The closer the time approached for us to leave the life we'd made together in Virginia, the more depressed I grew.

When the packers came I watched in despair as they quickly wrapped up bits and pieces of our home in sheets of paper and stuffed them into boxes. Then they pulled out rolls of tape and sealed up the cardboard. A few words scrawled on the side of the box, "baby's room — toys," "kitchen — silverware," and the comfortable life we'd had was stuffed out of sight.

That night I sat at the kitchen table and called my mother-in-law. She'd been a self-described "corporate nomad" for most of her married life, never living anywhere for longer than three years. I figured if anyone could understand my anxiety, she could.

"How are you holding up?" she asked.

My gaze drifted over the stacks of boxes now filling the living room. "I don't know how you did it."

"Did what?"

"Moved so many times. This is killing me."

"Physically?"

"No." I sighed. "Mentally. I don't want to leave. I love it here."

"Good."

Her enthusiastic reply surprised me. "You're happy that I'm sad?"

Her warm chuckle brought a smile to my face, even though I was confused. "Let me tell you something, I've lived in more houses, in more states than I can count, and I listened to a lot of the corporate wives moan and groan with each new transfer. I decided early on not to be one of them."

"How'd you do that?"

"Think of each move as a new adventure. I vowed to explore each place as much as I could with the kids. They knew more about every new state than people who had lived there their whole lives because we didn't take anything for granted. Every vacation we'd take a road trip to some new corner or historic site."

My heart lightened as my mother-in-law continued, "I always said, 'If I don't cry when I move away, I wasted my time.' I don't know about you, but life's too short to waste any of it, don't you think?"

Her motto stuck with me through my twenty years as a military wife. We made the most of every new duty station. We've walked through Revolutionary War forts in New England, panned for gold in California and slept with the sharks in a Florida aquarium. I tried to instill in my kids the same view of life. Every move is an opportunity, a chance to see new things and make new friends. And even though I cried as I left each home, I celebrated the fact that I hadn't wasted my time.

~Kim Stokely

23

The Tiny Waist of the Fifties

Life is really simple, but we insist on
making it complicated.
~Confucius

S he looked like June Cleaver except for her red hair. Like
many young mothers in the fifties, mine often did housework in what she called a "housedress." It was nothing like
the slouchy sweats I wear today to tackle the toilet bowl, the
kitchen floor, and the cobwebs in the corners.

The housedresses our mothers wore then were unique. They were
cotton and had to be ironed. They buttoned down the front to about
six inches below the waist or nearly to the hem. The waistline of that
dress still amazes me after all these years. Mom's waist could not have
been more than twenty-two inches. The dress always had a belt that
defined her tiny waistline.

That housedress, with its tiny belt-covered waist, represents an
era when people didn't discuss or worry about weight control. It was
something that happened due to lifestyle. Diet programs and books
were much less prevalent.

Most of my adult life, I fought to keep my weight under control.
It was a struggle at which I had varying degrees of success. I tried fad
diets as well as healthy diets. The struggle occupied too much of my
time and thought, almost to the point of obsession.

About three years ago, the image of my mom's belted housedress began to flit across my mind frequently enough that I deemed it important. I decided to evaluate her lifestyle compared to mine. Surely there was something about how her generation lived that kept most of them trim even into their later years.

Here is what I found:

- We never ate more than one thin pork chop each. When Mom opened a can of vegetables, it was shared by four of us. Our hamburgers were probably about a sixth of a pound. Weekday breakfasts were a piece of toast, milk, and juice. Yet, I never remember passing out from hunger. Conclusion: If we eat smaller portions, we will survive until the next meal.

- We ate a wide variety of fruits and vegetables. Living in an agricultural community, we had access to fresh produce, which Mom canned. Although we had meat at most meals, produce dominated our plates. We always had some type of starch with our meals. Conclusion: Starch is not bad. Meat is not bad. The idea is to use them as additions to our meals rather than the mainstay.

- We ate food close to its source. We did not have packaged food until I was in high school. About that time, the infamous frozen potpie arrived. It was totally disgusting, so we seldom ate it. Conclusion: There's something about real food that promotes good health.

- Neither of my parents ever obsessed about food. If we had homemade ice cream, we all enjoyed it. I suspect Mom's bowl was smaller than Dad's, but she never mentioned the fact. We all enjoyed the ice cream guilt-free. I think my mom's idea was that if she could get enough veggies into us during the meal, there wouldn't be a lot of room for dessert. Besides, most of our desserts came from the fruit bowl. Conclusion: No food is bad. And, it may be that spending too much time analyzing one's diet causes problems.

- Mom and Dad did all their own work. Mom did the shopping, cleaning, laundry, cooking, sewing, and childcare. Dad did the yard and repair work. They raised chickens and put them in the freezer to enjoy through the year. Together, they painted and papered walls, waxed floors, and cleaned rugs. Conclusion: There was no need for a gym membership when there was so much to do at home.

- Television and computers didn't dominate our lives. Even after we bought a TV, we chose to be active. Although we weren't jogging or working out on a piece of machinery, we were moving most of the time. Even our winter taffy pulls burned more calories than sitting in front of a screen. Conclusion: An active lifestyle is conducive to trim waists and good health.

- We ate supper at six o'clock and had nothing else to eat until breakfast. That gave us about a twelve-hour fast each night. Conclusion: Bodies do well not having a continual inflow of food.

After I looked at how a family of the fifties lived, it was apparent that our twenty-first-century lifestyle was responsible for the differences in our waistlines. I decided to make some changes.

I knew any modifications needed to be gradual so I could fully embrace them. Drastic changes usually end in failure.

I set up these guidelines, knowing it would take time to totally adopt them:

- Decrease portion sizes drastically. Picture the one-fourth-can serving size of my youth.
- Plan for my plate to be two-thirds plant-based food, light on white starches.
- Quit talking and thinking about food and diets.
- Increase the amount of work I do in the house and yard. Include regular gym-type exercise because I use work-saving devices not available fifty years ago.

- Decrease screen time.
- Eat supper early and then fast until breakfast.

Has it worked? It has been three years. During that time, I have very gradually lost fifteen pounds. That is not the "fifteen pounds in two weeks" many fad diets advertise. But slow is okay, because I know I am changing.

I changed how I think about food. I know that I will not fall over if I eat a light meal. It's okay to leave food on my plate. I learned that a meal heavy on meat makes me feel sluggish, so I look for ways to get more vegetables on my plate. I eat my larger meal at noon and try to have a light supper early.

I changed how I feel about exercise. It is now like the air I breathe — necessary for my wellbeing, rather than something I force on myself. I do some weight training and yoga. I walk outside if the weather is nice, or I watch the news while I'm on the treadmill. I have a shelf for my computer in front of the treadmill, allowing me to watch inspiring or educational videos.

What is in my future? I may never totally adhere to my guidelines. I sometimes eat too much. There are times when I eat late. I don't think about food and diets as much as I once did, but here I am writing about them now.

However, I don't believe I will ever again have an issue with weight. I expect to slowly lose a few more pounds until I am where I should be. I doubt I will wear housedresses with belted waists even if they do come back in style. It is enough to be strong and healthy, and to have more pleasant things on my mind than the number of calories in a food or whether or not it is "on my diet."

~Carole A. Bell

for Mom, with love

Thanks for Being There

Best friends come and go, boyfriends and girlfriends love and move on, bosses hire and fire but the only person present through it all is a mother. Thanks for always being there for me.
~Author Unknown

24

A Child Like Me?

There are no unwanted children, just unfound families.
~The National Adoption Center

With saddened eyes and head bent low,
It's damaged goods most see.
With my unclear past and broken heart,
Who would want a child like me?

I watch her walk into the room.
From a distance I can see.
But dare I take a closer step?
Who would want a child like me?

And then I see her look my way.
She smiles so tenderly.
But do I even dare to dream,
She would want a child like me?

And then, as if I spoke out loud,
She approaches cautiously.
I try so hard to once believe,
She will want a child like me.

But dare I once let down my guard,
And trust that she will see,
Hiding beneath this old stained shirt,
Is a beautiful child like me?

My smile, they say, lights up a room.
I'll be good as good can be.
Oh, please, dear God, let her want
A special child like me.

I feel her hand reach out for mine,
And within her eyes I see,
A single, tiny, shining tear.
Could she want a child like me?

And when she takes me in her arms,
With a warmth so pure and new,
She says the words I've prayed to hear,
"The child I want is *you*."

~Lisa J. Schlitt

25

My Mother, My Father, My Everything

She raised us with humor, and she raised us to
understand that not everything was going to be
great — but how to laugh through it.
~Liza Minnelli

t was the happiest day of my life. I was dressed in a long, white gown with a train that filled the room and glass slippers on my feet like Cinderella on her way to the ball. My mother's pearls floated around my neck and an old handkerchief made by my great grandmother resided on my heart. A new veil with scattered pearls to match my dress was tucked into my twists and curls; a borrowed tiara was the perfect accessory and a blue garter was hidden under the layers of fabric, beads and crinoline.

My mother stood where a father should be, beaming with pride. Although I did not have a father to walk me down the aisle, give me away or share the traditional father/daughter dance, I did not feel slighted. My mother had always played both roles as a mother and a father to my brothers and me. She hugged and disciplined us. She helped with homework and shared our joy when we passed a test. She taught us how to love each other even when we were pulling hair or fighting over a toy. She taught us the importance of family. She was, to us, our everything — and still is today.

My husband, Nick, proposed to me when I was twenty-five. My

mother asked if I would like my older brother or my uncle to walk me down the aisle. I responded with, "No Mom, you have always been my mom and my dad and you are the only one who can give me away."

The morning of my wedding day passed quickly. My mother never left my side. She was there for hair, make-up, and helping me put my gown on. Once I was ready, my mom and I stood alone. She was dressed in a long, pale blue spaghetti-strapped dress that made her look thirty years younger and more like a bridesmaid than the mother of a twenty-six-year-old bride. She was beautiful. She knew all the right words to say to calm my nerves and assure me that everything would be okay. No one else could have taken her place.

The tears did not begin for either of us until my pastor said it was time for her to give me away. At that moment it became real to both of us; I was really getting married. As we embraced, the room full of people disappeared and it was only my mom and me. Silent promises were exchanged. This is not a farewell, Mom, this is not the end; this is a new beginning and I am not leaving you behind.

Since my mom and I broke all the traditional rules, we kept the theme going with our mother/daughter dance. It was a medley of a few songs that told our story. Starting with "Shall We Dance," a song we often danced to in the kitchen at home, moving onto "Girls Just Want to Have Fun," and finishing with "Last Dance."

My wedding, much like my life, was not ordinary or normal. Thank you, Mom, for teaching me how to laugh when I wanted to cry, encouraging me to write even though I was shy, for loving me with the strength of two parents and above all, for being there.

~Natalie Scott

Coming Home

Having a place to go — is a home. Having someone to
love — is a family. Having both — is a blessing.
~Donna Hedges

A vibrant blaze of autumn colors swept by my window as we drove down the road. My grandpa, hands tight on the steering wheel, was telling me a story about his childhood. I smiled, but as hard as I tried to pay attention, my mind was on other things. This was my first trip home as a college freshman. My grandparents had made the two-hour drive to my school so that I could come home for fall break.

I should have felt relaxed and free from my heavy class load, but instead I was weighed down by a different burden. What if home didn't feel like home anymore? I had only been away for a couple of months, but my whole world had changed. Most of them were good changes, but I needed home to be somewhere familiar, a solid foundation to anchor myself. What if this part of my life had changed too?

"Are you okay, honey?" My grandma patted my arm. "You seem quiet."

"I'm fine, just tired from late-night studying," I said.

"Well you should get plenty of time to rest soon. We're just about at your house," she said.

We rounded the last corner and I could see our big house peeking around the maple tree in the front yard. Everything looked exactly as it should. The fence my dad and I had built wrapped around the lawn. I could see the worn picnic table and my childhood swingset in the yard. My brothers' bikes were abandoned on the driveway. It all looked the same. It should have felt the same too. It didn't.

For some reason, I felt like I was looking at somebody else's home. It seemed like the life I had lived in that house belonged to another person. Everything was so different now. How had that happened in such a short time?

Before the van was even in park, a jumble of blond heads raced across the driveway. I opened the car door and scooped up my two smallest brothers. We passed around hugs and smiles as my parents came out to join us.

"It's good to see you," my dad said as he laid his hand on my shoulder.

My mom had tears in her eyes. "We're so happy that you're back," she said. "Let's head inside. I have some homemade chocolate chip cookies fresh out of the oven."

As we moved into the house I tried to shake off my unease. It was silly for me to feel this way. I didn't want these doubts to ruin my time with my family, so I pushed them as far back in my mind as I could. We gathered around the dining room table. The boys hit me with a barrage of excited questions.

"What kind of food do you eat at college?"

"What does your dorm room look like?"

"Do you have to make your bed?"

I shot back answers to all of their questions, but I couldn't help but feel strange about it. Like I was a visitor sharing about my life somewhere else. I felt even more disconnected when I heard about all of the things I had missed in the last two months. They talked about new family friends whom I hadn't met and new activities they were involved in. Things I hadn't heard in our phone calls and read in e-mails.

The afternoon slipped by as we swapped stories. When the darkness started to sneak in through the picture window my grandparents decided they should head home. We walked them to their car.

"It's such a blessing to have you back for the weekend," my mom shared quietly.

"I'm so glad to be here," I replied. Silently, I wondered if my family saw me as a guest for the weekend. I just wanted this place to still be my home.

My mom had made my favorite dinner. We ate it together and then watched a movie in the living room. Then it was time to go to bed, and the lights flipped off one by one while I heard as many "goodnights" as John-Boy Walton.

I brushed my teeth and got a drink of water before I headed to my room. When I opened the door, I found everything where it should be. Which was weird. Because nothing was ever where it should be in my room. Tonight, it looked so nice and tidy. I knew right away that my mom had straightened up, and I was grateful. But it still felt like somebody else's room. I walked over to my bed. The sheets were crisply folded and the comforter smooth. The kind of smooth that belonged in a movie or a magazine. Something else stood out as unusual. A simple brown envelope propped against my pillow. I carefully broke the seal and slid out a note that said:

Logan,
I'm so happy for where you've been, but I am so glad to have you home.
Love,
Mom

And suddenly, the doubt was gone. I knew I was home. It didn't matter how much time I spent here. It didn't matter what things I missed out on. As long as I was part of this family, I knew this house would be my home. No matter what had changed or would change in my life, this was a constant. Something that I could always count on. So, as I stood there in my room, holding that handwritten note, I let go of my fear and confusion. Then I mussed up my bed sheets just for good measure.

~Logan Eliasen

27

Always a Mother

Mother is a verb, not a noun.
~Proverb

I had just heard two of the most dreaded words in the English language: "It's cancer." My husband gripped my hand, as I struggled not to dissolve into tears. "I want my mother," my inner child wailed. I craved the reassurance, the support that only a mother could give.

But she was the one person I couldn't turn to. Her home was hundreds of miles away, and she lived in the fog of Alzheimer's.

For more than five years the dementia had stalked her, ripping away memory and severing logic, leaving confusion and fear in its wake. During those years, she'd become the child. I mothered her through bouts of panic, when she couldn't remember where her home was. I comforted her when she cried as she relived her own mother's death. I calmed her when dementia-induced fear erupted in a temper tantrum. I metaphorically tucked her into bed each night, sending her kisses over the phone line while my own heart fractured.

Now, when dementia gnawed on her mind and cancer ate away at my body, numb hopelessness enveloped me. I didn't dare let the word cancer slip into the daily conversations with my mother.

Yet she knew things weren't right, and the protective wall I'd built around her began to crumble. At first it was a tiny chink, brought about by her insistence that something was wrong with me. The chink cracked and widened until the wall crashed down. She demanded I tell her my secrets. I stopped holding back and shared the news of my impending surgery—still careful not to use the "C" word, but admitting my other fears.

She asked if I'd have a scar.

Yes, I would.

"Well," she said, "I think a diamond necklace should cover it nicely."

I smiled.

Together with my stepfather, she made the 500-mile trek to my house to "help" me through the treatments. On the eve of my surgery, family surrounded me.

At the hospital, as the team prepared to wheel me away, my mother pushed past my husband to grab my hand. "I love you," she whispered fiercely, her eyes blazing as she bent close and kissed my cheek. In that moment, the tears I'd held at bay for months broke free and the fear loosened its grip.

By some miracle, my mother had thrown off the dementia, fighting her way through the fog to be at my side. She'd come to me when I needed her most. Her spirit was stronger than the disease.

The moment of grace lasted through the hours of surgery and beyond. During the night, my husband sat at my bedside, while my mother and stepfather managed alone in my house, without the benefit of their routine. They stayed with us through the days of recovery until I was home and safe.

Then, the fog descended again. Dementia locked my mother away and I returned to parenting her. But with a difference.

She'd taught me something. This, her last and best lesson, was that the mind might fail. The body may deteriorate. But the spirit will remain strong.

As she slipped further away from us in mind and body, I began to watch for glimpses of that indomitable spirit. Sometimes, it tiptoed in with flashes of humor. Once, while visiting, I lost my train of thought. "I'm sorry, sweetheart," she said as she smiled and patted my hand. "I didn't know it was contagious."

At other times it stomped in with a stubborn declaration. "You're not the boss of me!" my mother shouted when I encouraged her to take a hated medicine.

But mostly, it appeared in her constant determination to live life on her terms. She fought to stay with her family, surrendering to death only on her terms, and in her time. She left surrounded by her children, husband, and friends — that spirit still intact.

Even today, her spirit whispers to me that nothing — neither death nor dementia — can stand in the way of love.

~Kelle Z. Riley

28

Happy Birthday, My Sunshine

Coincidence is God's way of remaining anonymous.
~Albert Einstein

It was my fiftieth birthday. Fifty! And no one seemed to think it was a big deal, except for me. Well, Mom would have thought it was a big deal, I told myself. And she would have made a big deal out of it, too, that's for sure.

Where birthdays were concerned, my mother's motto was always "bigger is better." The first time my brother requested a birthday party, she insisted on inviting each of his classmates, accompanied by a parent, for a birthday bash that has become part of our neighborhood history. When I turned fifteen, a very special age in the Latin culture, a party at home wouldn't suffice according to Mom. We celebrated by visiting family in my mother's South American hometown so that I could have an authentic experience. Even when times were lean, as they often were, I was guaranteed whatever small gift my parents could afford, my favorite cake, a special card, and the largest bouquet of wildflowers Mom could pluck from her garden.

It was no surprise to my family then, that after Mom's passing several years ago, I continued her tradition of celebrating big. I began hosting birthdays for my father and brother while also extending the tradition to my own family. I must admit, though, that at first these get-togethers were not the fun times they once were. These occasions just felt so empty without Mom — the driving force in our family, the cheerleader always at the ready with her round-faced smile, corny jokes, and off-key rendition of "The Birthday Song." It took a while for the rest of us to recapture our spirit after her passing but eventually, with the help of time and determination, we did. So why, now, did I feel the emptiness of her loss so deeply once again?

I sat down at my piano in search of a distraction. Perhaps I was feeling so melancholy because I was experiencing what I thought of as a milestone. Mom had been with me for all my other milestones, big steps, little steps, tears, and triumphs, and this was the first such event I was not sharing with her. I lifted my hands from the keyboard, then reached into the wicker basket full of sheet music in search of an uplifting selection. There, between my collection of classics and show tunes, I found an old manila file folder. Odd, I thought, what is this doing here? I opened it and found nothing much of interest — a few yellowed newspaper clippings, old recipes, and long-expired grocery coupons. I stood, folder in hand, then walked to my kitchen trashcan. Just as I was about to drop it into the pail, a card slid out. There on the front of the card was a painting of a wildflower bouquet similar to those Mom often presented to me from her garden. Inside, written in my mother's familiar scrawl, were greetings in honor of my fortieth birthday.

That night, after my husband Bill and I were seated at my favorite restaurant for a special birthday dinner, conversation inevitably turned to the long-lost card. I so wanted to believe that somehow the card was more than mere coincidence and turned to Bill for confirmation. "I mean, what are the chances of finding that card today of all days?" I asked him.

Bill just shrugged his shoulders, noncommittally.

Still, the question haunted me.

Later that evening, after Bill and I got home, I sat down at my computer to check the last of my e-mails. There were several birthday greetings among the advertisements and other junk mail. I opened them and read each one, finally scrolling down to the daily newsletter I receive from Chicken Soup for the Soul. The featured story of the day was "What Is Your Feather?" — my contribution to one of their books, *Chicken Soup for the Soul: A Book of Miracles*. It was a story I had written about dealing with the initial grief of my mother's loss. A story I wrote about my mom, included in that newsletter on my actual birthday? Now that was eerie.

Surely, Bill would have to admit this was more than coincidence. My heart racing, I printed the newsletter and sprinted down the stairs to the first floor where Bill readied for bed. "Look at this," I said as I thrust the papers toward him. "Now this can not be a coincidence," I insisted. I watched as Bill remained cool. Hmph! Now I knew for certain my mom was contacting me. What would it take to convince my husband?

Frustrated, I went into my bedroom and flipped on my radio to listen for the weather report as I did each evening. Static. I ran the tuner up and down the band. Nothing but static. Finally, I tuned in to the only station that came in loud and clear to hear Willie Nelson warbling a country tune in his inimitable style. Now, I'm not necessarily the biggest fan of country music. But my mind was so distracted by the events of the day, I sat on my bed, closed my eyes, listened, and tried to make sense of it all. Still with a glimmer of doubt in my mind, I asked myself: Could the card I found and my story posted on the Internet really be signs from my mother? Could those passed on to the next realm of existence really communicate with those of us left behind on Earth? No matter how much I wanted to believe that my mother could still send me greetings from beyond, really, was something like that possible?

Then I got my answer.

Strains of Johnny Cash's rich baritone came through the airwaves singing the old folk song, "You Are My Sunshine," the very same song that was my mother's childhood lullaby to me. Right there, I broke down. I started to sob deep and hard, but not in sadness, in gratitude for my mother and for the love we shared that was so powerful it could travel across the realms. When I opened my eyes, I found my husband hunched over me, his hand covering mine. "It looks like your mom did remember your birthday," he said.

Yes, my mother did remember my birthday. And she did it in the same grand style she always did. After all, she sent me not one but three signs that day. Of course. My mother always did do birthdays in a big way.

~Monica A. Andermann

29

Pizza Night

A grandmother is a little bit parent, a little bit teacher,
and a little bit best friend.
~Author Unknown

My first week at college was rough. I already had two quizzes to study for, a project to begin, and a pile of lecture notes to review. My financial aid was a mess, and my roommate wouldn't speak to me. Everything was unfamiliar, and I didn't know anyone. This was not how I had planned things.

While I was only three hours from home, it seemed much farther. I couldn't wait until the weekend.

Finally, it was Friday. I told my roommate I was going home. He actually acknowledged me by nodding his head once. If Western had a degree in video games, this guy would get an A. As I drove home, I prayed and asked the Lord to please take my mess and take control over it.

I got home and no one was there. "Great," I thought. "Just when I need them the most." Then, out of the blue, it occurred to me that I hadn't seen my grandmother in weeks even though she only lived ten minutes away.

As she was expecting no company, Grandma's porch light was out. I could see the light of the TV flickering in the window. I knocked at the door and heard Grandma coming to the door. Suddenly, I was blinded by the porch light and the door swung open. "Well, hello there! I sure didn't expect to see you," she exclaimed.

Pictures of all the grandkids crowded the mantel and every available space on every shelf in the living room. The ceramic pig that had given Grandpa the last smile I saw him smile sat on a shelf across the room from me. I still remembered giving it to him for Christmas more than fifteen years ago. The wooden duck our last pastor had carved for Grandma and Grandpa sat on yet another shelf. I could see into the kitchen from where I sat and noticed the door to the stairwell. That stairwell led to an upstairs adventure paradise for us grandkids for so many years.

I was already glad I had come to see Grandma. We talked about my week. I had so much to tell. I had been there for over an hour when Grandma asked me something I never thought I'd hear her ask. "I have a pizza in the freezer. You in the mood for pizza?" she asked.

"You like pizza, Grandma?"

"I love pizza, especially after I doctor it up!"

Grandma is well known for her cooking. I couldn't imagine what doctoring up a pizza meant to her.

As we added extra cheese, pepperoni, and peppers to the pizza, I realized I had never really had a conversation with Grandma until that night. My grandfather had passed away nearly fifteen years earlier, and I always regretted that I never really got to talk to Grandpa. I suddenly felt so blessed to have this evening with Grandma. The pizza turned out awesome. The best pizza I had ever had, in fact.

The thing I noticed about Grandma was that she really listened to me. Often, I find myself interrupting people to give advice. I realized that sometimes we just need to listen. Grandma would only occasionally say, "Just pray about it."

So I prayed about my situation all weekend. The next week was so much better. I didn't even go home that next weekend. I hadn't even realized that Western had such a beautiful campus. I had been blinded by my troubles but Jesus had removed the trouble. Now I could see.

I started making a point to get to Grandma's at least once a month for pizza. We still have those pizza nights four years later. I'm just thankful that the Lord led me to Grandma when I needed an ear. As the ways of the Lord often turn out, I got so much more.

~William Mark Baldwin

30

A True Mother

Gratitude makes sense of our past, brings peace for
today, and creates a vision for tomorrow.
~Melody Beattie

I remember well the day I realized I had a true mother here in the United States, so far from my home in Germany. I had packed the last of the dishes for the move, when she called. Oh no, I thought. I can't talk to her right now. My heart was bleeding and I had no idea how to start a new life with my six children—without my husband. I was sure Grandma Towne would give me a hard time. After all, I was leaving her only son. Maybe I shouldn't say anything. I didn't want to lose her support and friendship. I had already lost so much. But I did tell her.

"Gary and I have separated. I'm filing for divorce."

Silence.

"Are you there, Mom?"

"Yes. I don't know what to say. Are you sure that's the right thing?"

"I've thought and prayed about it. I can't raise the kids with them knowing about the details of our troubled marriage." My voice broke.

"It's all right, Sonja. I understand," Grandma Towne said. "Do you need any help?"

That caught me by surprise. Mom Towne wasn't mad or upset. Instead, she offered me help. "Sonja? Don't think you are divorcing me, too. If there's anything I can do to help you, I would like that."

Suddenly the sky wasn't as dark. I took a deep breath to steady my voice, but tears rolled down my cheeks, anyway. "Oh, Mom…" I said and couldn't say anything else.

"Why don't you bring the kids? I can keep them until you have your stuff together."

I wiped my eyes with the back of my hand. "That would make it so much easier. And… thanks."

"Everything will turn out okay. The divorce shouldn't make a difference in our relationship. You're like my daughter. Your children are my grandchildren, and that can never be taken from us. Go ahead and bring them. I'll keep them until your summer classes are over." And that's what I did.

Grandma kept the kids at her home in Colorado, while I finished summer courses at the university.

As time passed, Grandma Towne was always there for me. When the engine in my car exploded, she drove three hours to pick me and the kids up, and helped us to find a new car. She came to my graduation and helped me find a good teaching job not too far away. When I got remarried, she embraced my new husband and called him "son," just like she had taken me in as a daughter so many years ago when I had first married her own son.

~Sonja Herbert

Mom to the Rescue

A mother's heart is a patchwork of love.
~Author Unknown

I think my friends and I started planning our senior prom when we were freshmen. Seriously. We talked for hours about what we'd wear, how we'd do our hair, how we'd pose for our pictures — as couples, then in a group, just the girls, then just the guys — where we'd eat, even rehearsed what we might talk about at the restaurant. I know. Get a life. But it was that huge to us. We painstakingly choreographed every minute and, with all that planning, we expected nothing short of an idyllic prom experience.

The big day arrived and we started getting ready before lunch. Between phone calls to each other, we worked on our hair, nails, make-up, shoes, dresses and purses. The restaurant where we'd made our reservations — three months ahead of time — was forty miles away. Ten of us were to meet there, three hours before the prom, eat together, then convoy to the dance.

The time came for my boyfriend, Rusty, to pick me up. No Rusty. Ten minutes passed. Still no sign of him. Twenty minutes. This was before cell phones so all I could do was wait — wait and experience a major meltdown. Thirty minutes. Forty. How could he do this to me? This was my only senior prom. He'd better be dead, I thought, or seriously injured. As my friends gathered in the restaurant, I paced the family room, burning a hole through the clock with my eyes. How could this happen? I'd planned everything so perfectly.

When Rusty finally peeled into our drive — an hour late — his tuxedo was rumpled and mottled with grease. The ruffled shirt was plastered to his chest with sweat. His face was flushed and his hair was tousled. He'd had a blowout on the interstate and had his first-ever tire changing experience only inches from rushing traffic. I tried to muster some sympathy for him but all I could see was my perfect prom night going down the toilet.

Little did I know that, while I was pacing the front room, my mom had been hard at work. She'd defrosted two steaks and roused my father to light the backyard grill. She'd gathered my grandmother's best china, crystal and lace tablecloth, thrown together an elegant dinner and then sent my little sister and nephew upstairs to don their Sunday best and serve as waiter and waitress.

By the time Rusty arrived, she'd transformed our living room into a private dining hall complete with candlelight and music. As our friends were returning from their formal dining experience, we were just sitting down to ours. I never saw Mama that night. She sent my sister and nephew through the door with dish after dish, from salad all the way to dessert. And while we ate, she washed, dried and ironed Rusty's tuxedo shirt.

We made it to prom with time to spare and a story to tell. Looking back now, I can't remember if I ever thanked my mom. I was probably more concerned with not spilling anything on my dress and making sure we got to the dance on time. She was content to remain in the shadows remedying yet another mini trauma in my life. By the way, thanks Mom.

~Mimi Greenwood Knight

32

Chicken Soup for the Soul

A Pink Dress and a Promise

I miss thee, my Mother! Thy image is still
the deepest impressed on my heart.
~Eliza Cook

I was sixteen and more than anything else in the world I wanted my mother to attend my high school graduation the following year. She was suffering from ovarian cancer, and although the expressions on the faces of other family members didn't offer much hope, I firmly believed she would recover and be there.

My mother and I had always enjoyed a special bond, perhaps because I'd been her only child for the first thirteen years of her married life. We shared a passionate love of books and reading. She'd read to me every day until I learned to master the skill myself. Afterwards she continued to share my love of stories by enthusing over my attempts at authorship. An amateur actress, she appeared in numerous local theatre productions. I grew up attending rehearsals and on opening night I was able to mouth every one of her lines.

I especially recall a small party held for the cast and crew one evening after a performance. My mother had bought a new pink dress for the occasion. In my six-year-old eyes, she looked like an angel.

When I was fourteen, my brother was born. Ten months later my mother was diagnosed with cancer. At first I didn't worry. After all, she was my mother. She'd never die and leave me. But as one year stretched to two and she grew thinner and often despondent due to heavy medication, I began to worry.

Two weeks before Christmas the year I was sixteen her condition worsened. I tried to deny the despair I saw in my father's face as we sat by her hospital bed. To strengthen the reality of her recovery I talked to her of the future, a future we'd share.

"And when you come to my graduation, will you wear your pink dress?" I asked her as she lay weak and thin on December 9th.

"Oh, honey, I don't know." She forced a thin smile. "That old thing? Really?"

"Yes, yes, please promise."

"All right, if that's what you really want… I promise." The words were barely above a whisper.

An hour later she passed away.

Somehow I forced myself through the next year and a half of school. My father had drifted away in his own world of grief and my aunt who came to take care of my two-year-old brother had no time for me. When graduation finally rolled around, both declined to attend.

As I sat on the platform with the other graduates, I felt hollow and utterly alone. I'd believed my mother would get well; I'd believed she'd be there for this milestone in my life. No one could possibly feel as bereft of happiness as I did at that moment.

Then the principal was announcing the prize for literature, for outstanding work in creative writing and the student on my right was prodding me. "You won, you won!" she hissed.

Stunned, I remained seated. And then I saw her. Standing at the back right hand corner of the auditorium, my mother was clapping with more vehemence than she'd taught me was ladylike. She was wearing the pink dress.

I stood and made my way to the podium to collect my award, all but staggering under the overwhelming sense of joy. She'd come. She'd promised and she'd come. And she was wearing the pink dress. The moments fluttered wildly in my heart, a beautiful butterfly of joy. In a cloud of happiness so intense I could barely control my movements, I returned to my seat. But when I looked at the back right hand corner of the room she was gone.

Later as I walked home alone in the soft, warm darkness of the spring evening, my award and diploma clasped in my hand, my attitude changed and anger suffused me. Why had she come only for an instant? Why couldn't she have stayed?

I sat down on a park bench by the river and stared at the calm water, and slowly understanding came. She couldn't always be with me, not anymore, but she would be there when I needed her most. She'd kept her promise. She'd come to my graduation and she'd worn the pink dress.

~Gail MacMillan

33

The Matriarch

A woman is the full circle. Within her is the power to
create, nurture and transform.
~Diane Mariechild

Young men who attempt to date one of my three beautiful daughters must first make it past my mother alive. We call her The Matriarch.

At first glance, she doesn't appear that intimidating. She's short and pale, and her red hair is never the same shade two months running. Nevertheless, she interviews the trembling novitiate with her blue eyes narrowed and a pitiless smile barely curving her lips.

"So, Daniel… what makes you worthy of our Rachel? How do you plan to earn a living? What do you love best about her? Just what makes you think you deserve her?" If she's in a generous mood that day, she might let the unfortunate beau off with a mere forty-five minute grilling.

My mother's frightening feminine force has apparently passed on to her daughters and granddaughters, if we are to believe the men in the family. Recently, a young husband was heard quietly coaching a newcomer, whose wide eyes looked as though he'd accidentally stumbled upon a tribe of Amazon warriors preparing for the hunt: "Concentrate on the mother. The power flows from there."

Let me hasten to explain that my mother has a noble purpose, greater than toying with the fragile egos of young suitors, amusing as that may be. She takes her role as tribal elder seriously. Over her seventy years, she has learned the value of prudence, primarily by making mistakes. She considers it her sacred duty to impart hard-won wisdom to those she loves, hoping to save them from wrong turns they might otherwise take in life. And so she stands guard at life's crossroads, posing hard questions intended to make her loved ones pause and think before proceeding.

My mother wasn't always a sphinx-lady swathed in bright, flamboyant clothing. Back in the early sixties, she was a small town teenager "in trouble." Friends turned their backs on her, and her new mother-in-law did everything she could to assure that the terrified girl would never forget her shame.

Life as an eighteen-year-old mother is never easy. But my mom had to face it without help or mercy. I didn't realize until I was grown that Mom had suffered from depression for most of my childhood, although it didn't surprise me when she admitted it. Having now raised my own four kids as a single mother, with my mom always nearby to help and support, I appreciate even more the strength she exerted just to get through each day on her own with her four young children.

"The only thing that kept me from killing myself," she confided to me once, "was knowing that you kids would be brought up by your grandmother if I wasn't there."

"Do you wish your life had taken a different turn back then?" I asked. "Do you ever wish you'd gone to Paris like you wanted to, instead of getting married and having kids so young?"

She answered without a moment's hesitation. "Never. I could have made lots of different choices at any time. You kids are the best thing I ever did. Anything more that I do in my life is just frosting on the cake."

I used to think Mom was easily distracted. No sooner would she get a degree or start a new job than she'd be looking at the requirements for the next one. In addition to her eclectic studies and many jobs, she owned and operated a plethora of businesses, made beautiful art, wrote a couple of books, got her real estate license, and filled her home with a gallery of interesting finds from estate sales and nature. Her hair got redder, her clothes got brighter, and she kept blooming in surprising new directions.

"The world is just such an interesting place!" she enthused. "With so much to learn and do and see, who could be content with just one life? I'm determined to cram as many as I can into this one."

Mom's stubborn refusal to bow down to circumstance was the example I needed. My own marriage was singularly unfortunate. My husband's ability to squirm out of his responsibility to our children and simultaneously cause us to live in fear and poverty was truly impressive... to most people. My mother was not impressed.

Late one night, at a time when I had packed up my kids in a panic and run home to Mom, looking for a refuge, my husband showed up. He immediately began browbeating me, convincing me that all of our difficulties were my fault, and that I needed to get back home where I belonged. At the time, I was too emotionally confused and physically weakened to protect myself. My mother heard the harangue from her room and descended the stairs like a night-gowned Valkyrie, red hair shooting out from her head like righteous flames. She ordered him from her house, backed him out of the door, and slammed it in his face, warning him not to come back. We had considerably less trouble with him after that.

I understand her ferocity better now, having grown children of my own. I can hardly imagine the pain she must have felt, watching me suffer through unwise life decisions, unable to fix them the way she did when I was little. What she could do, however, was be present, and be a proper, rollicking grandma to her grandchildren, even though she had a full life and interesting work of her own to tend to. Like everything else, my mother did her grandmothering with flair.

For years, my kids spent Fridays with Grandma Cindy while I worked. I would come to collect them at the end of the day, invariably finding them pink-cheeked and flecked with fabric paint from the sweatshirts they'd been decorating with fabulous designs, or their clothes blotched with homemade play-dough. One day, I found them out on the back porch, plastering multi-colored handprints on white, plastic chairs. More often than not, however, they would all be cuddled up together on the big, comfy couch, stuffing their faces with cookies, blowing bubbles, and watching cartoons—Mom, too.

With Grandma nearby, my kids learned that they were safe and loved, and maybe the world wasn't such a scary place, after all. In her own unpredictable way, she's still teaching them. Just recently, I came home from work to find my three grown daughters and my mother dressed in flowing gowns, boots, and floppy hats, having a tea party. Mom clutched a wizard's staff.

"Oh, good! You're just in time for tea!"

The manner in which my mother has lived her life is a great example to the rest of us: "Never stop learning; never stop reinventing yourself; don't be afraid to try something new; never give up; be loyal to the ones you love; for heaven's sake, color outside of the lines; and always… always do all things with passion."

~Rhonda Brunea

34

Motherhood: Not Quite a Stroll in the Park

*Mothers and daughters are closest, when daughters
become mothers.*
~Author Unknown

As a young woman, I used to work at a pharmacy right in the middle of London's affluent neighbourhood of Holland Park. At the same time every morning, I would look out of the shop to see a particular mother out on a stroll with her pretty baby propped up cosily in what must have been the latest state-of-the-art pram. Sometimes, she would grace the pharmacy with her presence. On some days, she would glide in dressed in a very feminine, floaty dress. Other days, she would be smartly attired in a casual designer suit. Her hair was always immaculately coiffured. Invariably, she looked elegant, like a woman in full possession of her mental and emotional faculties. She would look around the shop and peruse the shelves for the latest beauty products. She looked like she did not have a care in the world. Most impressively, she manoeuvred the baby and the pram around effortlessly, as though they were merely fashion accessories.

Fast forward four years later, in a different continent altogether. In that reality, I have become a mother myself. I could not have been a more stark contrast to that calm and collected Holland Park mom who I imagined must have had a whole army of nannies and other support staff to manage her baby, household and wardrobe for her. For a start, I would never be dressed in anything other than a crease-proof T-shirt and the most comfortable pair of jeans. I dressed for the sole purpose of ensuring that the main source of nourishment for my baby — my breasts — could be easily accessed. The accompanying accessories to my outfits were often some stain or lingering smell of something the baby had regurgitated. My hair would always be carelessly pinned back in no particular fashion, strictly to keep loose strands from getting into my baby's face as I bent down to kiss him for the thousandth time.

I could not have loved my precious newborn more, and I wanted to spend all my waking and sleeping hours with him by my side. In those early days when I walked around bleary-eyed and dishevelled from surviving on perhaps three or four hours of sleep each night, I cared about nothing but the wellbeing of my baby. When I wasn't cradling, changing, feeding or burping him, I would be poring over parenting books and magazines in a frenzied search for the answers to questions that were crowding my already addled head. Why did my baby constantly need to be breastfed with hardly any respite between each feed? Was it natural for every single feed to shoot straight out of the other end? What if his cognitive or physical development did not quite meet the milestone markers clearly laid out in parenting books? I had also become a constant fixture in the paediatrician's office, furnishing soiled diapers with faeces of questionable colour or consistency for him to examine and tirelessly besieging him with one query after another about all manner of things related to the baby and parenting. Bless that lovely man, for he never once judged me or let on that he felt I was making a beeline for the funny farm.

Yet whilst I was completely immersed in the world of motherhood, I could feel a rift widening between my husband and me. Soon after the birth of our baby, he started being given greater responsibilities at work. This required him to travel out of the country quite frequently. If he were to come home at night, I would already be deep in slumberland, quite often with the baby still in my arms. At times, I would just pretend to be asleep. I had begun to develop a slight resentment for how his life had not changed in the least after the baby.

The increasingly fewer conversations we had would inevitably end up with me launching into a tirade about how exhausted I was and how yet another one of his relatives had visited. The trouble with those visitors is they could never resist dishing out unsolicited advice about parenting, which predictably questioned the way I was caring for my baby. They were also fond of making comparisons between my little angel and so-and-so's child of a similar age. In any case, their visits were never something I looked forward to.

Then one day whilst on the phone with my mother, I broke down in hysterics and told her how I often felt frustrated about not coping as a mother. My mother listened very attentively throughout and then spoke: "It's only natural to be experiencing all these feelings that you are having right now. I'm still discovering new things about mother-hood at my age. I now have to learn to be a mother to someone who has become a mother herself." I just had to chuckle at that. She then added, "I know how busy the baby keeps you, but you must make the time to enjoy the things that you did before the baby came along. And you must make the effort to keep the spark in your marriage alive."

I kept thinking about what my mother had said. A couple of days later, my old boss rang me and asked if I would be interested in helping out with some mini projects that she was working on. I did not hesitate to call my mom straightaway and ask if she could babysit for a couple of days a week. In the end, it was not just those couple of days that I would turn up at my mom's.

My mom had insisted that I keep a set of baby clothes, a pack of diapers, toiletries, feeding bowls and a sterilizer at her house. That way, I could just strap my baby in the car seat straight after breakfast and literally deposit him at her doorstep whenever I was running late for the classes I had agreed to teach. My mom was truly a godsend. When my baby showed little interest in eating his pureed vegetables, my mom taught me that by sweetening them with a little fruit puree, we could make him eat every last drop. When my baby started babbling, my mom sang songs and read wonderful books to him to boost his speech development. My mom bought him his very first Thomas the Tank Engine toy, which grew into a large collection of trains, tracks and books. It was so apparent that Grandma and baby delighted and flourished in the company of one another. Although the travelling to and from my mom's was a little tiring, we were all infinitely happier.

With Mom ever willing to volunteer her babysitting services, I managed to find the time for the occasional hair treatment, pampering massages and, most importantly, the romantic nights out my husband and I had missed and sorely needed. I never quite got my act together enough to dress and carry myself with the admirable composure of the Holland Park mom I had encountered in my youth. But there were actually days when I caught myself in the mirror and smiled at what I saw. I realized that motherhood is seldom a stroll in the park. It is not something you gain mastery of overnight. However, if you can accept that and reach out to ask a trusted person for help along the way, it makes motherhood so much more manageable and enjoyable. Getting my mother involved in the caring of my firstborn was the best thing I ever did for myself, my baby, and my marriage.

By the way, my husband has become an incredibly supportive and amazing father since those early days of parenthood. We now have two kids, and they both put him on a pedestal where he rightly belongs. My mother continues to be the best grandmother any child could ever ask for.

~Maizura Abas

35

Wreath Rivalry

A mother's love for her child is like nothing else in the
world. It knows no law, no pity. It dares all things and
crushes down remorselessly all that stands in its path.
~Agatha Christie

I t was a wreath only a mother could love. The program promised "100 holiday ideas for a total of $100." As with virtually
every designer show on cable, I was completely sold at the first
airy wave of the hostess. Beautifully dressed interior design-
ers frolicked through their demonstrations of ideas, many of which
required a master's degree in glue guns and access to esoteric waxes
from India. But then a handsome, delicate man in a black turtleneck
with an air of bored superiority showed how anyone could make a
wreath with drycleaner bags. By tying shredded strips of the plastic
bags around a disassembled coat hanger, you could create a shiny,
ecologically friendly wreath.

We rarely went to the dry cleaner, but our mountain of un-recycled
grocery bags looked like decent substitutes. So I started cutting and
tying strips around a wire circle of an old coat hanger. A few hours
later, I was astonished. It looked pretty good.

This is what cable does to you. You actually come to believe that
plastic bags tied around a coat hanger look pretty good.

I added a few ribbons and ornaments and decided I'd give this
to my mother to add to the huge number of decorations around her
house. She loved to decorate, would set a beautiful table at the holidays,

and I thought this would be a fun addition to a window somewhere.

When I delivered it on one of our family visits early in December, it was fourth grade all over again. She loved it and promptly displayed it on the mantel. I was a little embarrassed, but also ridiculously proud.

As the holidays reached their fever pitch, we returned to her house for the big dinner. Everyone was there, and we were a bit late, having had a few meltdowns with the kids along the way. After we finished hugging and getting rid of coats and shoes, I walked into the formal dining room.

On the mantel was a huge wreath, practically encompassing the fireplace, filled with glimmering ribbons, bells, and ornaments. It was gorgeous, the greenery absolutely perfect, the colors flowing in a holiday harmony that would have silenced any decent choir. I was in awe.

And there, on the little music stand next to the mantel, was my recycled bag wreath.

"Oh! Did you see the wreath Christy sent me?" my mother said, walking into the room behind me.

Of course. My sister. From across the Midwest she had reached into our open-ended game of sibling rivalry blackjack and tossed down a big, fat ace right here, in my mother's house. Like a typical little sister, I didn't even see it coming.

"Wow. It's amazing," I said, hoping there was as little animosity in my voice as was possible under the circumstances.

"And see? I put yours right there. I wanted everyone to see the wreaths my daughters gave me."

There had to be a dagger somewhere. Something sharp I could pluck out my eyes with before I saw the look on everyone's face. I was mortified.

I turned to look at my mother, to try and apologize for my sad little homemade wreath. But one look at her brought me up short. She had no idea. She had no idea of the vast gulf that lay between my wreath with the ripped grocery bags and the epic salute to the spirits of yuletide through the ages on the mantel. In her eyes, they were somehow THE SAME.

I was floored. First and foremost, I realized I'd have no chance to ditch my plastic ring of Christmas in the closet, sparing myself from the inevitable comparisons that would race across the faces of every relative at the table. Then, it dawned on me.

My mother is incredible.

For her there was no difference. Forget the white shredded plastic versus glossy greenery and silk ribbons. Never mind the cheap ornaments versus hand-painted porcelain from Europe. So what that one was small and insignificant versus the other, large enough to rival the tree itself. None of that mattered. In her heart, in her eyes, they were from her daughters. They were our love shaped into circles and she cherished them both.

I looked at my own daughters, who were busy running from room to room at my mother's house, squealing with energy. My eyes burned with love and I hoped when the day came, they would see this beautiful blindness in me.

As a daughter, I'm still completely mortified by the memory of the wreath rivalry where I was so completely left in the dust. Yet I take considerable comfort in knowing that to my mother, there was no contest — and there never has been.

~Winter Prosapio

Chapter 4

for Mom, with love

Thanks for Your Strength

*You gave up the most important things in your life
so that I could take on the most important things in
mine. Mom, thanks for all the sacrifices you
have made.*
~Author Unknown

36

Worth More than Money

All that I am or ever hope to be, I owe to my
angel Mother.
~Abraham Lincoln

I slid my arms into my old gray coat and buttoned it as I looked at the wear around the sleeves. I hated that coat. Hated having hand-me-downs that neighbors had discarded as not good enough for themselves.

Biting my tongue, I forced a smile as Mom handed me my school lunch. "You could use a new coat," she said. "We'll have to see what we can do about that." She patted my shoulder as I hurried out the door, hoping she didn't see the tears in my eyes.

Seeing what she could do about it meant she'd find another old, used-up coat for me. I brushed the tears away and took a deep breath. The fall air was getting crisper. Soon winter would be upon us. I shivered, pulling my coat tightly around me. It did little good to wish that my parents had money like my friends' parents had. With six kids to feed, there was little cash left to spend on clothes and I couldn't remember when my mother had ever had a new coat. I told myself that I'd better get used to wearing castoffs. At least I had a coat, even if it wasn't fancy.

"Look what the neighbors sent over," Mom said, a few days later. She was beaming as she caressed a soft, short-sleeved sweater. She handed it to me. "This will look lovely on you. The collar is so soft."

I ran my fingers over the white angora collar. It was the softest thing I'd ever felt and added a beautiful touch to the bright red of the sweater.

"And look at these," she continued, as she lay two skirts side-by-side on the sofa.

My jaw dropped. One skirt was pink and the other was light blue. My older sister and I could each have one.

There were other things too, but these were my favorites. I lay awake a long time that night, suddenly grateful that our neighbors grew tired of their clothes.

The next morning I put on my old gray coat. I buttoned it, kissed Mom goodbye and turned toward the door. She was smiling. "Yes," she said, almost to herself, "you definitely need a new coat."

Mom had a twinkle in her eye and a hum on her lips for the next few days. She was up to something, but what?

The weather suddenly turned cold. I put an extra sweater under my old coat and tied a scarf around my neck, but the wind chilled me to the bone, long before I ever reached school. I was still shivering when I went to bed that night, and Mom looked worried.

I had a fitful sleep. My room was upstairs and therefore usually quiet, but that night I thought I heard a sewing machine whirring all night. I pulled the covers up to my neck and put the pillow over my head. Finally, I dozed off.

Wind whistled, blowing snow into drifts. I groaned the next morning as I looked out the window. I had to go to school and I shivered at the thought of another cold walk in my threadbare coat.

Mom looked tired as she made us breakfast. But there was a twinkle in her eye and she was back to humming.

As usual, I was the last one to leave for school. As I sullenly slid into my gray coat and began buttoning it, Mom said, "Why don't you leave that old thing at home?" Then, before I could answer she slipped into the living room, returning with a beautiful green coat that sported a real fur collar. "Try this on," she said proudly.

It fit perfectly. I marveled at the softness of the green wool fabric, the heavy lining and the light-brown fur of the collar. "Where did you get it?" I was in awe.

She smiled. "It was in the box of clothes that we were given. I altered it to fit you."

"You mean, it was for a lady, and it would have fit you, Mom?"

"I suppose it might have," she nodded, reaching out to help me button the coat. "But you need a coat more than I do. And look how lovely it looks on you. Now hurry up, slowpoke, or you'll be late for school."

I wrapped my arms around my mother; my heart so filled will love for this woman who had always put her family's needs above her own. Who could ever ask for more than that? My friends' families might be better off financially than we were. But I had Mom, and she was worth far more than any amount of money.

~Chris Mikalson

37

Return to Heart Mountain

I will permit no man to narrow and degrade my soul
by making me hate him.
~Booker T. Washington

ike a little kid who gets too excited waiting to ride a roller coaster, I feel like I might throw up. I have been looking forward to this and yet my emotions alternate between complete euphoria and an overwhelming desire to turn the car around. I'm scared, but I can't turn back. There is too much riding on this venture and so I continue driving into the unknown at sixty-five miles per hour.

It feels like my husband, Mike, and I have been driving on this rural Wyoming highway for hours, when in reality barely twenty minutes have passed since we left our motel in Cody. The land before me is beautiful, but I am unable to appreciate it because I am so preoccupied with what is about to happen. My hands take on a life of their own, fidgeting with the seatbelt, the window, my sunglasses. My eyes search the road for any sign of our destination. In my hand I hold the directions given to me by my grandma. The frayed edges are becoming damp in my sweaty hands.

"Is that it?" Mike asks. I follow his gaze and almost miss seeing a small brown sign with faded white lettering on the side of the road.

This is Heart Mountain Relocation Camp. This is our destination and the reason for our trip. We have come to visit the site of the internment camp where my grandma spent three years of her life locked up like a prisoner during World War II simply because she was the "wrong" race.

"That's it!" I yell, but we have already missed our turn.

"Don't worry, I'm turning around," Mike says. He reaches over and pats my leg, both to reassure me and to make me sit back down in my seat.

"Here it is," Mike says as he exits onto a small dirt road. I stare at the land, devoid of any markers that would hint at its importance, as we slowly make our way toward the camp.

The humming sound of gravel under the tires of our car has a calming effect, but it can't drown the sound of my heartbeat in my ears or ease the tightness in my throat. I catch myself leaning forward, silently urging the car to go faster. The remnants of the camp come into view and I want to be there now. I need to be there.

We pull off onto what might have once been a dirt road, but is now nothing more than a path overgrown with weeds. There are no other cars around and even the birds that chirped non-stop since we arrived in Cody seem to have disappeared. As we park the car I sink back into my seat, unable to move.

Three buildings loom before me, the remains of my grandma's former prison, fenced in by a chain link fence. A thin line of barbed wire tops the fence and the sight of it sickens me.

They were fenced in like cattle, I think. And guarded like criminals in their own country.

The buildings are predictably worn down, but after years of staring at pictures of the camp in textbooks, I recognize them. I recognize the black tar paper that barely kept out the wind and snow. I recognize the tiny windows in the walls.

In the far distance, I can see a tower made of bricks. I know from my grandma's stories that it used to be a part of the internee hospital. It is infamous in my family because it is in that hospital that my grandma's first daughter died when she was less than a day old, a baby whose only day on earth was spent behind barbed wire fences.

I am no longer afraid. Instead, I feel the resentment my grandma has been holding onto for half a century collect in a lump in my throat. The reality of what happened to her so many years ago hits me harder as I stare at the same landscape my grandma stared at for three long years. I am angry. Big salty tears blur my vision and I lose sight of my surroundings.

"Are you ready?" Mike asks quietly when minutes after we have parked we are still sitting in the car.

I nod my head, but still don't move. Mike gets out of the car and I take little notice of him as he rummages through the trunk. My eyes are glued to the tower. Mike opens my car door and I jump at the sound.

"Come on," he urges as he pushes my camera into my hands. Suddenly, I am out of the car, brushing past Mike and running toward the buildings. I remember why I am here. This place, so desolate and rundown, is a piece of my history. I am here to remember those who lost their lives and lost their years in this place. I am here to document what's left of their prison. I have brought years of resentment and anger with me and I intend to leave them here. I have come in my grandma's stead to make peace with the past that has held our family captive for too long. I have come for closure.

The land feels empty and eerie, but in a strange way it also feels welcoming, like it has been waiting for me. I move reverently among the buildings, snapping photographs and lightly tracing my fingers over the walls. I try to wrap my head around what I am feeling, but words escape me. I feel pain. I feel connected. I feel peace.

As I look through the lens of my camera I feel myself willing the buildings to give up their stories. For an hour I silently wander back and forth, taking pictures and taking it all in. As I walk, I can literally feel myself change. I unclench my fists and the anger that Grandma had felt, the anger that she had passed on to me, seems to drop to the ground like pebbles.

I close my eyes and take a breath.

"We forgive you," I whisper, and as my words are carried away with the breeze the roots of resentment that kept my family tied to Heart Mountain begin to untangle themselves from the ground. I bend down and pick up two small white rocks from the dirt. I am taking home a piece of this place: one rock for me and one for Grandma.

As we slowly drive away from the site, I turn around in my seat and stick my head out the window desperate to watch it until it completely disappears. The wind whips my hair around my head in a frenzied dance. Years ago my grandma had lived here as a prisoner in her own country, forced to give up everything she owned. Today, I had walked the grounds offering forgiveness for the past and gaining closure in return. I did it for myself. I did it for my family. I did it for Grandma.

~Jessie Miyeko Santala

38

To My Other Mother

I would maintain that thanks are the highest
form of thought, and that gratitude is happiness
doubled by wonder.
~G.K. Chesterton

When you married my dad, I was twelve. We didn't meet then, you and I, for I lived with my mother. Dad emerged occasionally, a shadow from the past — a smiling face in a photo in Mom's cedar chest.

You made no difference in my life. You and Dad inhabited one corner of the earth, Mom and us kids another. We still ate peanut butter sandwiches for lunch every day, and wore holes through the soles of our shoes.

That first year, the shadow I knew as Dad visited; you waited in the car outside. For a long time afterwards, I cherished the memory of Dad's hug as we sat together on the sofa. Soon after that first visit, black patent leather shoes appeared in my closet. At first I wondered where they came from… until Mom said Dad had sent them. How special those shoes were! No laces to tie; instead, small pearl buttons decorated the clasps on the narrow straps. I thought of Dad whenever I wore them.

Six months later, when Dad visited, he took my face in his hands, studied my smile, and concluded that I needed braces on my teeth. Embarrassed, my smile shriveled; then Dad tickled my lips again, and I giggled. Once again, you waited in the car outside. That was the day we met. Mom practically dragged me to the car. "Can't you say hello?" she prodded. I dropped my head in adolescent shyness, and squeaked, "Hi."

You turned into a smile with a name that day, not just a lady in the car. As you and Mom chattered away like old friends, I wrestled with the problem of what I was supposed to call you.

Several weeks later, Mom made an appointment with the dentist. That dreaded dentist trip, a weekly worry, stretched into a two-month ordeal, but at least I didn't need braces.

Then there was the coat. Dad had never given me an Easter present, but shortly after I met you, a large box wrapped with brown grocery bags and string was delivered just in time for Easter. When Mom lifted the lid, I squealed with delight. There was the prettiest, softest, pink coat I'd ever seen — and it was mine. With the cool satin lining caressing my skin, I buried my hands in the deep pockets, and twirled around the living room. As if that wasn't enough, later that same day the florist delivered a pink and lavender corsage of flowers, which was also from Dad. It's funny that Dad had never thought of these things before marrying you.

Mom said this called for a celebration, and we went shopping together. Now that Mom didn't have to buy the coat I needed, she used the money instead for my very first new Easter outfit — a navy blue dress with a white lace collar.

Time passed. I graduated from high school, got my first job, married, had children, and eventually pursued a career. Contact with you was sporadic during these years. Although you didn't know it, I enjoyed the occasional times we spent together. I'm not sure why — perhaps I was curious about you back then. Of course, Mom was first in my life as always, but you never seemed to mind.

You were patient. Because you understood Mom's need to be my only mom, you waited behind the curtain, and whispered the cues to Dad. Many times in the midst of trouble and turmoil in my own home, Dad appeared on the scene just in time to make a difference. I remember the urgent financial crisis that resulted from my husband's incarceration, and Dad's help. About this time, God stepped into my life, bringing peace to quiet the storm. When a special delivery letter arrived from Dad with a generous check enclosed, my faith surged. Knowing you now, I can't help but wonder what role you played in each intervention.

My faith was shaken when my brother died, but I had to be strong for Mom's sake. When we gathered at the funeral parlor to stand at the casket, you stepped back again. Yet we were on one level. Grief only crawls; it cannot climb. You stood among the backdrop of my friends that day, waiting to help if you were needed.

Seven years later, my mother died. We stood together at the grave to mourn my loss. This time you were at my side.

Eventually, my own nest had emptied and I was alone. Because of my growing relationship with God over the years, I didn't mind the solitude so much. But you and Dad were there for me. I watched you shower gifts upon my grandchildren; if I tried to refuse the folded bill that Dad slipped into my hand, you protested. It didn't take long for me to discover that the "care packages" containing groceries, favorite junk foods, and treats for my doggie were your idea, and not Dad's. I could always depend on you for licorice and cheddar cheese crackers when I attended an out-of-town conference.

Dad and I grew closer in recent years thanks to you. You urged him to call if we hadn't been in touch; you planned your vacations to coincide with mine. In a way, you were still whispering the cues, right up to the time of his death, when again you and I stood together at a gravesite. I no longer stumble over the word "stepmother." You're my friend, and you have made a difference in my life.

~Penny Smith

39

The Girls on the Bus

*There are many wonderful things that will never be
done if you do not do them.*
~Charles D. Gill

As I backed my car out of Mom's driveway, I asked her a question. "Have you taken the senior bus yet?" I held my breath as I waited for her answer.

Mom adjusted her seatbelt and stared straight ahead. Emphasizing each word, she said, "Oh-yes-I-did."

There was an uncomfortable silence.

Finally, I asked, "How was it?" I said the words as cheerfully as I could manage, even though I sensed the answer was not going to be positive.

"Well," she said, once again with emphasis, "I called the Senior Center and made the arrangements for the bus to take me to the grocery store. When they came to the house the next morning, I climbed on and looked down the aisle. And what do you think I saw? I'll tell you what." She clenched her hands. "I saw about thirteen depressing little old ladies and one depressing old man."

Something clutched my stomach, and I didn't know if it was sympathy for her plight, fear that she'd refuse to use this helpful transportation, or anger that she maligned what she needed desperately.

More silence. It didn't take a genius to figure out that in her own mind she thought that now she was one of them. My dad had recently passed away after six weeks in the hospital. He had been in a coma after surgery for an aortic aneurysm that burst while he was having an MRI. The long hours of waiting and hoping all those weeks had taken a toll on my mother and the rest of the family, too.

Mom had seemed to wear down a little more each day as she watched and waited in the hospital, but she got through the many decisions each time another crisis arose and finally agreed to disconnect life support. Then, surrounded by her children, their spouses and her grandchildren, she reigned graciously at the visitation and funeral.

When the family left to go back to their own lives, she was suddenly alone and frightened. For fifty-seven years, my dad had walked by her side. He had always told her, "Don't worry about it. I'll take care of it."

Dad took an early retirement twenty years before his death. These were years my parents were always together. Mom never learned to drive, so Dad chauffeured her everywhere, on errands to the grocery store, to get her hair cut, or whatever she needed. Now, her wheels were gone, as one grandchild so aptly described her situation.

I spent the week after the funeral helping Mom with paperwork and other chores, and I contacted the local Senior Center to inquire about transportation for her. I teased her, saying she could now see her tax dollars at work and get some real benefit from them. She agreed, although reluctantly, that she'd need to use the senior bus since I lived an hour and a half away.

Now, as we drove to the shopping center, I thought about what courage it had taken for her to call that first time and then to ride the bus with other seniors. As I wove in and out of traffic, Mom changed the subject. We didn't discuss the bus again that day.

The following weeks, when I came to visit, she would mention the bus and often end by saying, "No one ever talks on that bus. They all sit there staring into space and looking sad." Her mouth turned downward, and she heaved a great sigh.

I thought to myself that surely couldn't last too long, not with my mother on board. Mom grew up in a small coal-mining town in Iowa where she knew everyone. She often waited for her father at the mine at the end of his shift and chattered constantly on the long walk home. Even as an adult, living in a large metropolitan area, she chatted to clerks in the stores or the mailman walking down the street as if she'd known them forever. I couldn't imagine her sitting silently on the bus, but her life had changed so drastically, and she wasn't the same person anymore. I so hoped to see a spark of life in her on one of my visits, but how to bring it about escaped me.

I worried needlessly, for after several more weeks went by, I noticed that many of Mom's sentences began with "The girls on the bus told me…" After hearing the same phrase on several visits, I dared to hope.

One day, as she made tea for us, I asked, "So, they talk to you now?"

She smiled and there was a sparkle in her eye, the first real sign of life I'd seen in her for many months. She poured the steaming tea into my cup and picked up a cookie before she answered. "I decided one day that it was silly, all of us sitting there saying nothing. So I climbed on the bus one morning and greeted them all. Then I remarked on what a nice day it was. I think I scared them at first. It took a few tries, but little by little they began to respond. And now we have some good conversations, and it makes everyone's life a little nicer."

She slid the plate of homemade cookies to my side of the table, and in my great relief, I ate several.

My mother had little formal education and had done very little on her own while Dad was alive. Nevertheless, she held the key to open the hearts of the other lonely people on that bus. A smile and a friendly word or two was all it took. She sowed tiny seeds of happiness for herself and the girls on the bus.

~Nancy Julien Kopp

40

Her Turn

Kindness, like a boomerang, always returns.
~Author Unknown

The first time I met them, I was nervous. I didn't know what to expect but I desperately wanted their approval. The prospect of meeting my future in-laws was enough to make me seriously doubt my qualifications. Would they like me? Would they measure me against the possibility of better offers for their grandson? Would they secretly wish for someone else, or would they actually welcome me into the family? Instead of sizing me up and down, Jack pulled me in for a great big hug and Joan handed me a beautiful afghan — handmade, with special colors and patterns chosen just for me.

I have to admit; at first their gestures were a little foreign to me. Not having spent much time with my own grandparents growing up, I didn't quite know how to respond to their generosity. The time and energy Joan had poured into my blanket both honored and inspired me. No one had ever given me a gift like that and I was humbled by the weight of the warmth it offered. Each stitch symbolized a moment of time she had spent thinking of me, and every intricate design embodied another gesture of unexpected kindness.

Jack and Joan were no strangers to welcoming others into their family. After raising five children of their own, they adopted another little boy — their grandson, my future husband. Selflessly putting aside plans for retirement, they took on another generation of PTA meetings, slumber parties, Boy Scouts, and private school tuition.

The kitchen table became another neighborhood hangout, and the stove rarely cooled between indulgent homemade feasts. Love wafted through the air in the form of lingering aromas of fried chicken, biscuits and gravy, and Joan's infamous coffee-glazed doughnuts. I've been told several stories of late night doughnut feeds that would have provided enough nourishment for a small country.

While they'd only say, "He was no trouble at all," I'm forever indebted to them for their years of servitude and self-sacrifice. Their lessons of love shaped my husband into the man he is now. Together, the two of them showed him what a home founded on grace and unlimited acceptance looks like. They taught him to have integrity and helped him create unending memories of laughter and adventure. Their faith provided an anchor of hope and their patience formed a foundation of gentle leadership that guides our marriage today.

Over thirty years ago, they stepped into a difficult situation, and altered history. With no regard for themselves, they created a potential that will reach generations to come. When they chose to take in their grandson, they chose to adopt me as well. When they changed his life, they forever transformed mine too. I couldn't be more thankful for the example they have given us. They have shown us what it looks like to stand firm in conviction, persevere with patience, and commit in spite of uncertainty. I'm always moved by their gracious understanding and constant support, and our children and grandchildren will be blessed because of a decision Jack and Joan made decades before they existed.

This last year Jack lost his battle with heart disease and medical complications, and left Joan to carry on without him. The house is empty now, and Joan is alone for the first time in her life — without the responsibility of caring for children, grandchildren, or an ailing husband. Her tears are many and her heartache is raw and unbearable at times. Still, she remains steadfast in expectation and confident in hope. Somehow, her care and concern for her family continues, as she prays blessings and guidance over all of us. She daily seeks to wrap her tenderness and attention around us, and never ceases to offer encouragement and support when we need it most.

Although we could never come close to repaying the depth of her compassion and affection, it's her turn to be adopted now. It's her turn to be pulled in and comforted; and like the afghans she has meticulously stitched for others, it's her turn to be wrapped in the safety and security of those who cherish her. When the chill of love lost pierces her heart, it's her turn to be taken in and consoled. Jack's departure is an experience that can't be mended this side of Heaven, but my fervent prayer is that her years of unconditional love and moments of immeasurable pain will be met by a blanket of peace that wraps around her soul and gently begins to heal her heart.

Thank you Joan, for adopting your grandson, for welcoming me into the family, and for faithfully standing beside us. But, now, it's our turn to return the favor.

~Kara Johnson

Urban Cowgirl

*We cannot destroy kindred: our chains stretch a little
sometimes, but they never break.*
~Marquise de Sévigné

I don't remember being told I was adopted. I feel like the knowledge has always been there. The sky is blue, the grass is green and I'm adopted. When I was a kid I didn't understand why I would tell people that and get a response of "That must be so hard for you." I wondered why. My parents hugged me and kissed me and read me stories and took care of me when I was sick. They loved me. What's so hard about that? I couldn't see a difference between the way my parents treated me and the way my non-adopted friends' parents treated them. Family is family.

My mother used to tell me stories about how they heard I was coming and piled everyone onto a plane to get there, how they flew to Texas to get me, and how she started crying when she first held me. My parents had been trying hard to have a child, without success, and were in their early forties when they decided to adopt. When I was four years old they decided to adopt again, and I got a brother. I don't think I could love him any more if we were related by blood.

My parents divorced when I was five. It was awful. I still remember my dad coming into my room to say goodbye. I was lying in my bed and he sat down and wrapped his hand around my ankle. He said he was leaving but he loved me and would see me soon. The memory that stays with me the most is the image of a long line of boxes filled with his belongings in the hallway. I was a kid who wanted my parents together and my world had shattered. But, at no point did I ever wish that they had not adopted me, at no point did I yearn for my biological mother. My parents were my parents and that was that.

Just as I've always known I was adopted, I've always known my birth mother's name. I've always known that I have two older siblings, and I knew that I was originally from Texas. When I was four and rode a pony for the first time, I told my mom that I wanted to be a cowgirl because cowgirls were from Texas. We lived in Chelsea on the west side of Manhattan, definitely not cowgirl territory.

I was about ten when I spoke to my birth mother on the phone for the first time. My mother made the call from her office. I was so excited! I sat in my mom's lap, even though I was a little big to sit there comfortably, and I chatted with my birth mother. I told her all about the summer camp and the horses I rode. I don't remember her responses or how the call ended, but I remember liking her voice. She sounded kind and she laughed.

My mom got very sick not long after that. Cancer. Somehow in the hell of treatments and hospitals and surgeries and more treatments, talking to my birth mother didn't seem that important, and between one thing and the next my connection to her faded. I still knew her of course, her name and general location. I had always thought that maybe when I was eighteen I'd see her. I'd fly down to Texas with my dad and meet her. I had always heard people saying that they looked like their parents and I wanted to know if I looked like her, if I looked like my older siblings. But then I started thinking: What if I didn't meet her expectations? What if I wasn't girly enough or pretty enough? What if I was too quirky? I let eighteen come and go without comment, without trying to get in contact. Between starting college, my new stepmother and baby sister, it all seemed too much — too many things in the air.

I spent a weekend the summer before I turned twenty-one obsessively researching online. I had my birth mother's name, the name of the hospital where I was born and the names of my siblings, and using that I was able to find her. I had her address and phone number.

I could call her, but what would I say? "Hey, this is the kid you gave up for adoption? Remember when we talked when I was ten? Sorry I didn't get in touch with you when I was eighteen?"

I let my insecurities call the shots and did nothing but stick the torn paper up on a bulletin board in my room, half hidden behind a picture my mom had painted. I did spend some time after that looking at various ancestry websites and was tickled to finally learn my roots. My parents' families had both emigrated from Russia in the late 1890s, but even though they were my parents and grandparents, I didn't feel attached to the family history. I wanted my own. And I found it, though the realization that they fought for the Confederacy gave me pause.

But I let it go, other than holding on to that paper and a family tree I had mocked up. I didn't want to be a disappointment and I didn't want it to be awkward.

Then, two years ago, my birth mother found me on social media. She said it was up to me if I wanted to respond; there was absolutely no pressure.

I had a panic attack. What if she didn't like me? I was now twenty-six, and had lost my mother to cancer only two years before. I sat on the floor trying to breathe. What if I was too fat or not pretty enough or didn't meet her expectations? What if I wasn't enough? But then I thought about how brave she had been to reach out to me. It took me twenty minutes to pull myself together and reach back out to her.

I have not regretted it.

I developed a relationship with one of my older siblings. It turns out that he shares a lot of my interests and a lot of my quirks. It's an odd case for nature versus nurture. I've connected with my birthmother and we exchange birthday gifts. She didn't replace my mom in the least, but having her as a support helped me cope with my grief. She posted a picture of herself recently and I wanted to laugh. We look a lot alike.

My parents are both gone now, my mother in 2009 and my father in the autumn of 2013. I don't think it could hurt any more than this. I don't think that I would be grieving any more if I had been their birth child. I don't think I could have loved them more if they had been my birth parents. I am my parents' daughter. I loved them and they loved me, and I will take that and the lessons they taught me and carry them with me for the rest of my life.

~Isabel Harris

42

Racing with Heart

*The most important thing in illness is never
to lose heart.*
~Nikolai Lenin

"I just want you to know where the AED is in case anything happens to me." My mom pointed out the box on the wall.

I rolled my eyes. I did not think that Mom would need CPR or an AED during the triathlon.

At fifty-seven, my mom would be participating in her first triathlon. I would be competing in my third.

I must have made it look fun the first time she had come and cheered me on, because ever since then she had been talking about signing up for one herself. She signed up for an indoor triathlon at my gym.

We talked over the phone as we prepared for the event. We would both be participating in the mini distance. I was very excited to be in the same race with my mom.

We started our training while still on a waiting list. We were not even sure there would be spots for us in the race but we trained anyway. Two weeks before the race we each got a phone call letting us know that there would be spots open for us. We would be in the same heat.

My mom has always been an inspiration to me for fitness. She made fitness a part of her life and tried to pass that on to us. Every year we got a family gym membership. My sister and I were active on the swim team and my mom swam laps or ran while we practiced.

When my mom took up running we went to races with her and cheered her on and ran in the kids run. I was excited to compete in an event with her.

When I went home to visit we trained together at her gym.

"I'm so proud of you," she told me while we were swimming laps.

My mom is a strong swimmer. She was concerned about the stationary bike portion and she decided to walk because she had not run in a long time.

On race day she felt ready but nervous.

"I don't want you to wait for me. That makes me nervous because then I feel like I have to keep up with you," Mom said. "Just do your race and I will see you at the finish line."

I finished before my mom and was able to watch her cross the finish line. She had a big smile on her face and she had even run some of her laps around the track.

I was so proud of my mom for participating in the event. I was proud of both of us.

At the end of the race we cooled down and waited for our results to come in.

The next day my mom left to drive back to her home six hours away and I went to work. Later that day I got a phone call from my mom. "I'm in the hospital. I had a heart attack. I don't want you to be worried about me."

Driving home the day after the event my mom felt nauseous and decided to pull over at a hospital. Her work as a cardiac nurse gave her the knowledge that her symptoms might be more than just a stomach flu.

I was shocked. I didn't understand how this had happened. My mom is a fit person. She eats healthy and exercises. She doesn't smoke or drink. She had just completed a triathlon yet here she was in a hospital with a heart attack.

"The doctor said that this was not caused by the triathlon," my sister called later to assure me. It gave me some comfort to know that the event that I had encouraged my mom to sign up for was not the cause of her heart attack.

She spent the next week in the hospital recovering and learning what had caused her heart attack. What she learned is that her heart disease is hereditary. She has low HDLs, which is the good cholesterol. This meant that even though her overall cholesterol number looked okay, the LDLs were high because the HDLs were low. This is a condition that she has even though she exercises and eats right and does all the things that she is supposed to do.

"I guess my triathlon career is on hold for now," she said.

My mom took her time recovering and used her experience to educate her kids about their risks. Exercise was important in her recovery but she had to take it slow at first.

She made sure that we knew that this was hereditary and that we would need to keep an eye on our numbers. She makes sure that we know the importance of exercise and eating right.

I have been able to educate myself and know that heart disease is the number one killer of women. I participate in races that raise money for this cause.

I continue to race in triathlons and running races. It is more important than ever for me to lead a healthy lifestyle.

As for Mom's triathlon career, it isn't over. My mom was back participating in triathlons within a year. She found an event called the Lazyman Triathlon at her gym. Over the course of six weeks my mom swims, bikes and walks the distance of an Ironman triathlon.

~Carrie Monroe

43

Finding Christmas

Because that's what kindness is. It's not doing
something for someone else because they can't, but
because you can.
~Andrew Iskander

The sound of my infant daughter's crying burst through the baby monitor. "She can't be awake already," I sighed, glancing at the clock. Only fifteen minutes had passed since I'd put her down for a nap. Caring for her and my six-year-old son, coupled with suffering from a bad case of the baby blues, had turned my days into blurs of diapers, bottles, crying, and whining. To make matters worse, Christmas was approaching. I had no idea how I would finish my shopping and gift-wrapping or bake the three dozen cookies I had promised my son's teacher for his class party.

I was lucky if I managed to take a shower each day. With my mom living only ten minutes away, I desperately wanted to turn to her for support. But she was in another state caring for my grandmother, who was recovering from a heart attack. I battled tears as I gently lifted my daughter, red-faced from crying, out of her crib. I dropped heavily into the rocking chair and cradled her. And as I rocked her back to sleep, I let my tears flow. Without my mom, I was unsure how to quiet the apprehension and worry I felt.

My mother's stay with my grandmother was lasting longer than expected. "I'm not going to get home in time to put up my Christmas tree," she had told me on the phone. "Your dad is still on a business trip so he won't be around to do it either."

"Don't worry about it, Mom," I told her, hoping I sounded reassuring. "You'll get done what you can and the rest won't matter this year."

But I knew better. Mom always made Christmas at her house magical. Every year, the scents of cinnamon, sugar, and chocolate would mingle as she baked her special cookies and fudge. The fresh balsam wreaths she would hang on every door brought a sweet, woodsy scent to each entrance of her home. She'd also make sure the aging, handmade felt Santas and Styrofoam snowmen blended perfectly with the newer ornaments that adorned her tree. She'd spend hours finding the perfect gift for each person on her list and planning the menu for Christmas dinner.

It looked like this year would be different. As I had hung up the phone, I thought, "I should put up her tree this year." I quickly dismissed the idea. Who was I kidding? I could barely drag myself to the coffee pot each morning. I doubted I'd even finish decorating my own tree. But I couldn't get the idea out of my head. I couldn't stop thinking about the weariness I'd heard in my mother's voice. I became ashamed at my self-centeredness. I realized that I wasn't the only person who was tired and overwhelmed this year. My mother had always made Christmas special for me, and now it was time for me to make it special for her.

A few days before Christmas, my husband and I loaded the kids into the car and drove to my parents' home. Amazingly, my daughter fell asleep on the way there. When we arrived, I placed her — still strapped safely in her infant car seat — on the couch. We began to work. My husband brought the much-loved artificial Christmas tree up from the basement, along with box after box of tree ornaments and decorations. While he strung the lights on the tree, my son and I began looking through the boxes. It felt like Christmas morning had arrived early. Each decoration I found transported me to a wonderful childhood memory.

"I remember this! I made this in Girl Scouts," I exclaimed, as I pulled out a round ornament decked out in glitter and fabric scraps.

"And look at this one," I said, holding up a large, blue, hand-blown glass ball. "This was my grandma's ornament. I remember hanging it on her tree when I was a little girl."

"Mom, these are cool," my son said. His blue eyes sparkled as he studied several faded, red-and-white candy canes made of twisted pipe cleaners.

"I made those when I was about your age," I said.

"Can we make some for our tree?" he asked.

"Yes, that will be fun," I answered, smiling. My joy at watching his excitement canceled out any thoughts of my own exhaustion.

Miraculously, nothing went wrong. No knots were in the light strands, and each jewel-toned bulb shined brightly. No ornaments were dropped or broken, and my daughter enjoyed a rare and extended slumber while we worked. I forgot about my fatigue and depression because I was focused on how my mom would react when she saw our handiwork.

We worked for several hours hanging ornaments and arranging other holiday decorations around her house. Then it was time for the finishing touch. My son giggled as he was put on his dad's shoulders. My husband lifted him high above the tree's branches to put the star on the tree. I looked at my daughter, still sleeping, and smiled at her sweet, contented expression. I had to blink away the grateful tears that suddenly filled my eyes.

The next day, we made the three-hour trip to pick up my mother. I could see dark circles under her eyes and the worry lines etched in her forehead as she gazed out the car window.

"I can't believe Christmas is only a couple days away," she sighed. "I am never going to get my tree up. I still have shopping, wrapping and baking to do."

I simply nodded and smiled. My son bounced in his seat the entire way home, talking nonstop, but somehow managing to avoid blurting out our secret. When we arrived at my mom's home, he and I ran into the house ahead of everyone else and turned on the Christmas tree lights.

My mother walked in and he yelled, "Look, Grandma!"

Her gaze was drawn to the tree standing regally in the corner. Her eyes grew wide and she gasped, covering her mouth with her hand. She started to cry and then ran to me and held me tight. We laughed and cried at the same time.

"Thank you. I can't believe you did this," she whispered, choking back her tears.

It was one of the best moments of my life. What we did for my mother changed my whole attitude that Christmas. It shifted my focus from my troubles to my blessings and the feeling of pure joy I received by giving to another. I had truly found Christmas.

~Annette McDermott

44

Hair Is Overrated

A daughter is a little girl who grows up to be a friend.
~Author Unknown

"One thing I can tell you for certain is that you will lose your hair before your second treatment. And my advice is to buzz your head before it starts to fall out. If you wait until it starts coming out, it will be in your bed, it will be in your food, it will be in your shoes. Look me in the eye. Buzz your head while you still have the power. You take control." These words came straight from the mouth of a veteran chemo nurse, and were spoken directly to the ears of my mother, a sixty-year-old breast cancer patient. So what did we do? We did what all obedient Southern girls do. We got ready to cut some hair.

Mama got out the scissors, the hair-cutting ones, not the paper-cutting ones. Mama is particular about her scissors. Then she got out the clippers that she uses to cut Daddy's hair. Mama is also particular about Daddy. I spread a worn floral sheet on the kitchen floor and pulled Mama's chair in the middle of it. Mama tugged her white T-shirt over her head, exposing one bare droopy breast and one crooked angry scar.

"Are you okay with this? Can you do this?" Mama asked.

"I am and I can but I'm not promising I won't cry."

"No reason to cry. You know I've never liked my hair anyway."

I took a deep breath and started with the scissors. A clip here, a cut there, and short ash-blond hair landed on a bed of faded purple flowers. I worked diligently like an excited cosmetology student. Then

I plugged in the clippers and the loud buzz was more than Mama could stand. She insisted on wearing earplugs while I finished my masterpiece. So there she sat, nude from the waist up, with pink and yellow earplugs stuffed in her ears. She caught my eye and we giggled. I took a long swipe down the middle of her head. I methodically shaved off hair in perfect rows as if I'd done it a million times before. I told Mama how awesome her head looked but she couldn't hear me. I told her shaving heads was a piece of cake but she couldn't hear me. I told her I was fine and wasn't crying but she couldn't hear me.

And just as quickly as we started it was over. We were done. I ran my hands over the stubble. Mama removed her earplugs.

Questioning blue eyes stared up at me. "How do I look?"

"You look beautiful, just like my mama. See."

So there we were, side by side as we'd been so many times in so many situations. The mirror reflected two women who were much tougher than they gave themselves credit for. Two strong women. One with hair, one without. One a daughter, one a mother. And both with big wide matching smiles — and not a tear in sight.

~Janet H. Taylor

45

Wonder Mom

*Unconsciously, Canadians feel that any people can live
where the climate is gentle. It takes a special people to
prosper where nature makes it so hard.*
~Robert MacNeil

*I*t was a Friday morning in January of 1977. Gigantic snow-flakes swirled into drifts across the deck outside our kitchen window. I crunched my Flintstones vitamin and listened to the radio announcer list all the cancelled buses in Prince Edward County in southern Ontario, fingers crossed. At last he said, "6G."

I stopped listening. Craig and I jumped up and down, sloshing milk from our cereal bowls onto the table. Daddy declared he was off to work and later to the Oyster Stag at the Yacht Club in Picton. Mom frowned.

No doubt there would be a crowd of loud men, lots of food and an endless supply of Canadian on tap where Daddy was going. I pictured Fred Flintstone in a tall, furry hat on his way to the Lodge of the Loyal Order of Water Buffaloes, as Mom closed the front door with a bang. She sent Craig and me to the basement. In our pajamas. Without even brushing our teeth!

The morning unfolded in a series of game shows, cartoons and floor hockey downstairs. Bologna sandwiches with mustard in front of the television for lunch. I was over the moon. If only *Wonder Woman* had been on instead of *The Flintstones*.

Wanting to check on the snow, I skipped upstairs. Mom sat at the kitchen table, where I think she had been stationed since Daddy left, with a coffee mug glued to her hand. The windows rattled. Wind howled as it often did from across Lake Ontario and over the Sandbanks toward our house, only louder than I'd ever heard it. This was the best snowstorm ever!

Mom puffed one cigarette to its end and lit another. I leaned against her shoulder. "I thought you quit."

She crushed out the barely-smoked butt, reached for my hand and pulled me closer.

"Mom, is everything okay?" I asked.

She spoke into the top of my head, "Of course it is. How could it not be on a day like this?"

The house creaked as Mom got up and led me to my room. I took *Alligator Pie* from my bookshelf, and then Mom handed Mrs. Beasley to me as though the doll were real. I hugged her to my chest. A great sense of comfort wrapped around me like a blanket, and Mom headed back to the kitchen.

Hot dogs for supper without Daddy seemed wrong. As Mom tucked me into bed that night, she wrinkled her lips and said, "Your father is stranded in town. At the Oyster Stag." She kissed my forehead. "Sweet dreams."

I snuggled in deeper with Mrs. Beasley.

By Saturday morning, Daddy still wasn't home. I knew he'd be back. Nothing could stop him.

From her post, Mom said to my brother and me, "You two can have whatever you want for breakfast, downstairs."

I looked at Craig. Together we sang out, "Froot Loops!"

Mom agreed and reached for the bowls without hesitation. I made a face and she smiled back. "Special treat."

Life couldn't get any better than this.

That afternoon, dressed in Mom's nurse's cape, I sat on the basement floor in a pile of clothes from the dress-up closet. The phone rang and soon Mom called down, "Can you kids come up here, please?"

We clomped up the stairs. "Mom, what is it?" I asked.

She dragged her cross-country skis from the front hall closet. "I have to go out. The neighbours can't get home. They want me to go next door to see if their lights are still on. They're worried about the pipes freezing."

Eagerly I said, "I can go with you!" The scrunched look on her face said "no" before she opened her mouth.

Mom wriggled into her lime green and brown ski pants and jacket. Then she pulled on Daddy's balaclava over her goggle-sized glasses. I laughed. She looked ridiculous! When she opened the outer storm door, a drift as high as the doorknob spilled across the tiles to the edge of the carpet. Climbing up and over it, she shoved her way out into the storm.

There was nothing to see through the front picture window but a shifting wall of white. We waited. And waited. Finally, the front door burst open and Mom reappeared, covered. Snow cascaded across the floor and past the edge of the carpet. Mom leaned her skis in the corner by the door and slapped her hands on her hips, her eyes focused in a serious look. Just like Wonder Woman.

Wonder Mom to the rescue! "Did you see the lights?" I asked.

She rubbed her temples. "No, I got lost. I didn't even get out of our yard." Slowly she grinned.

Sunday arrived and still no Daddy. His phone calls were not enough. Mom seemed frazzled. Snow blocked every window and door in the house. Craig had become annoying and I was bored. Sunday afternoon TV was awful, and the stations didn't come in clearly no matter which way I turned the rotor. Daddy needed to get home before bedtime.

That evening, the sound of skidoos whined outside. The engines stopped. I rushed to the front hallway and waited with Mom and Craig. We opened the inner wooden door and heard the crunch-swish of shovels. At last I saw the tip of a shovel, then a boot, then Daddy's nose smooshed against the glass like a kid. Daddy was home!

A week after the storm hit, Mom held my gloved hand tight as the whole family headed to the end of the laneway. Joining with all our neighbours, we watched the huge snow blowers and plows from CFB Trenton clear the West Lake Road. As the soldiers worked and waved, above the groans of machinery came a collective cheer for the heroes who had come to free us from the remnants of the storm.

It wasn't until years later I discovered just how protective Mom had been. For her, the storm of 1977 was a time of immeasurable anxiety and fear. Would the power go out? Or the phones? Did we have enough oil in the tank? And food? Would we stay warm? She had never been so overwhelmed as a mother, or so alone.

Ever since then, Mom makes sure to always have at least a month's worth of supplies and food in the house, no matter what the season. Stocking up in case of emergencies became the norm. It still is. But the real lesson — the true gift she gave to me — came from a mom's love: During that storm, and for decades after, Mom preserved the innocence of the experience for me like a true superhero.

This is the memory I hold dear in my heart.

I think Wonder Mom deserves a new cape, and maybe some shiny red boots.

~Susan Blakeney

46

Tea in the Afternoon

So much has been given to me, I have not time to
ponder over that which has been denied.
~Helen Keller

I was born cold, small, and underweight in a country in South America, at a time when incubators were unheard of and the mortality rate for premature babies was devastatingly high. Lacking strength to even swallow small amounts of nourishment, I was not supposed to survive twenty-four hours. Everyone was resigned to let nature take its course... everyone except my grandmother. She had great faith, fierce determination, and bold ingenuity, an unbelievable mix of virtues for a simple woman who didn't read or write.

Lovingly, she took me to her home, tucked me in a shoebox, and placed light bulbs around it to keep me warm. She slowly and constantly fed milk to me with an eyedropper.

Under her care, I not only survived, but flourished physically, mentally, and spiritually.

For years, I thought she was my mother. Even today, when "mother" is mentioned, it is her I think of. She, however, would often remind me, "No, I am your grandma. Your mother is that lady who comes on Sundays and brings us groceries. Talk to her; she is lonely. Someday, you will have to live with her."

For me, it was inconceivable that such a severe-looking lady could be my mother. I felt as if I was the victim of fraud. When she visited,

I would hide behind a couch. In my child-mind, if she didn't see me, I didn't exist, and then I would not have to go with her. I wished life with Grandma would never end.

Even under that cloud, however, I lived a happy life. Our small family consisted of three: my grandmother, our dog, and me. My grandmother was a frail, spirited, clever, small woman with worn-out hands, a sweet grin, easy laughter, crow's feet deeply carved into her temples, and brown eyes that resembled mine. Her thinning white hair was pulled back in a tight bun. Most of the time, she dressed in a white shirt or sweater and brown skirt and shoes. My playmate was our old dog. Patient and almost blind, he would let me pull his tail. I completed our family, a skinny little girl about four or five years old, who liked paper dolls, picture books, pretty clothes, and had lots of simple questions requiring complicated answers. We were all snug in our humble home in a small town near the Andes Mountains. We didn't have many material conveniences, but always had enough food and a place to live. Our life was peaceful, quiet, and predictable.

Tea in the afternoon was our favorite routine. My grandmother, the perfectionist, enjoyed setting the best stage for our tea. It was not just the tea, but the position of the table holding the tea. It had to catch the sunlight coming in from the only window in the room. Together, we placed the small round table in the best location. On sunny days, we put it to the south and delighted in the brightness and warmth while shadows projected into our teacups. On cloudy days, we opened the worn-out window to maximize the light coming in. The sunlight made us feel special, fancy, and mischievous. Then, only when everything was just right, we would begin our very own tea ceremony.

My grandmother made my tea in her own special way. A half cup of tea, a half cup of warm milk, and two teaspoons of sugar. She called it *tecito*, Spanish for "little cup of tea." Our dog sat at our feet, lazily wagging his tail in quiet approval. Grandma sat in front of me with a twinkle in her eyes, sipping her tea ever so slowly.

I preferred to make it last longer, getting tiny teaspoonfuls, one from the lighter side of the cup, another from the darker side. I savored her company and the feeling of closeness, security, and love. I eagerly looked forward all day to that time of nourishment and affection. A very religious woman, Grandma talked to me about God's goodness and the angel assigned to protect me all my life. Graciously and wisely, she was preparing me for the rugged road ahead.

We didn't have a heater, and during winter our home was bitterly cold. Always worried about my health, she put me to bed early to prevent my catching a cold or worse. Then she brought me *tecito* in bed with her small, trembling hands. The warmth and the smoothness of the tea going down my throat, as well as her presence and devotion, warmed me body and soul.

Then, one day when I was nine years old, without any warning, Grandma peacefully died. My world crashed, and my life was forever parted into two: before and after Grandma.

I never realized how strong I had become under her guidance; her teachings kicked in, and I continued believing in God, my guardian angel, and sunshine.

Years have passed. Places have changed. People have gone. Painful memories have faded. But happy memories continue to live in me.

I live now in a different and faraway place. I honor her memory by living my life by the values she taught me. In return, I have been blessed with children, grandchildren, health, and life. And I am not cold anymore.

Sometimes, when I need to talk to Grandma, I wait for the afternoon and then deliberately, leisurely, playfully, and lovingly set myself a little table near a sunny window and pour myself a cup of tea. Then, I feel her love softly comforting my soul. It's the two of us again, and I secretly whisper, "Thank you, Mother."

~Nancy Bravo Creager

47

Dance Lessons

*There are shortcuts to happiness, and dancing
is one of them.*
~Vicki Baum

The feel of gliding around a dance floor gracefully performing a waltz or romantically moving in a samba is one of my greatest delights. In fact, dance has been a significant part of my entire life, and I have committed considerable time, money, energy, frustration and glowing success to mastering all different types of dance.

Would this passion have been ignited if not for the sacrifice of my mother? I doubt it. I grew up on the other side of the tracks in a very affluent town. What I mean is that while classmates were flying to Vail for the weekend to go skiing, my brothers and sister and I would get cafeteria trays to use as sleds on local golf courses. However, in our community, which is a suburb of a major metropolitan area, there were many benefits even us "townies" could enjoy. We attended outstanding schools and securely patrolled parks and streets and participated in extravagant town-directed summer activities.

But one activity that we could not enjoy by simply living in this town was dance lessons. In the early 1960s, my mother thought that dance lessons, table manners, polite behavior, and etiquette were important skills that her children needed to prepare themselves for their futures.

Her attempts at teaching us herself left her with bruised feet and left us frustrated and discouraged. Then one evening after dinner she presented us with our "church" clothes all freshly ironed and informed us that we were going to the dance school for lessons. There was such joy on her face that no one grumbled about putting on our Sunday best in the middle of the week.

For several weeks, each Thursday night we endured the sneers from our dance partners who commented on the fact that we always wore the same clothes. Their comments brushed right over me because within the first week of dance, I was hooked. The lights, the music and the intricate dance steps captivated me. For that one brief hour, I was transported to a life of gaiety that my wealthy neighbors took for granted.

At the end of the hour, my mother, who had been reading a book in the car during the lesson, would bring us home. There, she would clean up the house, make lunches for each of us for the next day, fold laundry, and review our homework. After we were tucked into bed, she would say, "I'll be back in a bit. Don't forget your prayers, and know that I love you."

This routine went on for weeks until one evening I realized that I had left my sneakers at the dance studio. Since I had gym the next day at school, I had to go back to get my sneakers. My father reluctantly drove me to the studio and just as I was about to knock on the door, I saw my mother on her hands and knees shining the hardwood floor. I was devastated; I banged on the door and my mother approached with a huge smile on her face. "Mama, what in the world…" I stammered, but before I could finish my sentence, she laughed and said, "Don't worry my precious girl, I saw your sneakers here and I was going to bring them home."

"But Mama, that is not what is upsetting me, I'm upset that you are working so hard so late at night," I wailed. She pulled me into her soft arms for a big hug and explained that the dance instructor was giving us the lessons in exchange for my mother cleaning the studio. "This is a wonderful solution, my baby girl," she stated firmly as she held me at arm's length. Looking me straight in the eye, she said, "Don't let anything take away the joy you have for dance. In fact, darling daughter of mine, never let anyone take joy away from you for anything."

As we walked arm in arm back to the car, I vowed then and there that I would honor my mother, I would honor my joy, and I would keep dancing—and I have.

~Judith Fitzsimmons

Chapter
5

for Mom, with love

Thanks for the Memories

*A memory is a photograph taken by the heart to
make a special moment last forever.*
~Author Unknown

48

A Glorious Ride

If wrinkles must be written on our brows, let them not
be written upon the heart. The spirit should
never grow old.
~James A. Garfield

Bold, wild, adventurous—not words I would use to describe my mother-in-law. I'd heard the stories about Gran as a young girl, daring to ride a calf back from the stream on her parents' farm and getting bucked off. But she grew up and calmed down. Marrying late in life, she lost her husband after only three years. Then she did the only thing she knew to do. She went back to work as a hairdresser and quietly raised her only child, my husband. After working more than forty years, she retired in her mid-seventies to settle into a semi-reclusive life. Sedate, solitary, dignified—now that was the Gran I knew.✓

So it surprised us all when she told my younger son, Jeremy, she wanted him to take her for a ride in his Jeep Wrangler—with the top down. Cautious Gran? The meticulous hair stylist?

For three years, Jeremy intended to grant his grandmother's wish, but something always got in the way. Finally, he picked up the phone one day just after her eighty-fifth birthday and called her. "We're coming up tomorrow. I'm going to take you for that ride in my Jeep."

Gran could barely contain her excitement. "I can't wait!"

The next morning, Jeremy and his dad hopped in the Jeep and drove the three-hour trip into the rolling foothills of middle Tennessee.

Making a brief stop at Gran's, they unsnapped the windows and pulled off the Jeep's top. Then they buckled Gran into the front passenger seat and headed for her seven-acre parcel of land near Sycamore Lake.

I saw the pictures of her later, perched on the leather seat with the sun shining on her face and the wind blowing through her hair. Well, sort of. Actually, she covered her head with a scarf and put Jeremy's golf cap on top for good measure. Gran is particular about her hair after all. But the wind didn't detract from her exhilaration. The ride down the bumpy dirt road to her property did nothing to spoil her excitement. Even the mud spewing past her windowless door when they got stuck on the trail couldn't diminish her joy.

Later that day Gran called me, tired but eager to talk about her adventure. "That was a long time coming but well worth the wait. It was a glorious ride!"

As I move into my senior years, I want to remember Gran's example. Raising my family, I often became so busy with work and church, home and activities that I forgot to take delight in the moment. Sometimes I let life rush past, like wind past a Jeep, or allowed the bumpy ride and the spewing mud to steal my joy. But Jeremy and Gran didn't. They took the chance at an adventure and made memories that weekend, sweet memories that will last across the years.

Thanks to Gran, I am learning how to make life a glorious ride.

~Tracy Crump

49

Momma's Christmas Cookies

What was silent in the father speaks in the son, and
often I found in the son the unveiled secret of the father.
~Friedrich Nietzsche

ecause I am the smartest man alive, I lived in my parents' basement until I was twenty-six years old. While I was still in school, my father and I would spend several hours each night hanging out in the basement spending time with one another. I was usually studying or reading something while he was on the computer playing games or checking e-mails.

One day during the holiday season my mother informed us that she was making a batch of cookies for work. She wanted to know if we would be her test-dummies. Yeah! Who would pass that up? However, my father, Tim, and I were quickly disappointed when she came downstairs with only one cookie for the both of us. After we begged and earnestly explained that half a cookie was not the appropriate size to adequately determine whether or not a cookie should enter a competition, my mother informed us that she only made twelve. This cookie meant she was going to work with eleven. Okay! We would share one.

To say that the spicy-gumball-gingerbread cookie was the worst thing I had ever eaten would be an understatement. It was terrible. After forcing myself to swallow, I saw my dad equally devastated by how terrible the cookie had turned out.

"We have to tell her," Timbo informed me.

"Heck, no! I'm not tellin' her."

"Son, we have to. She will be so upset if she hears it at work."

"She is your wife; you tell her."

"She's your mother; you tell her."

"Not by choice!"

Ha! This was my go-to move. I always resorted to that — I didn't choose my mother, but my father chose his wife. And I won!

If only the dog could tell her. She never got mad at the dog.

Later that night my lovely parents went out for dinner without me. This was normal, as my father believed that putting a roof over my head was more than enough to fulfill his fatherly duties. While they were at dinner, I decided to take a break from studying in order to play some video games.

During my game, I heard a loud thud from upstairs that sounded very similar to a cooking stone slamming against a kitchen floor. I didn't think too much of it — at least not until I was at a good stopping point in my game. Then I proceeded upstairs to investigate.

At that time, we only had one dog. Her name is Laci, and she is a Border Collie and Lab mix that we rescued in 2004. Laci is a great dog! But like all dogs, she won't turn down an opportunity to eat people-food. At least, that's what I thought.

I looked down at the kitchen floor to see the cooking stone just as I expected. But what I also saw were ten little spicy-gumball-gingerbread-cookies. Mind you, this was at least fifteen minutes from the time I heard the thud, so Laci had more than enough time to stuff her little face.

"Man," I said aloud. "Even the dog won't eat them."

My mother's potential humiliation factor went from a batch of bad cookies that some people might not like, to a batch of bad cookies that even a dog would not eat. But the fact that a dog wouldn't eat her cookies puts her in an elite group. I mean — how many people do you know who have made something that even a dog will refuse to eat? I know one — my mother — and I couldn't wait to tell her.

~Kevin J. Kraemer

50

Just the Way I Like It

It isn't so much what's on the table that matters, as
what's on the chairs.
~W.S. Gilbert

I was excited! I was going home to visit Aunt Marge. Marge lived in Kansas and I lived in Seattle so although I called her every week, I hadn't been home to visit her in years.

I'd been a neglected child from a broken home and the happiest memories of my childhood were the brief visits I spent with Marge. Spending a few weeks with Marge in the summer was an oasis in my life and I always thought of her as my "real" mother. She was cheerful and kind and patient and fun to be with and she was a fabulous cook. Every meal was delicious and even after all the food had been eaten, no one was anxious to leave the table, so we'd often sit and talk for an hour while the food dried on our plates and the ice cubes melted in our sweetened tea.

When I knocked on her door, I hollered, "Mom, I'm home!"

It was a happy and tearful reunion.

"I cooked all your favorite foods," Marge said.

She had cooked a meatloaf that was burned and crusty around the edges and she made lumpy mashed potatoes and half-cooked corn on the cob. She had sweetened iced tea, and she had sliced tomatoes and cucumbers and doused them in vinegar. For dessert, she had baked a chocolate cake that had fallen in the middle and was evened out with extra frosting.

It was the exact meal she'd cooked for me many times when I was a child. It was perfect, and she was right — it was my favorite meal, because Marge was my favorite person.

At Marge's table, burned meatloaf and lumpy potatoes were a banquet, because she loved me. I told her everything was delicious and perfect because I loved her. We sat at the table and talked about the old days, family, friends, and a hundred other things, because when you had a meal with Marge, you were never in a hurry to leave the table.

The next morning she fixed my favorite breakfast, coffee with cream and extra sugar and burned toast. She scraped most of the black crumbs off the toast and she covered the toast with extra butter and jelly to hide the burned parts.

We sat at the kitchen table watching the birds come and go at the birdfeeder outside the window.

"I like…" I started.

"Meadowlarks," Marge said, "When you were eight, you liked meadowlarks."

"I still do," I said. There wasn't another person in the world who knew or cared that I liked meadowlarks. Marge knew me better than anyone else and she was the only person beside myself who remembered my childhood.

That evening we sat on the front porch and listened to the locusts in the elm trees. I felt eight years old and although Marge's hair was now white, I remembered when it was dark auburn.

"Do you still have Suzie?" she asked.

"No, she got lost a long time ago," I said. Suzie was a doll with a cracked head and one missing eye. The rubber band holding her arms onto her body had rotted and her arms had fallen off, but she'd been my favorite doll when I was five.

"Too bad," Marge said. "I've really missed you. I wish you didn't live so far away."

"I've missed you, too," I said. I hadn't realized how much until now. "I'll come home more often, I promise."

The sun went down and we went inside to watch television.

"We should have a snack before we go to bed," Marge said. She went into the kitchen and returned a few minutes later with a bowl of ice cream for each of us. When I was a child, we always had a bowl of ice cream before we went to bed. Tonight it was strawberry ice cream with broken potato chips sprinkled on top because that was how I liked it the summer I was seven.

I knew the next day, and every day of my two-week visit, would be the same. The meals would only vary by which foods would be burned and which foods would be half-cooked. We'd scrape the black crusts off the meat, potatoes, rolls or toast. We'd reheat undercooked vegetables. We'd laugh and do whatever we needed to do to make it edible, whether it was just scooping out the middle and leaving the black edges stuck to the pan or if it meant covering something with gravy that was either as thin as water or thick enough to cut with a knife. When she accidentally dropped a hot pad into a boiling pot of chicken and dumplings she dug the hot pad out with a spoon and asked, "Do you think that will affect the flavor?"

I told her no, I didn't think so, and it didn't matter — it would taste like a feast to me.

Because with Marge, it was never about the food, it was about the love.

~April Knight

51

The Healing Power of Toilet Paper

With the fearful strain that is on me night and day, if I did not laugh I should die.
~Abraham Lincoln

A letter to the editor in our local newspaper complained about nocturnal pranksters stringing toilet paper on residents' trees. That letter brought a flurry of responses defending this act as being a harmless tribute to friends: "It's an honor to get toilet papered," admonished one writer, "and good clean fun for teenagers!"

Reading these letters brought me chuckles and then tears as they stirred up old memories of my mother's ninety-second year — a year Charles Dickens would describe as "the best of times, the worst of times." She was terminally ill that autumn. And I watched, powerless, as my mother's vigor and grit gave way to frailty and despair.

Mom's ninety-second year was also my tenth one as her caregiver. A decade before, I helped her, as she liked to call it, "break out" of the nursing home where she resided. It was a fine facility with a caring staff. But Mom didn't want or need skilled care; she wanted to live on her own and just needed some assistance to do so. Being in a more restrictive environment than was necessary had plunged her into a clinical depression; she got out of bed only at mealtimes and spent the rest of each day staring at the ceiling, disconnected.

And so I made a leap of faith. With her doctor's blessing and my determination to help Mom live independently, I found her an apartment, furnished it, and hired a few part-time caregivers to assist us.

The risk paid off, and I was abundantly rewarded by seeing my mother once again enjoying her life. Icing on the cake was Mom's eagerness to resume our fun-filled weekly outings — "adventures," we called them — exploring country roads to discover what lay around each bend: a field of flowers, an old barn or maybe a country café to stop at for pie and coffee.

It was during these years of Mom's need and my help that we became closer than we had ever been.

Though I still look back and wonder how I found the time and energy to manage Mom's home and helpers, along with my own home, family responsibilities and job, I did handle it — one day at a time. Mom was happy and thriving; that kept me strong and resolute.

Then, ten years later, Mom was diagnosed with cancer. Following on the heels of her chemotherapy, she suffered a series of strokes that made walking difficult.

As Mom's health declined, my caregiving duties increased, leaving little time for things like adventures. Those days the only unfamiliar roads we traveled were the ones leading to Mom's new symptoms and my corresponding duties. Who had time to even think about fun or outings?

Then, one balmy September evening, for some inexplicable reason, I invited my mother to do a thing neither of us had ever done: "Let's go toilet papering!"

I picked her up around twilight that evening and headed to a store to buy our double-ply ammunition. We devised a plan to paper the yards of her two other children, my brother and sister, and to hit a few of her grandchildren's homes, time and energy permitting.

This outing would push my mother to her physical limits. Was I making a mistake? Her usual bedtime was 9:00 p.m. and it was already 8:30; we always used the handicapped spaces, but this night, to avoid notice, I parked a full block from our first stop.

At that distance, we snuck arm-in-arm down the dark walk leading to my brother's home. Mom's steps were labored, but her attention was focused on the clear, star-studded sky and gentle autumn breezes.

Once in his back yard, I guided Mom to a small tree and handed her a roll of toilet paper from our canvas bag. Without hesitation, she shot it skyward. We watched the white ribbon sail over the crown and glide down the other side, leaving a streamer of well-placed Charmin.

I retrieved the roll and handed it back to Mom; she had both hands clasped over her mouth to keep from laughing out loud. Hugging each other, we glanced toward the patio doors and spotted my brother relaxing in his recliner. The sight of him so oblivious to our presence emboldened us to continue our shenanigans.

Bent over and leaning on me, Mom shuffled from tree to tree, gleefully pitching rolls like an ace. We were in a timeless cocoon where pain and burdens didn't exist. Finishing the last tree, we stood a while to survey our handiwork; the moonlit yard looked like a surreal wonderland of shimmering white streamers. Mission accomplished, we headed back to my car, giggling all the way like two schoolgirls. Mom was to paper a dozen trees in four family yards that unforgettable evening.

We both knew this would be one of our last outings, but the lesson we took from it would ultimately help carry us through the rough days that lay ahead. Mom and I resolved that night to make some play time every day, in whatever way we would be able; I added crayons and coloring books to our shopping list.

The day after our big adventure, Mom and I sent an anonymous card to each of our victims, signed, "From your EXTERIOR decorators." We laughed all the way home from the post office. In the coming weeks, Mom and I shared many more laughs after each of us received calls from puzzled family members wondering who had done those strange things.

Our family Thanksgiving gathering was at my home that November. To accommodate the thirty-some guests, I set dinner tables in my basement recreation room. My brother, sister and their families made many trips up and down the stairs that day to help carry food and dishes, and to use my first and second floor bathrooms.

That evening, my sister was the last to leave. At the door, she pulled an envelope from her purse, handed it to Mom and then kissed us goodbye. Baffled, Mom read the note: "From your INTERIOR decorators."

For the first time that day, I had a chance to go upstairs; the entire second floor was strewn, top to bottom, with toilet paper!

My mother's last year was marked by physical decline. Nevertheless, we kept our resolve to share some simple fun each day. Those light-hearted moments were like a salve on our stress, and they are the ones I'll always remember. Toilet papering had taught us that play is, indeed, powerful medicine!

~Toni Becker

52

Mom Didn't Play Fair

A man loves his sweetheart the most, his wife the
best, but his mother the longest.
~Irish Proverb

I checked my watch. Yeah, I had time to catch a quick break-fast at IHOP. So I exited my car, slammed the door shut, and leapt up on the curb. As soon as I pulled open the door, it hit me.

I flashed back forty-two years. During the cold Ohio winters of my youth, the last thing that I wanted to do was crawl out of my toasty cocoon and go to school. I remember being snugly curled in the fetal position beneath a mound of blankets. If I happened to awake, then I would intentionally flip the pillow over to get to the cold side, and curl up again. Mmmm… there was no way that I was getting up!

But my mom didn't play fair. She knew how to get my brothers and me up without the use of an alarm clock.

And Mom did so with a minimum of effort. She didn't stand in the bedroom doorway and yell. She didn't rudely turn on the bedroom lights and walk away. She didn't violently jostle the sleeping lumps under the blankets.

No, Mom would depart the kitchen to silently trudge down the long hallway of our single-story, ranch-style home. Upon arriving at my bedroom, she would simply open the door. Then Mom would turn around and silently traipse back down that hallway to the kitchen.

In a matter of minutes, I'd start sniffing. I'd roll over and face away from the open bedroom door. I'd place my pillow over my head. It was no use.

My brothers and I would kick off our blankets and roll out of our beds. Then we'd race down the hallway to the kitchen to find Mom's primary weapon: bacon that was perfectly fried — not too floppy and not too crispy.

From that effort, Mom always saved the bacon grease in an empty can of Maxwell House coffee. Placing it in the refrigerator, she would use it to fry the next day's eggs. Or she would use it to prepare her homemade mush on a giant griddle. Little more than fried cornmeal batter, those orange slices of mush were slathered with butter and then drenched with hot syrup.

That's right — Mom even heated the syrup. Yeah… Mom didn't play fair. And I love her for it.

~John M. Scanlan

53

Joy in an Unexpected Friendship

It's one of nature's ways that we often feel closer to distant generations than to the generation immediately preceding us.
~Igor Stravinsky

Our entire family was over at my parents' house for Thanksgiving—the scene was the same each year. The eight grandchildren were running around playing, arguing and playing some more. The adults were finished with the meal, lazing in the living room on the good couches, which were always covered with an old quilt when my family came to visit. We sat there watching the Cowboys game, chatting and trying to keep my dad from steering the conversation to politics.

I had always found the similarities between my grandmother and my daughter, Lizzie, who has autism, fascinating. Lizzie was about four years old and did not interact much with anyone; neither did my grandmother. My grandmother's grip on reality had slowly been sucked out of her as Alzheimer's took its toll; similarly, Lizzie seemed to lack any understanding of our day-to-day lives.

Both Lizzie and my grandmother were often in their own worlds. Lizzie would flap her arms and loudly recite all the words from *Dora the Explorer*. My grandmother would rub some sort of fabric in between her fingers and read a script from an earlier time in her life when she still had young children at home. They both seemed to wander around the house with no sense of purpose.

As the adults were chatting, I realized things had gotten very quiet. Eerily quiet. Way too quiet. Lizzie had either gotten into something she wasn't supposed to, or gotten out of the house.

I immediately jumped up and began my search.

Kitchen? Nope.

Den? Not there.

Bathroom? Oops, wrong person. Sorry.

Then I heard it... the sweet sound of young and old giggling together. I peeked around the corner and what did I see? Lizzie and Grandma had found the remote control for the lamp in the bedroom. Such a simple thing; how could this possibly be bringing so much joy to both of them? They would walk into the bedroom, push the button, watch the light turn on and break out laughing.

After they completed their immediate cause-and-effect thrill, they would turn the light off, walk out, and then Lizzie would grab Grandma's hand and pull her back into the room again. They would repeat this simple act over and over, again and again and again. Each time the light flipped on, they would laugh hysterically as if they had never experienced this phenomenon before.

The repetition of the light made sense to Lizzie, and she had found her perfect playmate — my grandma, a sweet old lady with no short-term memory! This was truly an unexpected friendship that brought joy to both of them.

~Julie Hornok

54

House of Sunshine and Tears

Youth is a crown of roses, old age a crown of willows.
~Jewish Proverb

I pulled my 1959 Plymouth into the driveway, fairly sure that I had the correct address. The "for rent" sign was still hanging in the downstairs window along with the monthly rent listing of $125 a month. To a college sophomore who'd already spent a fortune on tuition and books, this was pretty steep, especially back in the mid-1960s. Additionally, it was in a rundown section of San Jose, California. Row upon row of aging, dilapidated Victorian homes lined the streets that paralleled my college. As I got out of the car I gazed at this once-elegant home, which I guessed had to have been built before the turn of the twentieth century.

As I was about to knock, the door opened, and there stood a tiny, gray-haired woman of about seventy. She wore a pair of jeans and rain boots as well as a large apron that covered her entire torso. She smiled and asked, "Are you here about the rent?"

Her accent was clearly Germanic but pleasant. "Yes, ma'am," I responded. She must have noticed that I was gawking at her outfit because she tittered, saying, "Oh, I was about to do some gardening in the front. After last night's rain, it can get pretty messy."

"I understand. My mother does pretty much the same thing." She smiled, her eyes squinting at the early morning sun.

"My name is Ester Levinsky, and whom do I have the pleasure of meeting?"

"Oh… I'm sorry, I'm Jody Chaney. Uh… I go to school here at San Jose State."

"That's wonderful. Without an education, the world can be pretty harsh." There was a momentary pause until she added, "Well, why don't we take a look at the room, yah?" I nodded, and together we went inside and up the polished staircase. My eyes darted everywhere, from the faded photos on the wall to the two facing china cabinets on either side of the hallway, filled with glass crystals and vases of various sizes. Despite the bright morning, the house was dark, even with the flowered curtains that had been pulled back and tightened with bows. Everything seemed to be extremely tidy.

As we walked down the narrow hall, I couldn't help but notice a large portrait of a young man and woman in what appeared to be a wedding picture. "That was taken on my wedding day in the spring of 1917." She pointed to the man in the photo. "This was my husband, Isaac. He was a chemistry teacher." She spoke no further of him but continued to walk down the hall until we came upon the room at the far end of the house. As we entered I noticed it was a bit more modern than the rest. The paint on the walls appeared brighter, and light from the window shone down on a comfortable looking bed. Opposite the bed at the far end was an old writing desk and chair. Two rows of bookshelves hung over the desk.

"Be careful opening the door too wide. The radiator is right behind you. Now, let's see… oh, the bathroom is right across the hall and it has a full shower and bath. As far as meals are concerned, you're welcome to join me for dinner… that's included in the rent and you can keep your breakfast foods in the kitchen cupboard or refrigerator. I do require though that you wash your own dishes. Also, you can use the washer and dryer whenever you need it."

This is a great deal, I thought, especially with dinners thrown in. "I'll take the room," I said a bit too enthusiastically. "Would you like some references?"

Ester shook her head, her hair neatly pressed into a bun. "No, you seem like a good boy. My husband always told me sometimes instincts are more accurate than cold facts."

"Are there other rooms rented out here?" I queried.

"No, this is the first time I've ever rented out a room. I hope I'm doing the right thing you know, with all the crime going on. I think I'd feel safer knowing someone else was in the house, other than just myself."

The following week I moved in, bringing with me my little record player, clothes, lamp, 49ers poster, and my baseball glove and bat. Looking about the room, with its oddly shaped trapezoidal window, I wondered who had lived here in the past, what they were like, and whether they were as content in this room as I seemed to be. Within an hour I'd set everything in place and was off to my afternoon class.

Returning to my newly rented room, I smelled the delicious aroma of chicken and rice being prepared. "Supper's on in thirty minutes," shouted Ester. I smiled to myself, and my stomach rumbled.

"Thank you ma'am. I'll be down shortly."

It was during our first evening together that she told me about herself and her husband. They'd both been raised in Frankfurt, Germany where they met at the university. She was beginning her studies in English literature while Isaac was doing graduate work in chemistry. Soon after graduating he got a job working as a chemist for an agricultural company, but was later forced to leave once Hitler came to power. She remained at home, raising their only daughter, Sarah, who died of polio at seven. Once it appeared that they would eventually be sent to a concentration camp, they arranged to leave, smuggling themselves out through Switzerland and eventually landing in New York in 1938. Isaac found work, not as a chemist but as an assistant researcher for a beverage company. In 1942 his company moved him to San Jose where they purchased the Victorian. They lived there together until 1962 when he died of cancer.

Day after day we'd sit together, discussing history, politics, religion, literature — anything that we fancied. Through the wisdom of Mrs. Levinsky, I gained insight into life that no teacher could ever have imparted on me. I no longer looked at her as my landlady but as a grandmother.

As a history major, I was fascinated with her understanding of Germany in the 1930s, and we ended up talking for hours on the subject late into the night. When we were done, I'd climb the stairs to my little corner room and study until overcome with exhaustion.

For three years I remained in that house, helping her with her chores while she regaled me with stories from her childhood. When I finally graduated, I was offered a job in Nevada. Although excited, I felt a certain sadness at having to leave. When the time came to say goodbye, we hugged tearfully, promising to keep in touch. For over a dozen years we did just that — until I received word from a neighbor that she had suffered a stroke and died a few months later.

I will always remember that house and the enchanting times spent with this most remarkable woman.

~J.D. Chaney

55

Gifts to Keep

Grandma's heart is a Patchwork of Love.
~Author Unknown

Only three Christmas gifts were under the artificial fir tree. All the other presents had been opened. These three big packages were wrapped identically, green ribbon tied around red-and-white striped foil. Inside were gifts that my mom had planned to give her three grandchildren — my son, daughter, and niece. Gifts she had begun making, but didn't finish. A heart attack had ended her life in April.

Six months later, Dad sold the family home and moved into a one-bedroom apartment. The first Christmas without Mom was made even sadder as our family sat cramped in a small living room — so different from Mom and Dad's home where we'd always celebrated past Christmases.

Dad looked at his three teenage grandchildren. "Those presents are for you from your grannie," he said as my brother and I and our spouses sat nearby. Alicia and Sarah, age seventeen, and Eric, age fifteen, all frowned. "She was making something special for you to have this Christmas," Dad said. He looked at me as tears flooded his eyes and then he lowered his head.

Taking a deep breath, I said, "It's three almost identical gifts."

"Is it something we asked for?" Alicia asked.

"No," Dad said. "It's something you can use now. Your grannie hoped you'd each keep it and maybe even pass it on to your kids."

The teenagers sat up straight, pulled their shoulders back, raised their eyebrows, and looked at each other.

"Is it something that we've seen her working on?" Sarah asked.

"No, she kept it a secret from all of you. But your parents and I knew," Dad said.

"So, how do we know which box is ours?" asked Eric.

"By numbers. The same way Grannie always let you choose. Take one of those folded papers in the basket. They're numbered 1, 2, 3, and the presents have numbers on the bottom of them," Dad explained.

As Alicia, Sarah, and Eric held the unopened gifts, silence filled the small living room. They had quickly ripped into the other packages, but now they sat cross-legged on the floor beside Dad's chair. Silent and still. "Go ahead, open them," Dad said.

The teenagers paced themselves so that they saw their gifts at the same time. "A quilt!" Sarah and Alicia said, almost in unison. Eric stood and wrapped his quilt around his shoulders. It fell to the floor. The girls did the same, holding their quilts close around their bodies.

"I love it!" Sarah said, "But Grannie always said that she'd never make a quilt." She pulled her white and navy blue patchwork quilt tighter around herself.

"This is beautiful! My quilt is just like yours. Same colors. Same everything," Alicia said to Sarah. Then she turned to her brother. "Yours is the same, except it's dark red. Almost maroon." They held their quilts up and compared. The quilt pattern, with triangles and rectangles, was exactly the same. All three quilts had solid white pieces and some calico printed fabric; only the solid blue and maroon pieces were different.

"Grannie made so many things but this is the best." Eric lifted his quilt over his head and sat down on the floor. None of us adults said anything. We wiped tears, coughed, and took deep breaths.

"Yeah, this is the best. But don't forget all the matching outfits she made when we were little," said Alicia.

"Remember the stuffed Raggedy Ann and Andy dolls?" Eric said. "Wonder why she decided to make us quilts now?" Alicia and Sarah held their quilts in their laps as they, too, sat on the floor.

Dad blew his nose, wiped his eyes with his wet handkerchief

and said, "Your grannie wanted you to have something that you'd keep. You girls will be going off to college next year; maybe you can take your quilts with you. She began cutting and putting the pieces together about two years ago. She was determined to finish them for this Christmas, but…" Dad's voice faltered and he looked at me.

I continue the story. "She'd finished one, was quilting the second, and had pieced the third, but hadn't started quilting it."

"So who finished the quilts that Grannie didn't?" Sarah asked.

"Dad and I found a lady named Mrs. Horst who finished the last two. We really wanted you to all have your quilts for Christmas. Mrs. Horst is an excellent quilter and normally makes tiny stitches. When Grannie quilted, her stitches were much longer. Mrs. Horst wanted her quilting stitches to be exactly like Grannie's so the quilts would be the same," I said.

"She even wanted to do the binding exactly like the one your grannie did," Dad added. "She said quilters did bindings and corners differently and she did them the same way as the one that was finished." Alicia, Eric, and Sarah held the corners of their quilts close together.

"They look the same to me, " Eric said. All of us were silent — each in our own thoughts, as the lights on the tree twinkled in Dad's tiny apartment.

"Aunt Susan, do you know which one Grannie really made?" asked my niece Sarah. I shook my head and smiled.

"I'll answer that," said Dad. He blew his nose one more time. "She made them all. That wonderful lady stitched for your grannie. When we picked up the finished quilts, she told me that she'd said prayers of blessings as she quilted and she hoped that someday she could make such beautiful quilts for each of her five children."

The three quilts have been used and loved. They covered twin beds in college dormitory rooms and were moved to apartments when each of Mom's grandchildren married. And now, more than twenty years later, those quilts cover Mom's great-grandsons' beds.

Mom's quilts were gifts to keep.

~Susan R. Ray

56

Love You Forever

I cannot forget my mother. She is my bridge.
~Renita Weems

N o one is ever ready to say goodbye to a parent, and I was no exception. When my mother suddenly passed away at the age of fifty-five, it was devastating. The only way I knew how to cope was to write. When it came time to write her eulogy, I welcomed the chance to honor her. After reading the eulogy at her funeral, I folded it neatly and tucked it between the pages of her favorite children's book, *Love You Forever*. When it was time to pay final homage to her, I felt satisfied as I placed my only copy of the book in her arms and helped to lower her casket.

Shortly thereafter though, I broke down. I could think of nothing but my mother. I missed her with every cell in my body. But most overwhelmingly, I could no longer grasp the concept of where she had gone. I found it impossible to believe that she was watching over me. If she were, I thought, then she would surely make her presence known. I pleaded with the Heavens to show me she was there, that she was still sending her love, and keeping a watchful eye. No such luck.

Weeks went by. I became depressed and broken, unable to fulfill simple tasks and care for myself. I stayed home. People came in and out, checking on me at all hours of the day. Family and friends tried to coax me out of the house, but all I wanted to do was hide. I wanted to hide from my harsh reality: I would never see or hear from my mother again. Finally, those who cared about me had had enough.

One night, my best friend and her partner came over with a plan to get me out of the house. I debated with them for over an hour, pleading for them to leave me alone. Two hours and a million excuses later, we finally compromised and I allowed them to take me on a quick trip to Target.

As we walked through the aisles my feet dragged. I didn't want to be there. I didn't want to be anywhere. Nonetheless, we perused the make-up, electronics, and home goods aisles. They were there to offer me an outlet, and I was only there to placate them. After several more minutes of mindless meandering I was done. I told them I had to go back home, that I needed to get out of there.

"Alright, but first we have to stop by the candy section. A little sugar will give you a pick-me-up," they reasoned.

I swallowed my pain and continued. I picked out a piece of candy just to avoid my friends' concerned stares. At the checkout, we dropped our items on the conveyor belt and waited in line. I looked at the merchandise arrayed at the checkout. At the top of a shelf, on top of the candy, hair ties, and hand sanitizer, sat a book, a copy of *Love You Forever*! I snatched the copy and skimmed the pages, enjoying the pictures of a mother cradling her child. Tears welled in my eyes.

"Ma'am? Ma'am? How would you like to pay for this?" the cashier asked.

I snapped back to reality, but ignored her question. "Why is this book here?" I demanded to know.

"I'm not sure, ma'am. Maybe someone was planning to buy it but chose not to in the end? They were probably just too lazy to put it back... It happens all the time, unfortunately. Thanks for pointing it out."

I felt compelled to know more, and am still not sure why I asked my next question.

"Where are the rest of the copies of this book?"

"Wow. You sure love that book. The rest are probably in our book section, but I'll scan it just to make sure. Sometimes when a book is on promotion it is moved."

She scanned it. The machine made a loud, shrill beep.

"Huh. That's weird. It's not scanning. Let me see..."

The few moments I waited felt like eternity. A ball of excitement mixed with anxiety formed in my stomach.

"I'm sorry, ma'am. This book isn't scanning because we have no other copies in-store. In fact, we haven't for a while. It says the last time we had this book in stock was two and a half years ago. I'm not really sure why it was sitting there... If you'd like to buy it ma'am, I apologize because I guess it's not really available for purchase. But... I mean... I guess you can... Just take it? It's not really ours to sell."

My heart fluttered as I gingerly took back the book. I cradled it in my arms and as I did, I felt a sense of security envelop me. I knew this was a message from my mother. It was a message of love, support, and understanding. It was her way of saying, "I will love you forever, no matter what." And I've never doubted that since.

~A.B. Chesler

57

Early Mornings with God and Mom

Welcome every morning with a smile. Look on the new
day as another special gift from your Creator, another
golden opportunity to complete what you were unable
to finish yesterday.
~Og Mandino

Growing up, I went to church with my parents, attended Sunday school, and participated in youth groups and service projects. Although these activities supported my faith development, a daily routine I shared with my mother created the foundation for it.

In one of my early memories, a soft glow floated down the hallway from my parents' bedroom when I opened my eyes in the morning. The smell of coffee lingered in the air. During some months, it was still dark outside. I slipped out of bed, grabbed some books from the shelf close by, and padded down the hall in pajama feet.

After Mom saw Dad off to work at his sand and gravel business, she returned to bed. In her housecoat, she stretched out to read her Bible, daily devotions, and Sunday school lessons.

Mom smiled when I entered the room, calling out, "Hi, honey!" I climbed into bed with her, flopping down on my dad's pillow and snuggling up to her side.

While she finished the page and marked her place, I flipped

through a book, my brown hair splaying across the pillow like my mom's wavy locks did on hers.

Mom tugged a thick book from the pile on her bedside table. "Now, where were we?" she asked, as she opened the book of Bible stories for children.

I took out the marker and pointed to the page. "Here, Mom!"

After she finished the story, if we had time, she read from a book of children's prayers or one of the Golden Books I lugged from my room.

As I listened to the sound of her voice and the rhythm of the language, my hands ran up and down the ridges of the chenille bedspread. Words and pictures became stories, and stories became windows to understand a world that sounded different to me, a child with hearing impairments since birth.

We talked about the pictures as we looked at them. Mom listened patiently to my observations. Sometimes, my words didn't sound accurate — a concern greater than typical developmental errors for young children — but she didn't correct me. She simply repeated the word, and then said, "Let's say it together!"

The early morning quiet time I shared with Mom throughout my childhood gave me a significant lifelong routine. Reading together, interacting with Mom, and observing her daily life taught me about faith. She believed, no matter what, that things worked out — though not always in ways we first imagined. I gained confidence in a world understood through language, scriptures and stories of the Bible, as well as through people who acted on their faith. I began to believe that I, too, could live successfully in such a world.√

My mother followed her early morning routine until she died. During my college and career years, my quiet time took a less predictable path. Most days, I grabbed devotional time whenever I could and sometimes fell short. As years passed, I gravitated toward early morning again, by then recognizing more fully this piece of my mother's legacy — starting with a calm routine set a positive tone for the day. After life-altering surgery in my late forties, I began writing in the early mornings as well, not waiting to see if opportunities occurred later in the day.

Now, at age sixty — wrapped in a purple prayer shawl — I consistently read the Bible and daily devotions, much like my mother, and follow up with writing reflections. Sometimes, I use her Bible, engraved with her name "Marybelle Parks" on the front, and inscribed by my older sister who gave it to her for Christmas in 1955. The Bible embodies her presence because I left her penciled earmarks and notations and scraps of handwritten notes, prayers, and church programs stuck in it, just as they were when she died more than twenty years ago from cancer.

Mom gave me a foundation in language and faith, but more than that — the lifeline, the routine to anchor me. She lived her belief that faith nourished through all times and sustained through all times. Over my own lifetime, as I experienced handling tough situations, I grew in my understanding of a personal relationship with God — a pattern of ongoing reflection and conversation — and the realization that without it, life could well be chaos and restlessness, with no feeling of safe sanctuary. Whether life seemed happy, mundane, puzzling, or troubled, the comforting routine centered me.

My mom knew a firm faith meant gratefulness, spiritual growth, and willingness to witness by example. By sharing her routine and acting as a model, she gave me the foundation to nurture my faith through the joys and jolts of life. Thanks to her, I keep it growing strong every morning.

~Ronda Armstrong

58

Tables Turn

There are no seven wonders of the world in the eyes of
a child. There are seven million.
~Walt Streightiff

I t starts with a table. It's an old oak table, the strongest table I've ever known. Even though it stood only on one center post the table never, ever wobbled. Huge claw feet extend out from the center trunk, each one holding onto carved wooden balls with a visceral tenacity. This table is still my grandmother's, even if it is in my house now.

When I was a little girl I spent hours under that table, crawling around the feet of what I imagined were a pair of mated eagles, their big oaken wings a perfect circle over my head.

The table was huge in those days, and everyone I knew and loved in the world could sit around it. Their voices were distant as clouds, and as immutable. There were stories, murmurs, and many, many peals of laughter.

The table was in the middle of the biggest kitchen in the world, which was the center of my known universe. I'd guess ninety-five percent of our waking hours were spent in the kitchen, with light streaming in from every window, even on rainy days.

That was the magic of that kitchen at my grandmother's house.

The table held the best food in the world, all of it made from scratch, and the smell alone drew everyone in from outdoors no matter what they were doing. At each place setting was a cold Coca-Cola, the kind made with real sugar, sparkling tall glasses with condensation glistening on their sides like jewels. I dined below with ease, reaching up periodically for a few bits of flour tortillas and rice to hold me over until dinner.

The space under the table transformed so often that it surprised me that I was the only one who noticed. Some days it was a coral reef, with mermaids and neon colored fish swimming through. I'd swim through, sometimes quickly, as I evaded sharks, and sometimes just floating with graceful and gentle jellyfish.

Other times it was the front gate to the castle and was guarded by a beautiful white horse with a mane that nearly touched the ground. I'd hold court with salt and pepper shakers and potholders until someone needed to get some cooking done.

Sometimes, usually late in the day, it became a cave. Bystanders were often taken by surprise when bats would suddenly fly out from the cave, screeching and whirling around the kitchen right as the sun started to set outside and bedtime was announced.

I don't remember the day that I stopped spending most of my time below the table and began to sit in the chairs around it. But I do remember even then feeling those strong eagles' feet with my toes, my mind drifting back to oceans, castles, and caves.

Then, in a blink of an eye, the kitchen was gone, the table had to be moved and, with great anticipation and the help of many strong backs, it had come inside my house.

But something strange happened in transit. The oak table was much smaller. I looked at it in the corner of the room, not sure it was even the same table. I wondered if oak could shrink after thirty-five years. I theorized that when tables travel from cotton farms in El Paso to the Hill Country there was a miniaturizing effect.

The first day it was in our house I ran my hand over the golden wood, puzzled. Everyone I knew and loved in the world couldn't begin to sit around it. It hardly seemed big enough to serve a meal on. It stood in the corner of the room, dwarfed by everything around it.

Then, after a few weeks I spotted something from the corner of my eye. It was my child, crawling around the base, arranging stuffed animals and a few books around the eagles' claws. The next day there was a sign up next to the table, indicating when it was "open."

Right then, the table grew.

Today all I have to do is peek around it and I can see silvery mermaids jumping under the eagle's feet, a proud white horse galloping up the curved balls, and the bats hanging from underneath, blinking their eyes, waiting for dusk to fall.

There are new additions too — gallivanting snow leopards hunting in the mountains of Nepal, fashion divas working the runway in Paris, and a few artfully placed drawings in the Louvre.

It starts with a table. And from there it goes on — forever — making a kitchen into a magical home that will live forever in a child's mind.

~Winter Prosapio

59

Lillian's Daughter

The past is never dead, it is not even past.
~William Faulkner

Some months after my mother died, I was at the fish counter of her local supermarket, the place where she had always bought tiny amounts of fish for herself with the greatest concentration and intensity. The counterman had become something of a friend.

"So how's Mom doing? I haven't seen her in a while," he asked as he handed over my salmon and tilapia.

And there I stood, hand outstretched for my package, speechless. Despite how calm and collected I'd felt that afternoon, I dissolved into tears. "She died in December," I said, and bolted.

It was another of those post-loss ambushes that seemed to come in a steady, pummeling stream for those who are new at grieving. I could have — should have — expanded on my answer. Explained more gently. But that explaining was somehow just too daunting on an ordinary Tuesday afternoon when I had let down my guard.

I have had so many of those moments. And so, I'm sure, has anyone who's ever grieved for a loved one.

For me, the worst moments would come as dusk settled, the time when I would invariably be on the kitchen phone calling Mom on hers. Our conversations were so insignificant, so non-cosmic. They were about what each of us was making for dinner, about the weather, about the kids, the grandkids, and in her case the great-grandkids.

Nobody could have prepared me for the excruciating pain I felt in those early days when I reached for the phone... remembered... and stopped.

I would have given anything to hear my mother's voice, her laugh, even her grumbling about this or that. It was the "never again" part that was so overwhelming.

I spent days, weeks and probably months reviewing my sins of omission and commission in my relationship with Mom. I lamented the times I didn't visit her, take her grocery shopping, spend a Sunday afternoon keeping her company in her apartment when the weather, or her infirmities, made it impossible for a lady in her late nineties to go out.

The most overwhelming thing about loss is that there's no going back. No replaying the tape. It is what it is.

So when grief was still raw and new, there was that hollow feeling of guilt, especially in early morning or in the dark of night, and when I talked about it to my husband or my daughters, they assured me that I had been a good daughter, that I had done enough. How I wish I could have believed them.

But guilt is the handmaiden of death. Just ask anyone who's done that inevitable litany of "I should haves."

I adored my mother. But like most mothers and daughters, we had our differences and occasionally, our epic battles — many more when we were both younger and more volatile. We were very much alike, and that made our connection deeper — and more fragile.

The months — and now three years — have passed. I am no longer nearly as lost and sad as I was just after her graveside funeral, and through the Jewish custom of "sitting Shiva," receiving friends and family for that first week as we remembered and grieved together.

That earliest mourning left me dazed, drained and yes, relieved that Mom's struggle was over. Her last weeks were difficult, and in dark dreams, they return to me. My daughters tell me that they've had those dreams, too. Bedside vigils linger in the marrow, maybe forever.

One of the early hurdles was the final closing of Mom's apartment in a Philadelphia high-rise, the apartment that still carried her sweet smell in its walls. Going there for the inevitable cleanout was beyond painful. Just opening the door to that world, with the familiar furniture in place, the familiar pictures on the wall, the books, the amiable clutter, turned into a grotesque parody without my little blond mother there to greet us.

I still wince when somebody I haven't had contact with for these last years asks how Mom is doing.

I still sob when I hear certain music that reminds me of her, or when I come upon a note in her familiar handwriting. Those are the "gotcha" moments.

Grief, I am learning, is no neat process. And there are sometimes no words for the feelings.

But I count it as a blessing that I have absorbed this loss, and that the transition finally came when I realized that I am still Lillian's daughter, even though she is not here. I am still part of her, just as she is part of me — and always will be.

Sorrow is a wild and primitive place, and there are no neat schedules as to when it releases its grip.

It is a long and difficult journey, one that each of us must take alone.

But with it comes growth, wisdom, learning, healing and yes, that phase the experts call "acceptance."

Yes, I am still Lillian's daughter.

And so enormously proud to be.

~Sally Schwartz Friedman

Chapter 6

for Mom, with love

Thanks for Being My Role Model

Role modeling is the most basic responsibility of parents. Parents are handing life's scripts to their children, scripts that in all likelihood will be acted out for the rest of the children's lives.
~Stephen R. Covey

60

The Lady in the Mirror

As you age naturally, your mother shows more and
more on your face. If you deny that, you deny
your heritage.
~Frances Conroy

I rise in the morning and bounce out of bed,
Visions of chores and errands rush through my head.
In jammies and slippers, to the kitchen I shuffle,
Hot coffee to pour, a loud yawn to muffle.

I grope through the dark, to the table I walk,
A sight I must be, much too early to talk.
I reach for my purse, now where did it go?
My cell phone was ringing, but I was too slow.

A second cup of coffee, I'm beginning to see
The dust on the table, the bookshelves, the TV.
I pull up my jeans, and turn on the light,
The zipper is stuck again, could they just be too tight?

Brush in one hand, mascara in the other,
I look in the mirror — Oh my gosh, it's my mother!
She crept in while I slept, tippy-toed in my room,
Her hair sprinkled with gray, crow's feet starting to bloom.

When I smile, she smiles back; she blinks with me too!
She's still there if my hands move, when I play peek-a-boo.
I wonder what happened; I try to focus,
Someone's played a trick on me, a little hocus-pocus.

No matter which way I turn to get back on track,
She's still in the mirror, staring right back.
The more I gaze at her, I begin to recall,
Mother was very pretty, and I start to stand tall.

Shall I pull my hair up? A decision to make.
Mother used to wear it that way, like Veronica Lake.
I swish on some lipstick, some shadow and blush,
And now just like Mother, I'm off in a rush.

As I get dressed and ready to greet the day,
I say my good mornings to my family and go on my way.
But with each new morning I race to the bathroom to see,
My copycat mother staring right back at me!

~Terri Lacher

61

Father's Day

*A father may turn his back on his child, brothers and
sisters may become inveterate enemies, husbands
may desert their wives, wives their husbands. But a
mother's love endures through all.*
~Washington Irving

*T*here were loops and curves and long squiggly spirals;
rings and letters and bow ties. The pile of uncooked
pasta made a faint clicking sound as I sifted through it,
searching for the very best pieces for my art project. I
carefully dabbed glue onto each bit and attached it to the empty frozen–orange juice can I had brought from home. I tried to ensure that
every last inch of the can was covered; ziti and macaroni protruded
at jagged angles. When our masterpieces were finished they would
be pen and pencil holders, and they would serve as Father's Day gifts.
Our teacher, Ms. Z., told us to leave our cans on sheets of newspaper
at the back of the classroom. The projects would be spray painted
gold after school and left out to dry overnight.

We put our glue bottles away and settled down at our desks to
make Father's Day cards. I picked up a crayon and stared at the piece
of paper before me on the desk. On either side of me, my classmates
were drawing pictures of their fathers: stick figures with scruffy hair
and ties; smiling faces with and without beards; men holding baseball
gloves or footballs. I chose, instead, to draw a spring scene. Smiley
faces, rainbows, butterflies and a bright sun danced across my card. I

folded it in half and wrote my message on the interior:

"*To Mommy… Love Denise*"

There wasn't anything else I could write. I'd never met my father. I didn't know his name or what he looked like. He had actively and consciously chosen to be completely absent from my life, although I would not be aware of that detail for years to come. When I was in the first grade, all I knew was that he didn't exist for me. I was honestly fine with that, because I didn't miss someone I didn't know. I wasn't thinking about the things I didn't have; I was enjoying what was there. I had a mother and aunts and baby cousins; I had an uncle and a grandmother and a sweet German Shepherd dog named Cindy who liked to play catch. A few of my classmates lived with their grandparents; others had huge extended families. Some of my friends had siblings and others were only children, like me. One of my friends from dance school had a parent in the military who wasn't home very often. I knew that there were all kinds of families out there and that mine was just one more possible permutation.✓

For me, addressing my Father's Day card to my mother was simple logic: it was supposed to be a present for a parent, and my Mum certainly was one. Ms. Z didn't get it, unfortunately. She was somewhat unsettled, and she questioned me about it. It was the first time I'd ever encountered a teacher who didn't understand that I really meant it when I told her that I didn't have a father, but it would not be the last. As I progressed through my school career, I would meet other teachers who were perplexed that my family configuration did not mesh with their expectations. They would ask why my blue emergency card — which listed family contact information — wasn't completely filled out; why my Father's Day cards were addressed to my mother; and why I didn't talk about my father at all. Some of my classmates' parents would sneer at my mother behind her back. I was occasionally upset that people felt the need to judge me, but for the most part, I took it in stride. I knew that if anyone had a problem with my family, it was their issue, not mine.

At that moment, though, in first grade, my concern was with my art project. Part of me fretted that Ms. Z. would throw it away. What if she decided that if I didn't make a Father's Day gift, I couldn't make anything at all? I needn't have worried. When I returned to school the next morning my work was still on the newspaper, right where I had left it. It had been spray-painted gold along with all the other cans; it was sticky and tacky and it still reeked of fumes.

I gave the presents to my mother as soon as I brought them home. Mum loved my card and gift, and she kept the pencil holder in her office. Whenever I visited her at work that summer I smiled to see it, shimmery and sparkling, on her dark desk.

~Denise Reich

62

Midnight Grace

A mom forgives us all our faults, not to mention one or
two we don't even have.
~Robert Brault, www.robertbrault.com

Mom and I stood in the hallway, nose to nose. Her hands were on her hips and her feet peeped out from her long robe. Even her toes looked curled and angry.

"I think you'd better go to bed now," she said. "I'll be talking with your dad when he gets home. He'll be in to give you your consequence."

I spun around and stomped to my bedroom. Then I yanked the curtains shut, flipped the light switch, and plopped down on my bed. 10:15. The green digital numbers reported that my dad would be home from second shift soon. Dad was a gentle man, but I knew that I'd be in trouble. Worst of all, I deserved it.

I'd had the worst day at junior high school. My best friend, Mary Ellen, decided to join forces with cool-girl Regina. So there was no room for me at the lunch table. I ate my turkey-on-wheat alone, in the library, pretending to be immersed in a book. Then we square danced in P.E. class. I was nervous about holding hands with a boy. The boy was unkind, refused to hold my cold, clammy hand, and called me Trout for the rest of the day.

Of course, none of this had anything to do with my mom, except that I'd been terrible to her that afternoon. Years later I'd learn the terminology — misplaced anger — but on that day I'd just been hurt and mad and Mom was the retaliation target.

I watched the numbers morph until 10:30. "Might as well lie down," I muttered. I pulled back the comforter and slid between flannel sheets. As I lay there, I replayed the day's events through my mind.

Mom had baked cookies and they'd been fresh, piled on a plate, when I got home from school. Peanut butter. Sprinkled with sugar and imprinted with the tines of a fork.

"Couldn't you have made chocolate chip?" I said.

Mom looked up from the table where she helped my sister with her homework. "I could have," she said. "But I made peanut butter. Why don't you pour a glass of milk?" Then she smiled.

Later that night, when she pulled chicken from the oven, I balked again. Never mind that Dad was at work and Mom still put a nice meal on the table. I wanted hamburgers. "No one even likes that kind of chicken, Mom. Why didn't you make hamburgers?"

Mom breathed deep and ran her fingers through her long blond hair. "I made chicken and I've never heard anyone complain about it before," she said.

And it went downhill from there. I growled and complained until Mom hit her limit, lost her cool, and we had a shouting match in the hall.

By the time I heard the garage door open, I felt pretty bad about the whole thing.

I lay in bed and listened. The creak of the door. Dad's boots squeaking on the tile. Muffled voices in the kitchen. Then silence.

I wondered what my consequence would be. After soaking in the dark for a while, I didn't really care anymore. I'd hurt my mom. I'd seen it in her green eyes.

Why had I taken my troubles out on Mom? I knew that if I'd come home and shared what had happened, Mom would've listened. She would have offered encouragement and compassion. Then she would've said something funny and we'd have ended up laughing.

But I hadn't done that.

Before long, I heard Dad's quiet, bootless footfalls pass back down the hall. Then I heard the bathroom door shut. Then the rush of water. "Why is he taking his shower first?" I wondered.

The longer I waited, the heavier my heart felt. I considered getting up to apologize, but Mom didn't want to see me. I decided it was better to wait for Dad.

The sounds of the night were exaggerated in the dark. The rumble of the heater. The wind outside my window. Then a strange sound. A whirring from the kitchen. The clank of dishes. "What's going on?" I wondered.

The minutes stretched long, but finally my bedroom door creaked open. A shaft of light stretched across the room and stung my eyes. Soft footsteps to my bedside. Mom's hair slid past my cheek as she leaned over to whisper in my ear. "Why don't you come down to the kitchen?" she said.

I shimmied out of my bed and followed Mom through the bedroom and down the hall. As I passed the bathroom, I noticed the door was open. Dad had gone to bed. I was halfway to the kitchen when I smelled the thick, juicy scent of hamburgers.

I rounded the corner, puzzled, confused, and wondering if I'd fallen asleep and was dreaming. The kitchen table was set for two. "Have a seat," Mom said. She bent to lift a tray of French fries from the oven.

I sat.

Mom scooped the steamy fries to our plates and then poured thick, vanilla shakes into the tall glasses she'd set on the table. Then she slid two burgers from the griddle onto rolls and placed them on our plates. Then she sat down, too.

"Ketchup?" she asked. She tilted the bottle in my direction.

I reached out to grasp the bottle, but I couldn't. My eyes turned to my pajama-clad lap. "Mom, I've been awful to you today. I had a bad day at school and I came home and took it all out on you. You didn't deserve it. And I don't deserve this," I said. "I'm sorry."

I looked up.

Mom put the bottle down. She stretched her hand across the table. "You're in a tough spot, Shawnie. Halfway to being a woman. Halfway from being a girl. I remember those days." She smiled and tears welled in her eyes. "And I forgive you." She stretched her fingers toward me.

I reached out and took her hand, soft and comforting.

"Now," she said. "How about some ketchup for that burger?"

I wiped my own tears and nodded.

Mom and I sat in the kitchen and munched burgers while the night wrapped around our house. We slurped shakes, crunched fries, laughed and cried.

And I learned a lot about grace.

It's now twenty-seven years later, and I'm the mother of five sons. They are good boys, but there are many, many times when a hefty consequence is laid out for one of them. And rightly so.

But then there are the other times. The times when I remember that night. The silence of the dark broken by Mom's laughter. The warmth of her hand around mine. The sizzle of the burgers and the salty, crisp fries.

The night when I should've been served a consequence.

But instead, my precious mom pulled out the griddle, wiped the dust from the blender, and dished up a hearty portion of grace.

~Shawnelle Eliasen

63

No Complaints

*A woman is like a tea bag. You never know how strong
she is until she gets in hot water.*
~Eleanor Roosevelt

*M*acular degeneration didn't sound scary when Mom first mentioned it. She told me her cataract surgeries the previous fall had been successful. Her eyesight had grown worse over time though, not better. Her ophthalmologist had referred her to a retina specialist for more tests. She'd let me know what happened. No big deal.

Two months later, Mom called to share the test results. She'd been diagnosed with age-related macular degeneration, or AMD as it's known in medical circles. Her macula, the central part of her retina responsible for detailed vision, was deteriorating.

"Remember I told you about the two types of macular degeneration, dry and wet?" she asked. I remembered; I'd researched the condition online.

The "dry" version of AMD moves slowly. People with dry AMD may retain good vision with no other symptoms, or their central vision may gradually start to blur. The "wet" kind of macular degeneration moves fast. Abnormal blood vessels in the retina begin to leak and bleed, usually causing visual distortions and rapid vision loss.

"I've got the dry kind," Mom said, "so there's good news and bad news. Here's the bad news: Doctors have no viable treatments for the dry kind. There's nothing I can do about it. But the good news is I'll go blind less quickly."

Blind? I couldn't imagine my mother blind.

Images from the past raced through my mind: Mom devouring a new book with a mug of hot coffee in her hands; Mom reading her Bible in the early morning light; Mom glancing at a recipe card while she stood over a mixing bowl; Mom and Dad on the couch watching a football game; Mom reading a story to her grandchildren. I wondered what images the future would hold.

"I'm so sorry, Mom. I'm sorry you have to go through this."

I didn't know what else to say.

"Oh, sweetheart, you don't need to feel sorry for me," Mom replied. "God has blessed me so much. I've seen a world of beauty with these eyes. I've seen sights I never imagined I'd see. If I go blind, I'll have nothing to complain about."

Mom may have said more, but I heard nothing else for a few minutes. I was replaying her last four words: nothing to complain about.

Mom told me later she chose her response to AMD ahead of time — before she received the diagnosis. She knew the choice would be harder if she waited to see how the condition might change her life. And she wanted to focus on her blessings, not her losses.

When Mom's macular degeneration moved from dry to wet a few years ago, she didn't grumble. When her doctor recommended monthly eye injections, she took the plan in stride. She's received twenty-eight injections in her right eye so far. They're not fun, but they haven't slowed her down.

I can't imagine someone sticking a needle in my eyeball, but my mom handles the process with humor and grace. Her attitude isn't surprising, I guess. Why would you whine about a needle in the eye if you were okay with going blind?

~Donna F. Savage

64

Burned

Every day may not be good, but there's something
good in every day.
~Author Unknown

I had just finished watching the twentieth anniversary of *The Oprah Winfrey Show*. Previous guests appeared and picked their own favorite guests who inspired them, and in some cases, changed their lives.

I will never forget the woman who had face cancer. She said she used to feel sorry for herself, until she saw the show with a beautiful young girl who was hit by a drunk driver. The girl had caught on fire. Her face had literally melted away. The story really hit home.

My mother had been burned over seventy percent of her body in a house fire two years before. I'll never forget the phone call that I received at work that cold January morning.

"Is this Ms. Dixon?" The voice on the other end of the line sounded distant. "I'm calling from the Vineland Police Department." I lived in South Carolina. My mom and brother lived in Vineland, New Jersey. I knew it was something tragic.

"Your mother is Naomi Cook? I'm sorry to have to tell you this, but your mother has been flown by helicopter to Philadelphia… there was a fire in her house. She is critical."

The drive to New Jersey was the longest of my life. The whole way there it seemed that every memory of my childhood came back. Warm cookies and loads of love is the only way I could describe my childhood. I recalled how my mom walked me to school when I was very young. Once, there was this little boy who was taunting me. When she heard him calling me names, she went right up to his mother and in no uncertain terms told her that her son better knock it off. That's how she was. She didn't put up with any guff, not from anyone. She was tough, and she taught me how to be the same. Yet she had a heart of gold when it came to the ones she loved.

When I arrived at the burn center, I honestly didn't know if I was prepared for what I might see. I was right. My mom was wrapped from head to toe in bandaging. She looked like a mummy. All that was showing were her eyes and nose. I broke down and sobbed most of the night.

The next few months my mother fought her way back from the brink of death. She was kept in a drug-induced coma because of the pain from the burns. During this time, she survived two bouts of pneumonia, the constant infections that plague burn survivors, numerous operations, and skin grafts. The medical teams that kept her alive were incredible, and the fact that she hadn't succumbed to these horrific injuries was nothing short of a miracle.

Four months after the fire, the doctors felt it was time to bring my mother out of the coma. To help bring her around, the doctors suggested playing her favorite music and talking to her. The children from the Sunday School class that she taught all drew her pictures. I had them all over the cabinets in her room and explained each one to her in detail. After one particular long night at her bedside, and two weeks of waiting, I began to lose hope. Would she ever come out of this? Was all of this in vain?

The next morning, as I came down the hospital corridor, one of the nurses from the night crew jumped up when I went past her. "Good morning!" She was awfully cheerful.

One of the male nurses who especially watched over my mom came up to me. He linked his arm in mine. "Did you have a good night?" He was upbeat too. He pulled back the curtain that protected my mom's room. "She did." My eyes filled with tears. My mom was being helped into a wheelchair by two of the physical therapists. In the course of the night, she had awakened. When she looked up and saw me, her face lit up, and she smiled. Everyone present in the ward started to clap. "Mom! Oh, Mom." The tears streamed down my face.

It would be a long, long journey down the road of recovery. But, my mother did recover. To say it was a lot of hard work on her part would be a gross understatement. She had to re-learn how to walk, talk, eat, dress herself, all the things we take for granted. Not to mention living with the disfigurement of the burns. She did all of it.

I won't lie and say that there weren't times when it would have been easier for that fire to have taken her away from us. It was inhumanely painful dealing with the physical affects as well as the emotional. People often would stare at her. There was a time I took her to the grocery store. An insensitive man outside asked, "What happened to her?" I quickly rushed her inside. I just wanted her to have normalcy. I didn't want anyone to notice that there was anything different about her. I wanted people to only see the inside, to know how much this woman was loved.

While she was resting on a bench near the checkout line, a little girl, maybe five or so, came up to her. She had a Band-Aid on her finger. "What happened to you?" The little girl asked innocently. I was in a panic. I couldn't get to her from the line. Mom had to handle this one on her own. "Oh, I was in a fire, but I'm doing a lot better now." My mom smiled at the girl. Holding her bandaged finger up, the little girl said, "Do you need a Band-Aid? My mommy has more." The sincerity was heartwarming. "I think this boo-boo is too big for a Band-Aid, sweetie," Mom joked. Then she looked over at me and smiled. For a brief moment, she had that familiar twinkle in her eye that I'd missed so much since this whole nightmare started. She was Mom again. It was just a quick glimpse into the past, but all the love and memories poured into that one moment and it has stayed with me and sustained me after all this time.

That fire was never able to take away my mom's willing and determined spirit. In spite of her dire circumstances, Mom touched the heart of everyone she came in contact with. Whether they were young or old, healthy or sick, she would tell them her story of how

God spared her life from the fire.

I have tried, however difficult, to carry my mom's great attitude about the fire throughout these years. No matter what life brings to me, I try to remember to see the glass as half full. I owe it to my mom, who never gave up.

~Lisa Wright-Dixon

65

Hope for the Future

*...suffering produces endurance, and endurance
produces character, and character produces hope and
hope does not disappoint us.*
~Romans 5:3-5

Whﾍen I was born they named me Hope. Don't ask me who "they" were — I don't know. It could have been the college kids who had an "oops" one night and knew they couldn't keep me. Or maybe a secretary at the Department of Welfare who had to fill out my paperwork and figured I would need all the positive energy I could get. Maybe it was a foster parent. Obviously, my beginning wasn't the norm.

The way it all went down was very non-traditional. My adoptive mom, Patricia — Pattie for short — had given birth to three adorable young boys, all healthy and full of personality. Light-skinned, blue-eyed, towhead to mousy brown, and ages two to ten. Sam, the oldest, was named after a long line of Sams in the family, fifth in line to be exact. Andy was sixteen months younger than Sam, more fair-skinned and with a slighter build. He had an artistic eye and loved to perform. The youngest, Greg, was still toddling around at two years old, charming folks with his "gregarious" personality and his spontaneous nature.

Happily in love with these three boys, my mom had always wanted a girl. Really, what is the experience of having a baby without the ruffles and lace? Or playing dress up with the sassy, pink, little girl outfits and combing shiny smooth hair into ponytails and adorning it with ribbon? For my mom, the family would not be complete without a little sugar and spice.

Interestingly, and for many reasons, Mom was drawn to the idea of a bi-racial baby. First, she knew there were a lot out there who needed homes and she liked the idea of being able to share that and give one of these children a second chance. She also knew if she wanted to have a fair-skinned Caucasian child, she and Dad were capable of taking care of that themselves. And third, she had recently taken a course at the local women's college on black history and found herself fascinated with the trials, tribulations and strengths of the African American culture.

At this time, in the late sixties, there was an abundance of mixed-race children up for adoption. It was still a period when people of different races weren't encouraged to be together, when these relationships could even be considered taboo. When a child came along in one of these relationships, sometimes, in certain circumstances, the only choice was to give the child up for adoption. There were so many of these cases that the Department of Welfare ran announcements in the newspaper about particular children who needed caring families and a stable home.

And this is how my mother fell in love.

She found an article in the *Rocky Mountain News* about a little girl, Rene, who was available for adoption. The headline read "Alone in the World." It stated, "Rene is just six weeks old, but she already has a winning personality. She loves to be cuddled and shows curiosity about her surroundings. Because Rene is of Negro-Caucasian descent, it is difficult to find a home for this baby. She is one of about fifty children of special needs who have no prospects for adoption according to Denver Department of Welfare social workers." There was an address and contact person at the bottom of the article. My mother clipped it out of the paper and made up her mind. She was going to adopt a mixed-race baby girl. (Race never was an issue for Mom. Years later, when my brothers were teenagers, she put them on a bus to send them to high school in a predominantly black neighborhood.)

So my mom and dad began to fill out the forms, went through family interviews with social services and put in their request for the type of baby they wanted. Mom's only stipulation was that she wanted a baby between two and six months old. My father, an obstetrician, stipulated a healthy birth mom.

The application and interviews helped the social workers approve the candidates and match the babies with the families. But it was a process, and by the time the Downing clan was approved for a new addition, little Rene had been adopted elsewhere.

After starting the process in the heat of the July sun, six months later, in the dead of winter, my parents received the call. They had a five-and-a half-month-old baby girl just waiting to be taken home and loved. My family packed up a blanket and clothes, and the five of them piled into the car, knowing their lives were about to change.

It wasn't a ceremonious exchange, but more like, "Here's the little girl you ordered." The cost of the entire adoption was about twelve dollars. This was something my brother Greg used to like to tease me about when we were growing up. One of his favorite insults was to remind me that I wasn't even worth as much as a twenty-dollar bill.

My mother instantly fell in love. After she dropped my father back at the hospital to work, she took my brothers and me first to the hairdresser and then to the church to show me off. I had an olive skin tone and chocolate brown eyes, with a little tuft of curly black hair standing straight up on the top of my head. I looked nothing like anyone in my family, but if you really wanted to stretch the association, my father had black hair and brown eyes too.

You could say that I was my mom's birthday present. I arrived six days after she turned thirty-two. Although I had a name, Hope, which was fitting for my circumstances, my mom wanted one that would fit my new life. Even though I was never physically part of her, she wanted me to be an everlasting piece of who she is.

She is Patricia Carolyn. And since that day she picked me up at social services, I have been her second half. My name is Tricia Lynn.

~Tricia Downing

66

The Locket

A house needs a grandma in it.
~Louisa May Alcott

I had always been close to Grandma. Yet, the summer she moved in with our family it seemed as if my life had turned upside down. I was sixteen years old and suddenly all the house rules had changed, and with them, my relationship with my beloved grandmother.

In years past, Grandma had always been the industrious sort. A visit to her house always meant a fresh batch of cookies and an eager ear. Since my mom worked, it was Grandma who introduced me to many of my childhood pleasures. We grew snapdragons and sunflowers. She taught me how to make a beaded purse, coat candy apples, cross stitch a pillow. Then Grandma had a heart attack, and the robust woman of my youth was suddenly frail and old. When my father brought her to our house with her belongings, she reminded me of a pale, wilted flower.

It had already been a tough summer. My boyfriend of six months, Jared, had recently broken up with me. I'd like to say it was mutual, but in reality I felt dumped. Jared was the first boy I really loved, and even though I was only sixteen I felt a deep connection with him that, now broken, left me feeling less than whole. It's not as if I didn't have other opportunities either. Several guys had asked me out, and at least a few times I had accepted my girlfriends' invitations for a double date. But my heart wasn't in it, and it's no wonder they rarely asked me out a second time. Since I was spending more time at home these days, Grandma's intrusion into my life seemed especially difficult.

I groaned inwardly when my mom rapped on my bedroom door, calling me to dinner. "Can't I just grab some food later?" I asked.

"Donna. Your grandma's here. We're going to eat as a family."

Eat as a family. Since when was that a big priority? I couldn't even blame my grandmother, because it was my mom who suddenly seemed to get all kinds of ideas in her head. Turn off the TV, Grandma's napping. No friends over this afternoon, Grandma's tired. The list went on and on.

Ordinarily, I wouldn't have minded so much, maybe even welcomed the opportunity to spend time with Grandma. But that was before Jared. Now I just wanted to crawl into my room, listen to music, and not be disturbed.

I was downstairs buttering my toast, my iPod blaring, and I didn't hear Grandma enter the kitchen. I could tell she was just glad to see me, which made me feel instantly guilty.

"Hi Grandma," I said. "You look good this morning." She did. The pale cornflower blouse she wore complemented her complexion, and today she reminded me of her old self. "What can I get you for breakfast?"

"Is there any of that pumpernickel bread left? I'll have a slice of that with my morning coffee."

I brought Grandma her toast with her favorite marmalade that I knew she'd want. I joined her at the table, and it dawned on me that this was the first time since she'd arrived that I'd sat down with her without prodding from my mother. I sighed.

"I'm sorry I've been a bit distant lately," I said.

Grandma bit her toast. "You're sixteen. I was sixteen, too, once."

That was all she said, but I could see the reflection in her expression. Some people you can't possible imagine they were ever sixteen, but not my grandma. I can't explain why, but somehow I could truly picture her at sixteen, her skin smooth and the same bright blue eyes. On a date, perhaps. Maybe with a boy like Jared.

"I would like to show you something," she offered.

Grandma returned and first she showed me a music box carved from delicate rosewood. It was exquisite. When she opened the heavy lid, I could see a large spindle, the components of the music box, through a clear glass window. The spindle turned and the tune "Somewhere My Love" from *Dr. Zhivago* filled the dining room.

"It's beautiful, Grandma. What's in the other box?"

It was a heart-shaped blue velvet box, and Grandma opened it to reveal a small, etched silver locket. "Go ahead," she said. "Open it."

"It's Grandpa! You were so young."

"Yes. Very. Your grandpa gave this locket to me on our wedding day."

"It's pretty, but I especially love the music box. When did Grandpa give you that?" I asked.

"He didn't," she said. "It was a gift from my fiancé. My first fiancé, before your grandpa. We were engaged to be married when he was killed in a training accident on the army base." Grandma's face grew wistful. "It wasn't even war time. I wasn't prepared for the tragedy. Or the grief."

I whispered quietly, "I'm sorry. I didn't know."

"Of course you didn't, dear. I met your grandpa at church and he was always trying to cheer me up with a funny joke or just some kind words. I was grieving, and I'm afraid I wasn't very nice to him."

"But he didn't give up."

Grandma smiled. "No. He didn't give up. It took a while, but eventually I began to break out of my sorrow. There was so much to love about the world. And I grew to love your grandpa much more than I ever loved Stan. You see, Grandpa — Tom — we shared a life. We had children together. Grew old together. We shaped who each other became."

Unexpectedly I felt my lashes grow wet. Jared wasn't my fiancé, only a boyfriend. Why couldn't I let go? "How did you know?" I asked.

"I can see it in your face."

"I guess you think I'm being pretty silly about Jared. It's not like he's dead or anything."

Grandma folded her worn hand over mine. "I don't think you're being silly at all. You loved him and you no longer have him, and now you're hurting."

Suddenly I found myself telling Grandma everything. How I'd met Jared. All the fun times we had. And the painful break-up. We were still talking when the phone rang. It was my friend Melanie inviting me to go to the movies with her and Michael and Sean. I said yes.

When I returned home that night Grandma was in bed. I almost didn't see the object on my pillow in the darkness. It was the blue velvet box, the locket that Grandpa had given Grandma on their wedding day. There was a note with it as well. I turned on the light at my bedside and read Grandma's grand, scrawling penmanship: "To my dear Donna, wishing you a lifetime of love." Grandma had chosen to give me the locket instead of the music box I had so admired, the locket that was a gift from the man who gave her a second chance at love. It was a gift that represented the future and not the past. I couldn't wait to tell Grandma about my date the next morning.

~Donna Brothers

Forgiving the Unforgivable

The things that people in love do to each other they remember, and if they stay together it's not because they forget, it's because they forgive.
~Author Unknown

What is forgiveness? Why do we find it so hard to forgive? These questions were hard for me to understand until the events that started one Tuesday morning. Any other day, I would have been waking up to prepare for school, but that day I had a dentist appointment. My mom usually took me, but on this day my dad sat in the driver's seat, my mom nowhere to be found. As I began to wonder what was going on, in a shaky voice he began to talk.

"Your mother has left to go to your aunt's for a couple of weeks," he said. When I asked why, he began to cry as he told me the same story of his affair that he had told her the night before. Only thirteen at the time, I was shocked and devastated at the thought of having to choose between my mom and dad and possibly never being a family again.

Very little was said throughout the next two weeks. It was like time had stopped. Everything was in slow motion. Nothing felt right without Mom there. The middle school drama that had affected me before no longer mattered. I suddenly realized what was really important.

I wanted so badly to hate my father for what he had done to our family! I wanted to shut him out and hurt him the way he hurt us. But when I looked into his eyes, I saw that I didn't have to. I knew he would deal with the guilt for the rest of his life, and it was not my place to judge him or hate him. After all, he was my dad.

I chose to forgive him, not because it was easy, but because he needed it and I knew it was what I needed to do. I wanted him to see that even through his biggest mistakes and failures I still loved him just like he would me. That is what family is all about. I could not handle seeing his tears or the hurt in his eyes.

When my mother finally came home I was very happy to see her, but I was also just as scared as when she had left. I didn't know if she was coming home to stay or coming home to say she was leaving for good this time.

I could tell she had missed me too as she walked through the door and tears flowed down her face. I saw love and hurt at the same time. I had never seen my mother like that and it frightened me. The strong woman she had always been seemed so frail and broken. Nevertheless, she told us she was going to try to make it work. I was relieved, but it was not the end of the story, as I had hoped — it was only the beginning.

I watched her cry for months; I saw the pain in her eyes every day. She had to wear waterproof make-up because the tears became a normal, everyday occurrence. My dad tried and tried to make it right and to show her love, but it wasn't until she completely forgave him that the tears slowly stopped. Carrying the weight of his betrayal was hard on her until she just let it go. It took years to build their relationship back, but it is even stronger now and they have grown from their experience. My dad treats my mother like a princess, even to this day, as she deserves. He has worked to earn her love and trust since the day she came home.

Seeing my mom go through this taught me so much about forgiveness. I cannot imagine the pain of being betrayed by the one person she loved and trusted with all her heart. To have that completely torn apart, but be strong enough to start over and rebuild that trust takes a special person. My mom taught me how strong forgiveness really is by her actions. It's not easy to forgive, but she has shown me it is possible and it is worth it.

~Sheridan Kee

Focusing on What We Have

A happy person is not a person in a certain set of circumstances, but rather a person with a certain set of attitudes.
~Hugh Downs

As I entered the emergency room, she lay there motionless and vulnerable under a white sheet. The doctor turned around, introduced himself and said, "We think your mother had a stroke affecting her entire right side." My biggest fear was that she would have brain damage and not know who I was. I said, "It's Lisa" and held her left hand. She squeezed my hand tightly. We both cried as the priest said prayers over her partially paralyzed body. That night, feeling scared and helpless, I cried for hours until I finally fell asleep.

The next day in the ICU Mom began exercising her left hand, arm and leg in bed. She squeezed her hand open and shut, lifted her arm and leg up and down, all with a smile. Prior to her stroke, she took an exercise class at the local council of aging and knew that it was important to keep moving. Despite her limitations, she had a determined spark and it was contagious.

The neurologist told our family that she had a 30/30/30 chance. Broken down that meant a 30 percent chance that she would die, a 30 percent chance that she would stay the same, and a 30 percent chance of change. I remember thinking that was funny math. What was the other 10 percent for? I decided it was for miracles. And that was what I was going to focus on.

I focused on what we had rather than what we didn't. She could swallow, she was conscious, she understood everything going on, and she could write with her left hand when she had difficulties with speech. With rehabilitation, she learned how to feed herself and talk again. She regained a lot of her speech with only slight difficulties with finding the correct word or pronunciation. I prayed for my mother, gave her inspiring cards and read to her to maintain and support her positive mood. Most importantly, I was grateful that we still had each other.

One day I went to visit Mom at the skilled rehabilitation center and she told me she had pain and headaches every day but that she was at peace. I said to her, "How can you be at peace? You are in a wheelchair telling me you have pain and headaches every day and you need a catheter." She looked at me confidently and said, "I pray to God every day and thank him that I am alive." I had tears in my eyes because it was so beautiful that she could maintain such a positive and grateful attitude despite all the physical losses.

I thought when she was told her physical therapy was to end that she would have a setback, yet she accepted it gracefully. She understood that her right side was not regaining movement. She then focused on getting involved with the events at the nursing home. She circled events on the calendar and attended them every day. She was curious to find out what Chumba was and later told me that it was a chair version of Zumba exercise class. Using one arm and her head, she moved herself quickly from side to side and up and down, complete with imaginary music and a smile.

She did not allow the physical limitations to stop her. Although her body was handicapped, her will was not. One day, before I was about to leave the nursing home she wanted to show me how she could get to the dining hall. I said, "I will get you someone." She said no: "I'll do it myself." I stepped back and gave her some room. She used her left arm and hand to move the wheel of her chair and her left foot to propel herself forward. She got herself to the hallway where she pulled herself along using the handrails on the wall. It was a slow and steady movement. Some would say it wasn't perfect or smooth, but she was doing it. I'd say it was one of the best moments of my life. I watched proudly as she reached her intended destination.

Before she went to sleep at night, she told me that she rubbed her right arm and hand, believing that it would bring the circulation back into them and they would move again. Four months later, her right thumb did move. The last time she spoke with me, I asked her to show me. She lifted up her hand and thumb and I saw it move. I said, "It's a miracle," to which she said, "Yes."

After being through so much, I thought my mother would have felt angry, frustrated and stuck. Yet, she could not have been freer. She was grateful, happy to be alive, and easygoing. She was connected to her childlike sense of wonder, yet was still an adult woman who gave me wonderful advice.

Positive thinking, prayers and love did not change the experience or the aftermath of the stroke, but it certainly changed my life. My mother taught me to live in the moment. Her positive attitude helped me to keep going, to have faith and to remain connected to her, especially after her death. Everyone loved my mother. Who wouldn't? She was the one sitting in the wheelchair at the nursing home with a big smile on her face. I can't recall a time I visited her that she wasn't smiling.

~Lisa Hutchison

69

Adventures in Staying

Do not go where the path may lead, go instead where
there is no path and leave a trail.
~Ralph Waldo Emerson

ad embodied adventure. Mom focused on the ordinary. He tickled me nightly on the living room floor, while she finished up in the kitchen. He took me on his rounds on the farm to water the fields of sprouting cotton crops, to jump in the trailers of freshly picked cotton, or to slide into the irrigation canals and ride the current. She made sure I made my bed.

I never lacked for excitement with Dad. He taught me how to catch and bridle my horse, and to snow ski at a young age. He would invent new ways to scare the daylights out of us every Halloween. And on after-dark hikes, he would eagerly recite his menacing "Headless Horseman" tale, as his dimly lit buddy skidded down a nearby mountain, supposedly without a head.

Dad was larger than life to me. I thrived on watching him in action — aiding the roadside birth of a new calf, rescuing the bloody neighbor who ran through the sliding glass door, or capturing the wounded coyote to mend in the empty chicken pen. I loved adventure and he was the adventurer.

Near the end of my third grade year, the action screeched to a halt. A closed-door discussion between Dad and Mom ended with Dad making trips to his truck with all his personal belongings. I walked each painful load to the truck with Dad the night he left. I did not witness my siblings huddled around Mom crying in the living room. I was so focused on the one who left that I didn't think of the one who remained. But in the years since that night, I have had the opportunity to discover who the true adventurer was — the one who stayed.

A single mom with four small daughters and no job — that, in itself, set the stage for disaster to come. Who would have guessed that, instead, life would evolve into one huge adventure?

It started small as we adjusted — watching the black-and-white *Wizard of Oz* with green sunglasses, pulling to the side of the road to gape at the special Christmas star, investigating a flood at the ranch from which we had moved.

Mom became creative. In an electrical outage, a flashlight at the player piano kept us busy for hours. Our not-so-intelligent dogs fighting through the glass sliding door served as simple and silly entertainment. And somehow, saltine crackers crumbled into a bowl, topped with milk and sugar, became a delicacy we begged for at suppertime.

Then the adventure grew. Simple outings transformed into explorations of uncharted territory, usually on the nearby Native American reservations. We escaped falling walls in dilapidated and crumbling Native American ruins. We appeased haunted spirits in Native American graveyards with the eye of the Kabbalah. We hunted for buried treasure in the old Cooley Civil War mansion. Each escapade left us with memories and scars to prove its worth.

Ordinary hikes became grand conquests of terrain, often leaving wisdom and safety back home. One ten-hour spree landed us above the snow and timberline with no supplies other than a picnic lunch and no more protection than an eight-inch tall dog.

Another day's jaunt led us high atop the nearby Hopi mesa. In the history of the Hopi Nation, they had allowed the public to view their ceremonial snake dances only twice. We were there, sitting cross-legged with the Native Americans and scampering panic-stricken when a rattler escaped into our ranks. Our interest level always seemed to outweigh the liabilities and risks.

We no longer vacationed, but set out on investigations into the fascinating. The boiling mud pots at Yellowstone National Park made us all feel unsteady, but no more than Mom's reading of *The Night of the Grizzly* in the tent — a poor choice in travel literature.

It never mattered that there was no father, uncle, brother, grandpa, male cousin, male anything around — we would bait, gut, and untangle at the toughest trout streams anyway. It never occurred to us that we should have experience. We naively assumed we could learn how to erect a tent on the first night of the two-week camping trip to Canada. And we did — a two-hour task, compared to the fifteen-minute job we whittled it down to by the end.

So adventure characterized Mom after all. But the adventure was not always easy. It required night classes to finish her college degree, and the after-work trip each week to the ranch, now over an hour away, to make payroll. It included not always having the money to pay all the bills. It involved de-skunking the ripe aroma from our over-friendly dog, picking up pieces of the glass sliding door I kicked in, and a lot of broom swinging to dislodge bats from the rafters. Yet she stayed.

It entailed the endless disciplining of four girls, who could easily find trouble. It also included raising us with no relative to pick up the slack. Mom lived with a constant fear of her four girls being separated into foster homes if something were to happen to her. So she stayed.

But in staying, Mom got to see her girls grow up. She whooped and hollered when we made the team. She scoured the racks with us for the perfect prom dress. She endured every concert and musical we performed. And she was there to plan each of our weddings. Hers was an adventure of family, of relationship, of love. And it produced a lifetime bond among five women.

Her adventurous spirit became so ingrained in me that it affected my choices on a regular basis. It influenced the way I raised my own kids, who, in turn, were fascinated by treasure hunts that never took them beyond their own back yard, and amazed at what kind of critters they could find under a rock. I will never feel compelled to look for adventure out there. Mom has proven there is great adventure in staying.

~Ann Kronwald

70

A Life Lesson in Courage

*It was times like these when I thought my father, who
hated guns and had never been to any wars, was the
bravest man who ever lived.*
~Harper Lee, To Kill a Mockingbird

I was sixteen years old when my brilliant, undefeatable father
was diagnosed with multiple myeloma. At that time, it was
considered a rare form of bone cancer that caused bones to
become very brittle and easily broken. He was in the hospital
for months, semi conscious. His discouraged doctor told my mother
that we needed to get his affairs in order because he would probably
live for fewer than six months. As I slumped on the chair beside her
in the doctor's office in a state of shock, my mom graciously thanked
him for the information but asked that he not tell my father that he
had only a few months to live.

I adored my father and could not imagine a world without this
kind and thoughtful man, with his twinkling blue eyes, always ready
to help with advice or a hug. My father was still in the hospital when
prom time came. My date and I went to the hospital first to show my
dad how grown-up we looked. From his hospital bed, he charged my
prom date with being certain that I was home by midnight.

Mom was a teacher and the life lessons she taught my two younger
brothers and me as we were growing up were not the usual adolescent-
oriented life skills. She set out on a courageous campaign to help my
father fight for his life and we readily enlisted. Dad came home from

the hospital, though he was wheelchair-bound for the remainder of his life due to the frailty of his bones. He opted to use a push wheelchair, rather than the easier motor powered type, because he wished to keep at least part of his body strong. His doctor assured him that he would be able to build strength in the muscles of his arms, though he would tire more easily.

Mom's determination and grit helped him be present at every possible school and scouting event in which my two younger brothers and I were involved throughout our school years. He proudly attended each of our high school and college graduations, though his eyes often glazed over with the effort and his physical suffering. When Mom had to be away for the day, teaching at her school, we learned to give Dad the pain tolerance shots prescribed by his doctor. She taught us how by having us practice on whole oranges and grapefruits. Both she and my father made sure they had time for each of us whenever we needed their attention, no matter how exhausted or how much discomfort either of them were in. They strove to ensure that the three of us had as normal a life as possible, despite the illness, agony and often depression that surrounded us.

Both of my parents had dreamed of traveling their whole lives. Even though my father was ill, nothing deterred my mother from arranging trips for the two of them all over the U.S., including Hawaii, and Europe. They refused help from nurses or companions on any of these excursions. Armed with letters to regional specialists from my father's physicians, Mom's tiny 5'2" frame could be seen pushing Dad in his wheelchair up and down hills, across cobblestoned streets, off and on buses, trains and airplanes. These were not luxury tours they joined. The two of them rented cars and used public transportation to go wherever their wanderlust took them. From Pearl Harbor to Stonehenge and many places in between, they roamed the world with love, laughter and courage.

When I announced my engagement a few years into my father's illness, I hoped to see him coaxing his wheelchair down the aisle between the rows of brightly glowing flowers we were planning in our back garden. I chose to get married and have the reception at home so that my dad could rest in his room if necessary.

The day of my wedding, I stood erect in the ecru lace wedding dress my mother had sewn for me, ready to take my dad's hand as a family friend pushed the wheelchair. Then I heard a collective gasp from our 300 closest family and friends in attendance. When I turned toward my father's wheelchair, I found him standing next to me offering his arm to walk me down the grass-covered aisle. My handsome groom's eyes glistened as he watched us make our way slowly toward him.

We made it to the end of that long walk, and my father insisted on standing throughout the ceremony. After a brief rest in his wheelchair, this astonishing man once again stood and asked me to dance. As I accepted through a haze of tears, I could feel what it was costing him in pain and energy.

My brave, diligent mom stood there, delight radiating throughout her whole being as she watched her only daughter and beloved husband dance to the "Tennessee Waltz."

It was due to my mom, and her determination to help my father succeed, that the idea of him walking down the aisle with me was born. While I dreamily mulled over wedding showers and parties, she had been driving my father to the beach, over an hour away from our home, several days a week for three months before the wedding. Once parked, he walked in the sand with her support. They spent an hour or more each trip so that he could build up his leg muscles enough to support him for what had to be a torturous long walk down the winding grassy path with his only daughter. It was a secret that my mother kept until after my father had gone.

It was not the only secret that she kept. My father lived ten years longer than the timeframe the physician specialists had predicted. He never knew that they had predicted a life span of only six months. My mother lived many years longer, never remarrying. When her beautiful grandchildren came along, she never tired of telling them how much their grandfather would have loved them. She traveled the world by herself or occasionally with friends or family members well into her eighties, riding elephants in Thailand, spending nights in pyramids in Egypt, joining a cooking school in France. At her death, as we were preparing for her memorial service, we counted almost 300 foreign stamps in her well-thumbed passports. She carried her indefatigable courage into her own final illness, assuring me that we would be visiting Africa as soon as she "felt a little better."

Life without my parents left me feeling orphaned, though I was an older adult myself when Mom departed. Our family was so strong, so loving and so cohesive that it left us all a little adrift. Mom and Dad taught us to face whatever life may bring with extraordinary courage and compassion.

~Donia Moore

Turning Into My Mother

*Of all the haunting moments of motherhood, few rank
with hearing your own words come out of
your daughter's mouth.*
~Victoria Secunda

O kay, now it's official — I am turning into my mother! On
a recent airplane trip, not only did I put all the liquids
in my carry-on into the required quart-sized Ziploc, I
decided to carry my other toiletries in two other plastic
bags. In my defense, I was moving my purse contents hurriedly into
a laptop case, which had no dividers for small items. Even as I did it,
I could remember recoiling in horror when my mother used to reach
into her purse and pull things out of the plastic bags she carried
regularly (in public!), so much so that I bought her a set of attractive
cosmetic bags she could use instead. Sigh.

My relationship with my mother has never been black and white.
I don't know about you, but I've got separation issues. Being close is a
double-edged sword, I think, for girls and their mothers. All the years
I was growing up, Mom was prominent in our small town, civically
and socially. Townspeople were always calling me by her name and
telling me I looked just like her, which I found unnerving.

As an adolescent, I could not understand why my friends tolerated, and even invited, her presence when I would rather crawl
under a rock than be seen in public with her. She even dragged me
to a meeting of a new teen group. Okay, so the kids there ended up

becoming a wonderful group of friends. Don't you just hate it when your mother's right? Still, after finding my way through some rocky middle school years and through high school, I eagerly broke away from her sphere. After college, I moved hundreds of miles away to be clear of her influence.

Flash forward twenty years. Mom moved down here to my town and started going to the church of my newfound faith in my neighborhood. She started studying at our local college with the same undergraduate major I once had. I had an instant resurgence of the push-pull emotions of my childhood, of feeling eclipsed by her once again. My bristling defensiveness was magnified by the fact that I had my own child by then. And we had very different ideas about parenting—hers, typical of her generation, involved playpens and schedules and discipline. Mine, well... not.

My son, Sammy, knows that the single most effective way to push my buttons is to compare me with his Nana. Like when I was flipping the remote one day as we sat before the TV and I tried to stop on the *Meerkat Manor* show on Animal Planet, which my mom watches for hours at a time. He teased me mercilessly.

Like Mom's, my hair has thinned so that I now sunburn on my scalp. But I refuse (so far) to wear a hat every time I go out, partly because of my own personal sense of style, partly because Mom wears one. Shall I admit that sometimes now, when people are still saying I look like her, I can actually see the resemblance?

Recently, I have been caught phoning her about something special on TV I think she'd enjoy, though I roll my eyes when she does this to me. I still have a visceral spasm of distancing once in a while—like when I had to use a cane before and after knee surgery last year, and hurried to give it up so I would not seem like Mom. She used one regularly before graduating to a walker. Mother and daughter matching props—that was just too much, and hey, I'm twenty-eight years younger than she is!

All the defenses against turning into my mother that I have spent an adolescent and adult lifetime building are crumbling with age—hers or mine, I cannot say. What I do know is that I am grateful that I inherited her strength and resilience, even if it comes with the rest of it. And who knows? Perhaps one day I, too, will be a tough old broad.

~Karen Kullgren

Chapter 7

for Mom, with love

Thanks for the Laughter

A laugh is a smile that bursts.
~Mary H. Waldrip

72

Granny's Bible

A single conversation with a wise man is better
than ten years of study.
~Chinese Proverb

I will never forget the first time I heard my granny quote the Bible. No, not the King James version. You know which one I'm talking about. The one that you actually live by every day of your life.

I was about eight years old at the time and a real brat. I had been fighting with the little girl next door and she was almost as mean as I was. We were pretty deep into battle when she threw a rock and hit me square between the eyes. Clutching my head and sobbing, I ran straight into the house to tattle. Granny met me at the door after seeing me come running across the lawn and hearing my screams.

"What's wrong?" she asked in her usual gruff way.

"That little girl threw a rock and hit me in the head," I managed through the tears.

"Well," said Granny smugly, "you just go pick up the biggest rock you can find and hit her back!"

I stopped crying immediately. "But Granny," I stammered. "I don't think…"

"Listen," she interrupted. "The Bible says feed them out of the same spoon." I happily obeyed. I never realized it then, but that was only the beginning of a lifetime of "Bible quotes" that would help me through life's biggest obstacles.

Several years later, and before I had enough sense to realize it, I was engaged to be married. My fiancé left it up to me to pick our wedding date. I unknowingly picked the date on which his mother had died many years ago. Instead of telling me that he didn't want to get married on this particular day, he told me he didn't want to marry me at all! I was simply heartbroken. I wandered through the house until I found Granny sewing in the den. I fell on my knees, laid my head in her lap, and started to cry.

"Granny, my fiancé doesn't love me. He doesn't want to marry me," I said.

"Well, that no good punk," she said angrily. "You just go tell him that the Bible says what goes around comes around. Someday he'll want to marry a girl and she'll do him the way he's doing you."

"But Granny," I said, "I don't think that the…"

"Listen," she interrupted. "You just go tell him what I said. You'll get your feller back." I married him in two months.

After our first three months of married bliss, we had our first fight. Oh, how that broke my heart. Packing my bags, I decided to go back home. When Granny saw me coming up the walk, she met me at the door.

"Well, what's wrong?" she asked. I was already clenching my jaw to keep from crying.

"We had a huge fight and he called me a spoiled brat," I told her.

"Come here," she said wearily. Putting her arm around my shoulder, she guided me into the kitchen where she put water on for tea. "So he called you a spoiled brat," she said over the whistle of the kettle. She looked very thoughtful as she poured water into waiting cups. "Okay," she said. "You just go right back home and tell him that the Bible says it takes one to know one."

"But Granny," I started to say, "I don't think…"

"Listen," she interrupted, "I was reading the Bible before you were even a twinkle in your daddy's eye." I did as she said and that was our last fight for a long time.

Before long I was expecting my first baby. Granny put me right to work crocheting a baby blanket. I could crochet fairly well, but let's just say Martha Stewart would never hire me to make anything for her. I became extremely flustered and did a double loop when I should have done a single.

"Oh gosh," I wailed. "I'll never learn this." I showed her what I had done. "Granny, I'm just going to do another double and no one will ever know the difference." That was the wrong thing to say.

"Yes it will make a difference," she said sternly. "Besides, the Bible says that two wrongs don't make a right."

My mouth dropped to the floor. "But Granny," I said. "I don't think the Bible..."

"Listen," she interrupted, "do you want your baby bundled in a blanket that wasn't made properly?" I unraveled the whole thing and started over.

I took my son to see Granny a while ago. She was sitting on her front porch crocheting and drinking tea. She was getting old but her usual spunk was still there. I sat down in the chair beside her and poured myself some tea. My son toddled off into the house to find the treat that Granny always had for him. After a while, we got to talking and forgot all about him. "Oh no," I gasped at the realization. "I forgot all about that kid."

As I started to get up, Granny reached for my arm and gently pushed me back down into my chair.

"You think he's going to keep meddling when he hears you coming? No, he's smarter than that," she added, with pride in her eyes. "Besides, the Bible says that you have to lay over to catch a meddler."

"But Granny," I said, "I don't think," and then I stopped. All through my years Granny had been quoting me the Bible. Her Bible, and it had always solved whatever problems had been thrown in my path. Smiling and shaking my head, I went into the house to get my son. Carrying him out on the porch, I placed him in the chair beside Granny. "Well Granny," I said, "I think I'm going to run to the store and get us all some ice cream." Pointing to my son, I asked, "Do you mind if he stays here? I'll only be a minute."

"Sure," she nodded. As I turned the car around and headed down the drive, I stopped and looked in my rearview mirror. There they were, two of the most precious people in my life: she, leaning over and quoting her Bible and he, hanging on to every precious word. I knew how he felt. He'll question it someday, but when he grows up he'll realize everything he holds dear is because of the Bible — Granny's Unforgettable Bible.

~Robin Rylee Harderson

73

Sense of Humor Needed

*Laughter and tears are both responses to frustration
and exhaustion. I myself prefer to laugh, since there is
less cleaning up to do afterward.*
~Kurt Vonnegut

Mom is getting more difficult. Lately, we waste so much time arguing and not getting anywhere. I know it is impossible to reason with a person suffering from Alzheimer's, but sometimes I get so frustrated that I can't help myself.

This morning is one of those times. Mom is scheduled to go to adult day care, which gives me a respite for a couple of hours. I will be able to go to my dentist appointment and shopping. We are running late as I am trying to get her out the door.

"Come on, Mom. It's time to go," I say.

"Wait, I want to change my blouse," she says.

"You can't," I state. "It's too late. Besides, what you have on is fine."

"No," she insists. "I don't like this blouse."

"There's nothing wrong with what you have on," I say abruptly and then I shout "WE HAVE TO GO NOW!" as I pull on Mom's arm to get her out the door.

Mom is not happy. And neither am I, especially since I haven't had a good night's sleep for a couple of weeks.

Finally, I drop Mom off at the day care. I'll be able to have a few hours to myself.

I know Mom can't help being so difficult. I feel bitter, too, that Alzheimer's disease has kidnapped the wonderful mother who loved and cared for me all of my life and left this imposter.

The day flies by, and I feel satisfied with all I have accomplished. It's time to pick up Mom, and I brace myself to resume our futile arguments.

Mom is waiting for me when I arrive.

As we get in the car, I ask pleasantly, "Did you have a nice time today?"

"Yeah, it was fun," she says with excitement.

"That's good. Today was exercise class. I know you love that," I say.

"Yeah, that was fun."

"Did you have a good lunch?" I ask warmly.

"Yeah, it was good."

Then she spots the chocolate candy I have in the car. "Would you like some candy, Mom?"

"Yeah, I'll have a piece," she says, reaching for a miniature Hershey bar. Mom still has a good appetite. And she craves sweets.

Then Mom says, "I'm glad you picked me up instead of that lady who took me this morning. You're the nice one. That other lady who took me this morning is such a bitch."

I am a little shocked at her statement. Then I start to giggle.

"You are right. That woman is a bitch. Everyone says that about her."

"Well, what's wrong with her? Why is she so mean?" Mom asks.

"Oh, who knows? She probably has all kinds of aches and pains. And she just doesn't have a sense of humor like us," I say.

"Well, even if she has aches and pains, she should learn to be a little nicer," Mom says with indignation. Then we both start laughing at that bitchy woman.

"From now on, I'll try to be the one to take you and pick you up," I say.

"Oh, good, because I like you," Mom says.

"I like you, too," I say.

Mom smiles at me. Then I say, "Let's have another piece of candy."

"Good idea," she says.

For the rest of the way home, I find myself smiling at this situation. I vow to take my own advice. The best way to deal with unpleasant situations is with a sense of humor. Even with Alzheimer's, Mom's still teaching me so much about life. She makes me laugh at myself, which keeps me from taking the situation too seriously. Today, I learned not to be like that lady who drove Mom this morning — the one with no sense of humor.

~Lucille Engro DiPaolo

74

A Fist Full of Dollars

Most grandmas have a touch of the scallywag.
~Helen Thomson

My friend, Zelda, was about to have her forty-fifth birthday party. She was a kindergarten teacher, and I volunteered a couple of years in her classroom. Her coworkers and friends decided to throw her a party.

I was excited when I got the invitation. I had never been to a birthday party that was described as "Girls' Night Out." At the bottom of the invitation was written, "Lots of fun and games. Bring five one-dollar bills." I thought that was strange, but I was ready for the fun. Then I remembered that my eighty-two-year-old grandmother-in-law was coming to our home for the weekend. We were going to pick plums and peaches, and she was going to show me how to make preserves and jams.

Grandma is the perfect picture of her title. She's from Spain, but lived in San Francisco from her teen years. She's almost five feet tall and roly-poly, hair held in place with a hairnet, feet supported by orthopedic shoes. She always wore a dress with a full apron to protect it from whatever she was creating in the kitchen. It was Grandma's favorite place to be, next to sitting at her kitchen table enjoying watching all of us devour her delicious meals.

I called the lady hosting Zelda's birthday party to see if I could bring Grandma with me. She had been to other outings with this particular bunch of girls, so she wasn't a stranger. I was told, "Of course. Bring

Grandma, and make sure she brings her own five one-dollar bills." I gave Grandma the good news, and she was excited as I was. We put a birthday gift together consisting of gift certificates for two for dinner and a movie and dessert afterward.

The big day finally came. We had our wrapped gift and tucked our dollar bills in our pockets. As we entered the house for the party, we were given party hats to wear and noise makers. Grandma and I made our way to the corner of an L-shaped sofa. Soon, Zelda the party girl came, and she got a very nice cardboard crown designating her as the birthday princess. After greeting all her guests, she sat down next to Grandma. The host announced the beginning of the games and asked everyone to display their five one-dollar bills. Grandma and I were ready to win every game possible.

Soon, music started to play, and a young man came into the room from one of the back rooms. He was wearing a very nice suit and tie, and looked quite nice. His walk started keeping tune to the music, and the girls started getting louder, shouting at him. Slowly, he began to take off his clothes! I looked at Grandma, and her eyes were glued to this young man. The birthday girl began waving one of her dollar bills, and the boy danced over to her with much of his clothing gone except a dental-floss-sized pair of briefs.

I noticed that Grandma started bouncing to the rhythm of the music as the boy got closer. As Zelda deposited her dollar in his costume, Grandma was blowing on her party favor, making it unfurl to where the tip was touching the boy's bare stomach. She giggled so hard I could have sworn someone slipped alcohol in the birthday punch. We were drinking the same, yet our reactions were not similar. I don't know which was more embarrassing: seeing the young man's almost-nude body or watching Grandma with the net still in her hair, "letting her hair down." I was sure her support stockings were probably going to end up on the floor from all the dancing she was doing while sitting on the sofa. It wasn't long before she began grabbing for my dollar bills, and then anybody else's she could reach. She had everybody in stitches.

The young man stuck so close to Grandma, almost dancing in her lap, that Zelda switched hats with her, which she never knew. The host provided Grandma with more dollar bills. I was a little nervous trying to think how I was going to explain the birthday party to her grandson at home and her son in the next town.

As Grandma deposited her last dollar bill, her hand disappeared into the depths of the skimpy costume, and she burst out laughing. Zelda told her she couldn't leave her hand in there, to which Grandma replied, "I'm looking for change."

~Gail Eynon

The Cooking Lesson

Recipe: A series of step-by-step instructions for
preparing ingredients you forgot to buy, in utensils you
don't own, to make a dish the dog wouldn't eat.
~Author Unknown

*I*t was time to learn the family secret. The particulars had never been recorded on paper or even shared verbally. The silence needed to be broken, and I gathered up my courage to confront my mother.

I was nineteen years old and engaged to be married. The eldest of three daughters, I would be the first to leave the nest. However, I was not about to leave without the top-secret information. So I sat my mother down, took a deep breath, and blurted, "I want the recipe for your spaghetti sauce."

There, the words were out. Still, the worst was yet to come. I dreaded her response, because I knew what she would say.

"There is no recipe. It's in my head."

We set a date for the information transfer: Thursday night. While this event did not approach the level of national security, it was certainly important in my world. Ready-made sauce was not good enough for the love of my life. He was special, and that meant he deserved special meals — homemade meals — with such ingredients as my mother's world-renowned spaghetti sauce. This was an event worthy of clearing my calendar and bearding the lioness in her own den.

I wished it were a matter of simply watching Mom while she

cooked. Mom is a fantastic chef, but she did not like interlopers in her kitchen. She preferred to be left alone, and we girls knew better than to bother her while she was cooking up her culinary achievements. Even Dad steered clear when she was at work. My plan to sit in the kitchen and carefully document each step as she prepared her sauce meant that I would be entering uncharted and dangerous waters.

Thursday arrived accompanied by rising anticipation. I rushed home from work, quickly changed my clothes, and sat at the kitchen table with pad and pen. "Don't worry, Mom. I'll stay out of your way. You won't even know I'm here."

Mom gave me a look that said, "I already know you're here." She set an empty pot on the stove and began chopping an onion. I watched her and asked my first question. "How big is that onion?"

"What do you mean, 'How big?' It's an onion."

Her back was to me, but I was sure she rolled her eyes.

"I know it's an onion, but is it a small, medium, or large onion?"

She sighed. "Let's just say it's a medium one."

I wrote that down: one medium onion, finely diced.

Then she reached for the garlic, broke off a couple of cloves, and crushed them.

"How many cloves was that?"

"Two... unless of course they're large, then you only need one."

I wrote that down as well.

Mom poured some olive oil into the pot, and then added the onion and garlic.

"Wait! How much oil did you use?"

"I don't know. Enough for the pot."

I ignored the growing annoyance in her voice. "Well, how much is that?"

"It depends on the size of the pot. Just enough to coat the bottom. Use your judgment."

I didn't want to use my judgment. I wanted a recipe.

Mom emptied a can of pureed tomatoes into the blender. Then she added the blended mixture to the onions.

I grabbed the empty can and noted the size. "But why did you bother to blend tomatoes that are already pureed?"

"Because this is the way I make it. Are you here to tell me how to prepare my sauce, or to learn?"

Next, she poured one can each of tomato soup, tomato sauce, and tomato paste into the blender. I wrote down the size of each empty can when she finished.

While I wrote, Mom took a bunch of parsley and began chopping. Scooping up a handful of the chopped parsley, she moved toward the blender.

"Wait!" I jumped up and reached for her wrist. "How much parsley is that before you add it to the tomatoes?"

"A handful."

"But, Mom, how much is a handful? Your hands are smaller than mine!"

I grabbed a large measuring cup and had her empty the parsley into it, noting the amount. After blending the parsley and tomatoes, she added the mixture to the pot. I could see she was beginning to get a little rattled, but thankfully we seemed to be near the end.

"Mom, I forgot to ask. How long were the onions cooking before you added the other things?"

"Once the oil begins to bubble, simmer for about five minutes."

Then she sprinkled some oregano into the palm of her hand and walked over to the stove, only to be intercepted by me once again. I carefully emptied the contents of her hand into a measuring spoon. "Aha. Just about one teaspoon." I dashed back to my pad and wrote it down.

"That's it. Simmer the whole thing for about an hour."

"Uh... Mom? That's the second time you said 'simmer.' Exactly what does that mean?"

She counted to ten before she answered. "It means cook over a low flame."

The sauce was simmering, and so was Mom.

I waited a few moments before venturing to ask my final question. "Are we done?"

"Yes, we're done. Now it just cooks—simmers—for an hour.

There's nothing more for you to write down, so please get out of my kitchen before you drive me completely crazy!"

An hour later, we all sat down to dinner. My sister was the first to speak up. "Mom? This sauce doesn't taste like you usually make. Did you do something different?"

"Of course not. It has the same ingredients I always... wait a minute." Mom grimaced and shot me one of her patented looks. "I forgot the sugar... and the salt and pepper."

The rest of the family laughed as I shrunk down in my seat.

I learned an important lesson that day. We've now been married more than thirty years, and my very special husband has always been served a very special spaghetti sauce.

Ragu.

~Ava Pennington

The Little Woman

The only rock I know that stays steady, the only
institution I know that works is the family.
~Lee Iacocca

"Mom, is anything wrong?" My grandmother didn't answer. My dad gently took her hands in his and asked once more. "Mom, what's wrong?"

"Let me try," my mom said quietly. "Mother, can you hear me?" She reached for my grandmother's hands, but the second she touched them my grandmother brushed her away.

Even though my grandmother had dementia, she had been able to converse with people, although most of the time her words made little sense. But lately, my grandmother seemed indignant and reserved. As my parents searched for an answer, they had noticed that when Dad visited alone, Grandma would speak. Yet when Mom visited, Grandma seemed agitated.

The following week my parents arrived together. Dad slid Grandma's lunch tray in front of her, but my grandmother shoved it away.

"How dare you bring your little woman on our lunch date!" My grandmother glared at my mom, who looked completely devastated.

"What do you mean, Mom?" Dad asked patiently. "This is my wife, your daughter-in-law, don't you remember?"

"And you, little woman, how dare you come here with my husband!" With those words my grandmother flung her lunch on the floor.

Long ago my grandmother had affectionately called my mom

"little woman" because she was tiny, unlike Grandma, who was tall and big-framed. Perhaps she remembered the name, but had forgotten my mom.

It might have been funny, but Grandma had accused her of being the other woman. During the next visit, Mom tried enticing Grandma with a box of her favorite chocolates, but she refused to acknowledge her.

When my father told the staff what had happened they explained that some women with dementia, like my grandmother, become confused and believe their sons are their husbands. The staff suggested we allow a week to pass before my mom visited again.

Even though my parents kept a good sense of humor during this period, I know it disheartened Mom. She had always been close to my grandmother and now she couldn't visit her.

As the years passed, Grandma became silent, even with my dad. However the sight of my mom still disturbed her, so Mom and Dad gave up. Then one day the phone rang. It was the nursing home.

"We're sorry, but her body is shutting down. We thought you'd want to know so that you can call the family together to say goodbye."

Almost thirteen difficult years had passed. While my dad handled every emergency that concerned my grandmother, my mom had stood by helplessly. She yearned to see my grandmother one last time. She needed to express her love and say goodbye, even if it meant Grandma might become hostile.

As my mother approached the room she could see my grandmother on the bed. She had her eyes closed and each breath she took was slow and shallow.

"Mom? It's me, Mom," she whispered, "the little woman." She reached out and gently touched my grandmother's hand. She worried that Grandma might throw a fit, but instead my grandmother clasped my mother's hand tightly and squeezed it.

With a smile on her face, Mom reminisced about old times and updated my grandmother on the lives of her grandchildren. While she chuckled through some stories, she cried through others. Then she told Grandma how much everyone loved her and how much she would be missed.

Most of all, she thanked her for being such a wonderful mother and grandmother. My grandma held her hand the entire time, and though Grandma never said a word, my mother believed she knew and understood everything Mom had told her. These two beautiful women, who loved each other so much, were finally family again.

~Jill Burns

77

Answer the Phone

An amazing invention — but who would ever
want to use one?
~Rutherford B. Hayes

In this day and age, it's hard to believe a person doesn't own an answering machine; my mother is that person. She has never really grasped the concept of the answering machine. When she calls and leaves a message, it goes as follows: "Hello, anybody there? (This is followed by a short pause.) Hello! It's me (which is followed by a second short pause). Anybody? Alright! Don't pick up the phone! Well, if you're really not there, give me a call when you get in. Remember, I can always change my will."

To my mother, leaving a message is equivalent to a game of hide-and-seek when the kid looking chants, "Come out, come out, wherever you are." She's under the impression we're all hiding from her, and she's got to smoke us out.

Sometimes, her messages are longer than our conversations. The following is an example of a typical conversation with my mother.

Mother: "Hi. How are you?"

Me: "I'm fine."

Mother: "Still breathing?"

Me: "Yes, still breathing."

Mother: "Good, then you have nothing to complain about."

Me: "No, I can't complain."

Mother: "How's the family?"

Me: "Everybody's fine."

Mother: "Good. So, nobody can complain, can they? Good talking to you. Talk to you soon. Oh, one thing before I go. You may want to get that damn answering machine of yours fixed. The last time I called and started talking, nobody picked up. Find out what the problem is."

Me: "I'll look into it."

Should my mother have company, our two-minute conversation will be cut down to one as I'll be resigned to chat with whoever's visiting at the time.

Mother: "Your aunt's here. Want to talk to her? Of course, you do. Hold on. She answers her phone when I call, unlike some people."

Just as I'm about to say, "Had I really wanted to talk to so-and-so I would call them," my aunt gets on the line.

Aunt Ann: "Hello, Cindy, how are you?"

Me: "I'm fine."

Aunt Ann: "Still breathing?" (She's my mother's sister.)

Me: "Yes, I'm still breathing."

Aunt Ann: "Good, then you can't com… hold on a second, Cindy, your mother's yelling at me. Oh, your mother says I have to hang up now as this is the second time she's called today. The first time she got the machine, and nobody picked up. Oh, Cindy, that's not good. You really should find out what the problem is and get it fixed."

Me: "I'll look into it. Bye."

As I bang my head against the wall, I think — one phone call — double the aggravation.

~Cindy D'Ambroso-Argiento

78

The Cursed Jersey

Superstitions are, for the most part, but the
shadows of great truths.
~Tryon Edwards

Sports fans tend to be superstitious. Maybe it's crazy, but we can't help it. So much about sports comes down to luck, a good hit, a lucky catch, a bad angle. One can't help but believe in bad luck and good luck, and that certain rituals, like not shaving during playoff time or wearing socks of a certain colour, can affect the outcome of a game.

For my mother, it's the deep-rooted belief that her Toronto Maple Leafs jersey is cursed.

My father bought her the jersey in 1994, as an anniversary present. At the time, the Leafs were playing in the conference finals and she couldn't wait to wear her jersey as she watched her beloved Maple Leafs on television.

The first game she was able to watch, the Leafs lost and then the next. Suddenly, the Leafs were down three games in the series and on the verge of elimination. Every time she wore the jersey, they lost. My mom decided to not wear it and instead she left it in her room, on her bed.

The Leafs rallied and took the lead in the game; it began to look like all hope was not lost. I was eleven at the time and I happened to go into my parents' room. I saw the jersey there and I couldn't figure out why my mother wasn't wearing it, so I took it down to her. "Mom, you forgot to put on your jersey," I said, handing it to her.

My mother nervously took it and as soon as she did, the Vancouver Canucks scored. The tide of the game changed, and the Leafs were eliminated that night.

"It's the jersey," my mother declared to my father and me. "It's bad luck."

My father rolled his eyes at her and grumbled about how it was a wasted gift if she wouldn't wear it, but my mother was convinced and she banished the jersey to the back of a drawer. After all, it was a gift and she couldn't bear to throw it out. Besides she'd occasionally wear it in the summer when she decided that it could do no harm.

The Leafs had ups and downs over the next few years, but they never made it to the Stanley Cup finals. Even if the jersey was bad luck, banishing it didn't suddenly bring good luck. But my mom still wasn't going to risk taking it out again.

Years passed and then during the 2002 playoffs I was a teenager who was just starting to get into hockey. I brought the jersey out, partly because I found that all the boys at school flirted with me when I wore it.

My mother wasn't thrilled, but it had been a lot of years and she decided to let me wear it. The first time I wore it, the Leafs lost, badly. I figured it was a coincidence, but I couldn't quite forget my mother's old conviction that the jersey was cursed. So the next time I wore it, I took it off before the game started, but the Leafs still lost.

My mother forbade me from wearing the jersey again and I was spooked enough by the two losses that I did as she asked. My father thought I was as silly as my mother. "It's just a piece of clothing. There's no way it can influence a hockey game over a hundred kilometres away," he'd point out. But my mother didn't care and I thought she might be onto something. I didn't wear the jersey after that, but soon it didn't look like that decision mattered.

Game Six in the second round against the Ottawa Senators, the Leafs were down three games to two. The game started off badly for the Leafs, with the Senators scoring two goals in the first five minutes. It looked like it was going to be a humiliating end to the playoffs for the Leafs and that the jersey had no part in it at all — it was just silly superstition on my mother's part.

Then, I happened to notice that the jersey was sitting in a pile of laundry in the living room, right in front of the television. I knew I was being silly, but I decided to bring the jersey upstairs. As soon as I left the room, the Leafs scored a goal and the game no longer looked like a lost cause.

The Leafs ended up winning that game and they won the series. They lost in the next round to the Carolina Hurricanes. But we never claimed that banishing the jersey brought good luck, just that the jersey itself was bad luck.

My father was never convinced. And every time he hears the story, my husband rolls his eyes. But my mother and I both firmly believe that her jersey, lovingly given as a present by her non-Leafs fan husband, was cursed. Neither of us has ever worn it since then.

~Michelle McKague-Radic

79

Serious Business

At the height of laughter, the universe is flung into a
kaleidoscope of new possibilities.
~Jean Houston

"That's right, now shimmy a little. Bend forward and just kind of drop into it." My grandmother moved as she spoke, twitching her shoulders from side to side and leaning forward, pantomiming how to delicately plop one's chest into the cups of a waiting bra. Around us the pink dressing room glowed cheerfully. Standing there half-dressed, looking at Nan sitting like royalty on the tiny stool with a mountain of candy-colored bras draped across her, I caught the giggles.

"What's so funny?" she demanded, her wrinkled hands sorting deftly through the scraps of fabric on her lap. "And what is this?"

Nan held up a leopard print bra with black lace on the edges. At twenty-one I was still embarrassed for her to see my more risqué selections.

"I'm just trying that on for size," I muttered, grabbing it from her hand and throwing it over one of the hooks on the opposite wall. Turning my back, I pulled on another option, a turquoise bra with tiny white polka dots that reminded me of a bikini from the 1960s.

"Looks like a swimsuit," Nan decreed. "Next."

I slipped out of the offending underwear and put on a blue bra with tiny pink flowers embroidered across the bands.

"Bland," Nan opined, waving at me to take it off as soon as possible.

"Besides, those flowers will make your shirt look lumpy."

I tried on a bright white bra ("boring"), a lilac bra printed with bumblebees ("childish") and a mustard-colored bra ("downright ugly") before Nan stopped passing me any more options.

"It's time for the leopard print," she announced, still tucking the rejected garments back onto their hangers.

I looked up in surprise. Normally Nan was against anything even remotely tacky and, in her book, leopard print and lace were probably in that category.

"Every girl needs a racy little something," she winked. "Though heaven help you if you think leopard print and lace is the way to go. If you want my advice, I'd say pick up a little something in black silk and call it a day."

Then Nan snapped her gum decisively and made me laugh all over again. In the dressing room next to us a woman chuckled and from across the small hallway I heard a delicate snort. An unsuspecting saleswoman wandered into the fray and asked if anyone needed help.

"Do you have anything in black silk?" my grandmother called, setting us all off again.

"I don't know what you're laughing about," Nan stage-whispered. "Bras are serious business."

I nodded, trying so hard not to laugh hysterically that I didn't trust myself to speak. I reached out and hugged her, holding tight while tiny lingerie hangers stabbed my ribs. She was right, bras were serious business. But just like everything else they were certainly more fun when she was around.

~Beth Morrissey

80

A Simple Wedding Dress

Clothes make a statement. Costumes tell a story.
~Mason Cooley

My wedding wasn't exactly a typical wedding. My fiancé and I, young college students at the time, wanted a simple wedding. There was no rehearsal, no processional, no dinner, and no dance. We didn't go on a honeymoon. Instead of a warm Saturday afternoon in June, we set aside a Wednesday evening in November on what was sure to be a cold Wisconsin night.

We decided to get married in a Thanksgiving Eve church service. We'd stand at the altar and take our vows before the sermon, then enjoy the second half of the service as husband and wife with much to be thankful for.

With so few details to worry about, you'd think I would have had a goof-proof plan in place. But I haven't told you about The Dress yet.

Since this wasn't going to be a conventional wedding, I figured I could skip the traditional white gown and buy something nice that could be worn again.

And that was my first mistake.

I kept my eyes open wherever I went, looking for that perfect dress. One day, I was browsing through a sewing store and happened to see a dress pattern that I loved. The envelope showed a long, flowing dress with pretty, petite flowers printed on a pale pink material. It featured a fitted bodice and bell sleeves that flared gently from the elbows. I began to imagine myself walking down the aisle in this dress. I grabbed the pattern, bought it, and sang, "I found my dress! I found my dress!" all the way home.

That was my second mistake.

Now, who would sew this dress? I briefly thought of my sewing skills, but since a wedding dress is slightly more complicated than a throw pillow, I decided to ask my future mother-in-law. Not only was she excellent with a sewing machine, but it could be a nice way for us to bond over the coming wedding. Never mind that she lived 600 miles away, which would make fittings and alterations difficult.

That was my third mistake.

When it was time to purchase dress fabric, for some reason that understated pale pink flew out the window. In a fit of temporary insanity, I chose a smokey blue damask that would've been quite lovely as a set of curtains in our new home. But no. This was it. My dress material was promptly packaged and sent to my seamstress.

That was my fourth mistake.

It was October before I held the dress in my hands. Though not quite finished, it was close. Trembling with excitement, I took the dress into my bedroom and stepped into the blue folds for my first fitting. With my soon-to-be mother-in-law looking on with a tape measure and hopeful smile, I just couldn't say what I felt.

The dress was all wrong. Gaps of extra material at the waist coupled with seam-popping tightness in the arms. I looked like a cross between a large blue pear and a matronly lady-in-waiting. Something Maria von Trapp would have sewn had she married Robin Hood instead of the Captain.

Swallowing tears of disappointment, I asked if the arms could be let out at all as they were "a little snug." Pinching the waist on both sides, I suggested maybe "bringing this in a little." She promised to try, but didn't know if much could be done. "Whatever you can do," I said, hoping for a miracle.

That was my fifth mistake.

For the next month, I worried. How would I ever walk down the aisle in that dress? And what was I thinking with that blue material?

The smallest drop of sweat would stain it dark and quickly spread. To say I was anxious would be putting it mildly, but what choice did I have? I couldn't turn back now, especially after all the hard work his mom had done.

The final weeks melted away, and soon it was the day before our wedding. My in-laws arrived in town, and so did The Dress.

The first thing my mother-in-law said to me was, "There's a problem with the dress."

A surge of hope raced through me. "What's wrong?"

"Well, I was doing some hand stitching, and I pricked my finger," she explained. "Some blood got on the dress." This sounds promising, I thought.

She continued, "I wanted to get the blood out, so I used some of Dad's orange goo cleaner." She held up my dress. In the middle of the blue bodice were two washed-out grayish smudges. "It took the color right out!"

My hand flew to my mouth. To hide a relieved smile. I wanted to jump up and down and celebrate at the top of my lungs. I didn't feel nearly guilty enough that she was obviously misunderstanding my reaction.

"It's okay." I hugged her. "We'll figure something out."

Later that evening, with less than twenty-four hours to go, I went out to buy a wedding dress. At the first bridal shop we came to, I pulled a beautiful white satin dress off the rack and tried it on. It fit like a glove, cost $100, and I loved it.

That was my lucky break.

As for the original wedding dress, for which I had a sentimental fondness, I passed it on to my sister. Not to be worn at her wedding, of course, but as an excellent costume for her annual trips to the Renaissance Fair.

~Debra Mayhew

81

Cotton Balls

The trouble with always trying to preserve the health
of the body is that it is so difficult to do without
destroying the health of the mind.
~G.K. Chesterton

My mother calls from Florida every day. Today she asks, "Are you okay? Are the kids okay? Where are they?"

I make the mistake of telling her the kids are playing outside. Now she calls every five minutes. "Are they back yet?"

"No, Mom, they're still outside."

"Can you see them?"

"No, but they're fine."

"You can't see them? They're in the woods? With the bears?"

"Yeah."

We hang up. I am trying to read, but it's hard to concentrate when I'm constantly interrupted. The phone rings. I sigh and put the book away.

"Are they back YET?"

"I can see them, Mom. Sophie is by the pond. Max is on the swing."

"The pond? She'll fall in! Go get her."

"Mom, she's fine."

My kids are ten and twelve. Not likely to fall in ponds, get lost in the woods, or be eaten by bears. But she worries. She worries about us, but even more, she worries about herself.

"I ate a banana!"

"That's great, Mom. Hold on."

Now I am trying to help my daughter with her math homework while holding the phone and stirring a pan of veggies.

"I can't remember how to do that long division, Sophie. You'll have to ask Daddy when he gets home…. Hold on, Mom. Max, no computer until you finish your spelling. What was that, Mom?"

"I said I ate a banana!" Her voice is high, like it gets when she is anxious.

"Yeah," I say, "a banana. And the problem with that is…"

"I'm allergic to bananas!"

I want to say, "Then why did you eat it?" But I bite my tongue and say, "Are you okay?"

"I don't know. My stomach hurts."

Her stomach hurt for a week after that, but I am pretty sure she isn't really allergic. She just scared herself into believing she was.

The next week, it was a peach. "I ate a peach!"

"Are you allergic?"

"No, but the peach was on the counter, and I had just washed dishes. I think some dish soap got on the peach. Do you think it will hurt me?"

"Dish soap on the peach?" Now she's caught us in the middle of a rip-roaring game of *Monopoly*. I'm beating the pants off the kids, and I want to keep it that way, but I just landed on Kentucky Avenue and Max has a hotel on it.

"Hold on, Mom."

"Ha! Pay up!" my kid says. I don't want to, but I hand him the money.

"You're not listening to me!" my mom yells. "I ate a bottle of dish soap! I'm going to die!"

"You ate the whole bottle? Sophie, your turn."

"You're not taking me seriously! I'm going to call Poison Control."

"Okay, call me back."

Poison Control tells her she'll be fine. That's what they always tell her. She calls every day. It's often a dish soap kind of thing, but sometimes it's that she got some face cream on the side of her mouth and may have licked it. Many times, it's the chicken. She calls Poison Control because after she eats chicken, she thinks she might remember having seen a slight blue tinge on the tip of the wing. "When in doubt, throw it out," is their motto, or so she tells me, which means more than half her groceries end up in the trash.

The phone rings while my family is eating dinner.

"The cotton ball is missing!" my mom cries.

I had just dropped a beautiful chunk of butter on a steamy mound of mashed potatoes. With a sigh, I leave my plate of food and my family, and take the phone into the living room.

"Cotton ball?" I say as I plop onto the couch.

"It's gone!" Her voice is near hysterics. I pet the kitty, who rolls over for a tummy rub.

"It was a new bottle of medicine," she says. "You know how they have the cotton in them?"

"Yeah?" I haven't heard this one yet.

"The cotton is missing!" I can tell she is pacing her kitchen, going back to the bottle of medicine again and again, looking for the cotton.

I change the phone to my other ear. "Okay, so maybe this bottle never had the cotton in it."

"It had the cotton!" she practically yells at me.

"But if it's not there…"

"It's not there because I ATE IT!"

My family hears her yell through the phone. My husband raises his eyebrows, while my daughter points to my mashed potatoes and rubs her tummy. "Yum," she mouths. I shake my head.

"You really ate a cotton ball?" I ask.

"It's not in the bottle, is it? So, yeah, I must have eaten it!"

I take a deep breath and wonder what it must be like to worry so much. I also wonder what it must be like to have a normal mother, or at least one who doesn't think she eats cotton balls.

"I gotta go," she says. We hang up. I go back to my potatoes, which are cold. The butter is congealed, but I eat them anyway. The phone rings.

"Hi, Mom, what did Poison Control say?"

"They said that if I ate a cotton ball, I'd know it."

"And do you think that's true?" I ask.

"I don't know. Maybe."

She once asked Poison Control if she was their craziest client. They told her no, that there was a man who called every day, convinced that his dog was trying to poison him. We had a good laugh about that.

"I better go," she says. "My stomach feels funny."

So does mine, but I finish my cold dinner knowing the phone will ring again in a few minutes. And who knows what it will be this time?

~Lava Mueller

Chapter 8

for Mom, with love

Thanks for Being My Rock

*If you look into your mother's eyes, you know that is
the purest love you can find on this earth.*
~Mitch Albom

82

Nighttime Mothering

*The tie which links mother and child is of such pure
and immaculate strength as to be never violated.*
~Washington Irving

A cry in the night. Whimpering turns to desperate screams. I hear it, but I don't really want to hear it. It is dark and cold, and my bed is warm and soft.

I throw my feet over the side of the bed, as I grab my cell phone and give it a tap to light my way down the hall. The screaming sounds like death. Gruesome images flash in my mind. Broken limbs? Anaphylactic reaction? Chest pounding, I rush to the door and open it.

My silhouette is recognized in the doorway and the screaming instantly stops.

Once again, I cradle my child's head against my heart in the wee hours. I rock gently to soothe my tear-soaked baby back to sleep. My bare feet touch the cold, hardwood floors in rhythmic movement. My back starts to ache and my arms quiver from the strain, but I don't stop moving until I am sure it is safe to put him down, so that he does not notice he is no longer in my embrace.

I am tired.

As I make my way back to bed for the third time this night, images of my own mother fill my mind. She was there for me when I cried out in the night, too.

There was a time when I was sixteen and angry with my mother. She and I had not been on speaking terms for a while, even though she didn't know it. She had abandoned me. She did not show up for my school events, she didn't know my friends' names, and she didn't care if I came home at two o'clock in the morning. She had a new infant to wake her in the night, and her new husband. I was left to cry it out on my own. So, I lied to her that night. "Going to the movies, Mom."

Instead, I got into a 1978 yellow Peugeot, packed with teenaged girls and Olde English 800, and headed up a long abandoned logging road that ran alongside a cliff, hanging over the Snake River. The forty-minute switchback ride up the hill promised a kegger party at the top.

Our chauffeur was sixteen years old. A girl named Dorothy. She had just gotten her driver's license. She beamed at every twist and turn the road made, like she was playing the latest Atari game. But she wasn't at all familiar with navigating on slippery gravel. Sometimes our back tires didn't go straight as our front tires turned a harsh corner.

Our car fell off a cliff. The only cedar left on the clear-cut logging road twenty feet down caught it.

The fall threw my friend, Jana, from the car and her arm was pinned under the left front tire, broken, but keeping her from falling to her death. The children that remained in the car with me, although mildly injured, were covered in my blood. My face and torso slammed through the dash and front windshield. I shattered the glass with my cheekbones and rib cage.

Screams in the night for our mothers.

Out of a dead sleep, in the darkness, a ringing. My mother reached out to the sound, startled, as her feet hit the cold floor for the third time that night; but this time, it wasn't the scream of her infant. The voice on the other end of the phone said, "Your daughter Jennifer is in the ER. Hurry, we don't know if she will make it." My mother rushed out of the house, forgetting all details of the phone call. Gruesome images flashed through her mind as she drove.

Because I had lied to my mother and told her I was going to the movies, she went to the wrong ER demanding to see her baby girl who wasn't there. Confused, she went to another ER, and yet another, until she found me.

She was too late. I had already left my broken body behind to become one with the light. Surrounded in a warm glow that comforted me in a divine embrace, I felt no pain, just love.

I looked down on my naked body lying on a gurney. I watched a frantic emergency room doctor and three nurses pump an air bag on my face and do chest compressions while a blaring EKG flatlined. There was panic in the room.

Just then my mother burst through the ER double doors, exhausted, yelling, "My baby, my baby!" In an instant, my breath was back with a painful force, and I cried out for my mother.

She stayed by my side for days, picking the glass out of my face with tweezers for hours, feeding me ice chips, and telling me that everything would be okay, only slipping out of the room when I didn't realize that I was no longer in her embrace.

The night comes. Mothers get up and go to their children. My babies cry out for me and I cry out for my mother. It never stops being important. But it is more than that. Sometimes it feels like life and death and mothers help us choose life.

~Jennifer Knickerbocker

83

There All Along

What greater thing is there for human souls than to
feel that they are joined for life — to be with each other
in silent unspeakable memories.
~George Eliot

I wasn't sure what to think about my stepmother. She came into my life when I was a teenager, when I had more important things on my mind than becoming friends with her. I liked her and was always polite to her and we would chat at family gatherings, but I had friends and a social life miles away from where she and my dad lived. I was happy my dad had found someone who loved him as much as I did, but I really never took the time to really get to know her. Any communication she and I had was done through my dad. While he retired early, she continued working in a high profile career that left her very few free hours. This was just how it was and I never gave it a second thought.

As the years went by I would meet my dad for lunch during the week while she was at work. I would fill him in on the events in my life. I know he relayed my news to her but she and I never had one-on-one talks.

Then the unthinkable happened… my dad was diagnosed with cancer. Before we knew it, the cancer had become aggressive and my dad's remaining time with us was limited. I spent many long hours in my dad and stepmother's home those last few months, but most of the time it was to tag team with my stepmom so that she could run errands, take care of business, or just go get her hair done.

I know my dad worried that my stepmom would be alone once he passed away. He expressed his hope to me that our family would stay intact and that we would still look out for one another since he would no longer be able to fill that role. I told him we would. My stepmom and I sat together on either side of the bed and held my dad's hands as he took his last breath and died peacefully.

The turning point in our relationship came on the night of his death. I remember it as clearly as if it were yesterday. We were sitting at her kitchen counter waiting for the coroner to arrive when I finally asked, "Why did you not have children of your own?" With sudden clarity I realized that, although she had been a part of our family for more than twenty years, I never took the time to truly get to know her. Her goals, her dreams, her past. It was clear that we loved and cared about each other but did we really know each other? I stayed with her that night and we talked, laughed and cried.

Since that night she has become my biggest cheerleader and I hers. She is the person I call to discuss hardships, frustrations and joys and she listens. She encourages my son to achieve his goals and dreams and never misses an opportunity to tell me how proud she is of him and how proud she is of the job I have done as a parent. When I need advice or just a sympathetic ear she is always there. Our lunch and dinner dates are cherished moments that don't happen often enough.

It has been almost eight years since that night. Rather then look back on what we missed those early years I am so grateful for what we have created since then. I hope my dad is able to look down from heaven and be proud of the relationship we have created on our own. A terrible time in my life brought a blessing I never knew existed.

By the way, her response to my question that night so long ago was, "I never thought I would be any good at it." How wrong she was.

~D'ette Corona

84

Unconditional Love

There came a time when the risk to remain tight in the
bud was more painful than the risk it took to blossom.
~Anaïs Nin

My mother and I have always had a strong relationship, one of understanding, friendship, and trust. We have been there for each other through the most difficult of times, including our escape from our home to a battered women's shelter where we stayed for three months. In our old home we shared a room; my mother was (and still is) my greatest confidante. Although my mother and I have such a strong bond I had always questioned whether a parent's love truly is unconditional, as many say. Deep in the recesses of my mind was the notion that a parent's love could indeed be conditional if her child were to do something horrible enough — and at the time I was harboring a secret that I felt could be the end of our relationship.

It is safe to say that in the very small northern Maine town where I reside, my secret would not be very well received. The repercussions would be inevitable. Although I feared the reaction of those around me, most of all I feared hurting my mother. You see, for the better part of two months I had been in a passionate romance with someone — another woman. I was elated. I would spend nights composing sonnets and love letters.

In the beginning I had no plans to come out to my mother, a woman who is very strong in her Catholic faith. My girlfriend also had no plans to come out to her parents, who were known to be outwardly homophobic. However, fate had different plans. On a rainy Tuesday afternoon the summer of my first year in college, we made the mistake of allowing her next-door neighbors to see us holding hands, and of course a prompt phone call was made to her parents.

I went home that night in tears, barely able to form complete sentences. It was then that I knew I could no longer lie to my mother about why I did not have a boyfriend. I could no longer hide from her this vital part of my being. My mom was staying at her friend's house so I called her there.

"Mom, I don't know how to tell you this. I think I might be gay," I attempted to say through my tears.

The silence lasted only a few seconds, although it felt like hours, as I waited for the outrage and disappointment that I expected.

"I think you should be an actress; you're so dramatic. It isn't that big a deal. I love you and nothing can change that," she responded.

Suddenly, years of secrecy, years of feeling as though I were an abomination, an abnormality, evaporated. It was as if my mother's warm words melted the ice that had surrounded my heart for so long.

The road to self-acceptance continues to be rough, however I no longer doubt that a mother's love for her child is unconditional. My mother has been one of my biggest supporters. Whenever negative thoughts about myself creep up, I think back on my mother's words: "I love you and nothing can change that."

~Angel Therese Dionne

85

From Despair to Peace

Mother's love is peace. It need not be acquired,
it need not be deserved.
~Erich Fromm

My mother died at the age of thirty-six, leaving my brother and me, ages seven and six, to be raised primarily by relatives while my father remarried and divorced numerous times. By my early twenties, I had learned that my mother, who had polio as a young child, had not been expected to live past her early twenties.

After the tumultuous upbringing I'd had, I began to question why she chose to have children when she knew she was expected to die young. Why would she knowingly bring us into the world if she knew she would not be able to raise us? Finally, I gathered the courage to ask my aunt, who gave a simple reply: My mother had always defied the doctors' predictions. She had done so well with her health issues that she thought she would live long enough to raise us.

I remained obsessed with this, however, and I still felt profoundly wounded that my mother had left us in such difficult circumstances. And then the dream came:

There were no words spoken and no thoughts exchanged. There were only feelings. I recall no backdrop to the dream — no pastoral field, no heavenly mansion, no clouds — only the vision of my young, beautiful mother walking toward me. She was free of the severe scoliosis that had plagued her in life. She walked straight and came toward me with her arms open, her kind eyes shining even more so than I remembered, a beautiful smile on her face. She wrapped her arms around me and I returned her warm embrace. We held each other tightly and I could feel the softness of her hair against my cheek.

We simply stood, holding each other in that warmth as an overwhelming feeling of deep, unconditional love washed over me. In that dream moment I knew that my mother never intended to bring me into the world and then leave. She loved me then and she had kept loving me. She would continue to do so as long as I lived.

Thirty-five years ago I awoke from that dream with a profound peace. My despair had vanished. I have never since had a single moment of doubt as to my mother's hopes for my life. I have lived with the secure knowledge of my mother's unconditional love. It is the greatest gift she ever shared with me.

~Kimberly Ross

86

Granny's Cedar Chest

They say genes skip generations. Maybe that's why
grandparents find their grandchildren so likeable.
~Joan McIntosh

lthough the brass trim has tarnished over the decades, the wood of my grandmother's cedar chest retains a soft, warm glow and the faint scent of cedar still wafts upward when the lid opens. A treasure trove of family heirlooms lies within the cedar chest and my own talismans mingle with Granny's keepsakes. The worn baby shawl with hand-stitched edging remains within, along with a candy tin filled with dime store jewelry that a young Hazel Hayward wore when she worked as a telephone operator.

Yellowed, thin clippings and brittle photographs capture fragments of lives and preserve moments of the past. I can open any of the albums and thumb through to watch my own life unfold in Kodak clarity. Through these old photographs I can also catch a momentary glimpse of the past, of the world that once was reality.

There are too many items to count, to tally, but there is one artifact that is most important, a single item that has the most meaning for me because it sparked my career as a writer and sustains it. The manuscript is fragile and the ink is faded, the ink that was once stark, fresh black on new pages written over with great care. One corner of the faded manuscript remains tied with a red ribbon now softened to a dusky pink by time. I can read the title and the entire work with ease although my fingers handle the precious paper with a light touch so that I do not destroy my Granny's one work as a writer, the Class Prophecy she penned in 1912.

Class prophecies were the vogue in the year that the Titanic sank beneath the waters of the north Atlantic and hers is written in the flowery, delicious style of the times. Most graduating classes had one, the work of a single student that attempted to foretell the future of their classmates.

Written in the first person, my grandmother's work lives and breathes life into the long dead youth who finished school with her that spring. I was fourteen, little younger than she when I first read it. Then, as now, I was awed by the power of the words, the unknown gift of my grandmother.

My own yearning to become a writer came early and I scribbled stories as soon as I learned how to hold a pencil. As a teenager, I hoped that someday I might write words that could touch others but it was a secret dream I kept close.

Granny knew me, however, almost as well as her own heart and so she opened the cedar chest to reveal that old manuscript. I read it with amazement, unaware that the grandmother who wore aprons over her house dresses, the woman whose hands were gnarled and worn with years of toil, had once shared my dream. Dust motes floated in the afternoon sunlight that filled the bedroom that my father once shared with his brother, and tears burned in my eyes as I asked why she had not become a writer.

"I couldn't." Her words were soft and simple but they spoke volumes. She couldn't; she had gone to work soon after that eighth grade graduation. By the time that the World War involved America, she had been a telephone operator. Later, after dial phones eliminated many operators, she went to work in a hospital laundry, a job she held until soon after my birth. She had also raised three sons, sent two of them off to World War II, and buried a husband. She married again in an autumn romance to my beloved Pop, the grandfather connected to me through love if not blood.

I stared at this remarkable little woman, unable to speak... but she could. "I couldn't but you should."

Her words were both benediction and challenge. It was a gauntlet tossed down to spur me and it has. Had she been able to attend high school or college, she might have become a noted writer but there is no "might" or "could" in real life. She had not but I could.

My dream had once been hers and on that day the torch was passed from one generation to another. I made a promise that I would not marry until I finished my education — high school and college. And, I made a vow that I would strive to take words and make them sing, that I could succeed.

The road to becoming a full-time writer has been long and filled with obstacles, but when tempted to falter, I would remember that manuscript, that dream and press onward.

Granny's cedar chest now graces my living room. Within its burnished depths, that manuscript remains, testament to a dream and foundation to my career as a writer.

She couldn't but I have — because of her dream.

~Lee Ann Sontheimer Murphy

87

Finding Strength in Love

*You have to be brave with your life so that others can
be brave with theirs.*
~Katherine Center, The Gifts of Imperfection

My mother was my hero when I was a child. She was tiny in stature, but I looked up to her in so many ways. She was beautiful. It wasn't just the dusting of freckles across her button nose, or the curls that I loved to brush that smelled like powder when I kissed the top of her head. It wasn't just her shining blue eyes or the contagious smile that spread wide across her face that she bestowed upon everyone with whom she came in contact. She always called me "babe" and held my hand in the car. I never felt as special as when I got to spend time alone with her, without my brothers.

My mother is the kindest person I know. She is humble to a fault, and she has lived her life taking care of those she loves, even when she needs to find a way to take care of herself.

I don't know how old I was when I first realized that my mother was ill. Nobody came out and told me she had bipolar disorder, but I started to notice her mood swings. By then, she was single, working multiple jobs, and our trailer home was in shambles. My older brother was in charge of us more and more, and my special one-on-one time with my mom dwindled as she struggled to keep us afloat. But she made time to read to all of us, huddled on a mattress in the living room where she slept. Her voice made everything seem okay.

One morning, I woke up to find she had painted our entire kitchen pink. Another time, during an argument between her and us kids, she passed out. We panicked as she lay on the floor, not sure what to do. I slapped her across the face to wake her up. Her symptoms seemed to be escalating, and I knew no way to help.

Sometime after, we left our tiny farm and moved into a small house "in town." A friend of hers lived next door and helped to parent us while my mother started to work on getting better. She started college and seemed more stable and attentive. But with the move, the confusion of her illness, and the onset of teenage hormones, I was left angry and I lashed out at my mother with hurtful words and actions. We fought often, and I struggled with my own depression in silence, not wanting to admit that I might be ill in the same way as she. But though my mother had so much on her plate, she put me in counseling, showed up at my school for meetings and made sure my brother and I got fitted with the braces we needed.

On "Take Your Daughter to Work" day she allowed me to attend classes by her side. I sat quietly, proud to be included in this new world my mother had bravely entered to reclaim a life of her creation. I never had the ability to tell her what this meant to me.

When I was nineteen, I found myself single and pregnant. My mother moved 2,500 miles to be near me and help me raise my son. And though I had accepted this journey of single motherhood thinking I would be on my own, I knew I was capable because of how much my mother believed in me. Because of my mother's love, I was never once alone. She stood behind me through a series of misguided choices and failed relationships. She encouraged me to pursue a path of personal growth and to find my place in the world. Because of her example, I have monitored my mental health closely and learned to seek help without shame or apology.

A few years ago, my mother decided she wanted to train to be a Mental Health Peer Counselor. With the help of a close friend, she mapped out a plan to achieve this goal. She ventured out of town despite her social anxiety to attend courses. I was never more proud. More recently, she earned her college degree, the first in our family to graduate from college. It took her twenty years.

I will never forget when my mother told me she had become part of NAMI, the National Alliance of Mental Health. I felt joy in my heart that she had found a place where she could positively influence the course of others who faced challenges such as hers. The woman who once avoided crowds at all costs called me to ask for assistance setting up for a benefit concert, saying that she was the volunteer coordinator for the event. I enlisted my son to help take down chairs after the show. We enjoyed the concert and my mom even danced with my son for a bit. I smiled inside, overcome with emotion and thinking about how far she had come. When they called the members of the committee up to the stage for introductions, I was shocked to hear that my mother was Vice President. I had no idea.

I never knew all the struggles my mother faced as I was growing up. But I know it took courage and strength for her to power through her illness. She fought fiercely and chose to be the author of her own adventure. This is why my mother will forever be a hero to me.

~Holly Wilkinson

88

She Never Stopped Loving Me

Mother, the ribbons of your love are woven around
my heart.
~Author Unknown

T he police officer cleared his throat. "Ma'am — you okay?" Bent over, I wiped my face on the blood-soaked bandage covering my lacerated thigh. "No." Tears cascaded from my eyes as I pleaded to God with the desperation of a lost child. "I want my mommy." My voice broke. Trying to mimic my mother's hold, I curled my legs up and clung to them, then rocked myself back and forth. Never before had I understood how much her love meant.

I hoped she would still love me.

"You can call her once we get to the station."

A guttural sound loosed from within, and my weeping increased. "No. I can't. She's in Haiti."

"Oh," he said. "Sorry."

Was this really happening?

My mother always told me she'd love me no matter what, but I didn't believe her. Convinced she'd be disappointed and stop loving me if she knew all the terrible things I did, I hid myself from her. My life was full of secrets and lies.

Would she stop loving me now that she would know the truth?

At the station, I gave a false statement to the detective. Promising myself I'd be honest if he questioned my story, I searched for signs of disbelief, but receiving only assurances, my lies continued. I couldn't even think the truth, let alone say it out loud.

A knock interrupted us. "Her attorney's here," a voice said.

"My attorney?" Confused, I shook my head. "I don't have an attorney."

"Well, she says she's your attorney," the voice said. "She wants to talk to you."

The detective slammed his hand on the desk. "She doesn't need an attorney."

Startled, I looked up at him. "I don't?"

He furrowed his brow. "Why would you?"

My lips trembled. "I don't know." I thought for a moment. "Maybe I should see what she wants."

The detective scowled as the door opened and a woman appeared. She looked at the floor beneath my bleeding leg and pointed. "Is that her blood on the carpet?"

Looking down, I nodded.

The woman pointed at me. "Don't say another word." She turned to the detective and put her hands on her hips. "She needs to go to the hospital. Now!"

In the emergency room, she explained the seriousness of my predicament. "Your mother insisted you have an attorney."

"My mother?"

"Yes. Your sister called her and she told your family to get you an attorney. It's a good thing — it's very important you don't say another word."

After that, I didn't say anything to anyone. I was afraid the truth, that I shot and killed my husband, would make everyone stop loving me. I worried no one would believe that it was self-defense.

My mother took the first flight home to help me with funeral arrangements. She held my weary body up as I faced the man I once loved in his casket. She helped me clean my house, which had been a crime scene for two days, and never asked me what had happened that night.

It took months, but the phone call from my attorney came. "You've been indicted for murder. You need to be in court in the morning."

Hands shaking and knees bouncing, I nervously awaited the judge's ruling for bond. Then, with a thundering clang, I was behind bars.

I thought back to years before, and my mother's words echoed in my ears. "Don't get involved with him. He's bad news."

Although afraid she'd stop loving me, I had married him anyway. I loved him and needed his love.

"I'm so disappointed. Why do you make such choices?" she asked.

My heart deflated.

"Well," her voice held resignation, "I'm worried, but I still love you. You made your bed, now you can lie in it."

At least she still loved me.

Then I had a child of my own, and maternal love overwhelmed me. When my mother saw her grandson for the first time, her face lit up. "Oh! Oh my goodness! He's so wonderful." She stroked his head and ran her hand down his body, then wrapped him in her arms and brought his face close to hers.

Her love was overpowering; it flowed from her as she drew him into her chest and held him tight. She looked at me with tear-filled eyes. "He's so precious. He reminds me of you."

"Me?" I grimaced. "How's that?"

She looked at him. "Holding him reminds me of holding you when you were born. I love him, just like I love you."

Could she really love me like that?

As time went by, my husband's extreme jealousy grew into obsession, which evolved into emotional and verbal abuse. Then the abuse became physical. But what could I do? The old mantra danced in my head. Worried the truth would cause me to lose someone I loved, I kept my burdens to myself, even when his anger escalated to daily threats on my life with a knife held to my throat. As my mom said, I had made my bed; I had to lie in it.

One dreadful night, my husband spun out of control. He tortured me with a knife and threatened our son's life. Instinct to protect my child kicked in and I knew I had to do whatever it took. I would die for my son. With that resolve, I managed to get away from my abuser and ran for the hidden gun.

The metallic clatter of enormous keys startled me back to the reality of jail. In a letter to my mom, I mentioned how much joy it brought me to receive mail; after that, she wrote to me every day. With each letter, the realization that she just might love me after all, even though I'd done so many egregious things, began to sink in.

Although my mother lived in another country, she put taking care of my business and visiting me at the top on her list whenever she came to town. She did everything she could while I was incarcerated for over eight months, including managing my bankruptcy filing, hiring a high-powered attorney who got me out on bond, and taking custody of my son in an effort to keep me from losing him.

On the eve of my trial, fear besieged me. My mother hugged me tight and rocked me. "It's alright." She tucked me into bed and kissed my forehead. "I'm here for you, no matter what."

Her presence reassured me during every minute of testimony. At the end of each day, she held me and comforted me. She stayed by my side and loved me through it all. When my jurors spared me from prison, she gave me a thumbs-up and mouthed, "I love you."

A smile crossed my face — I believed her.

My mother loves me, no matter what.

~Leigh Ann Bryant

89

The Spelling Bee

The best way to conquer stage fright is to know what
you're talking about.
~Michael Mescon

S pelling was my favorite subject in fourth grade. Every week
I memorized my new words, and by Friday I was prepared
to take the spelling test. I usually got all the words right. My
teacher, Mrs. Casazza, wrote "100%" and "Excellent!" on the
top of my paper, and when she handed it back I felt so proud.

In the desk behind me, Donna Slocum would lean forward and
whisper, "What did you get?" and I'd show her my test paper. "Again?"
she'd ask, with a hint of jealousy in her voice.

One day Mrs. Casazza announced to the class that we would
have a spelling bee on Thursday, the day before our test. "It will be
a review for those who are having a difficult time remembering their
words," she said.

Oh, no, I thought. Last month when I had to stand up in front of
the class and give a book report, my arms shook so badly that it was
hard to read my paper. I was overly conscious of the twenty-seven
pairs of eyes on me, and all I wanted was to run back to my seat. A
spelling bee would be even worse. I wouldn't have a paper to read from!

After lunch on Thursday, Mrs. Casazza told us to line up by the
board, and she explained the rules. "Say the word, spell it, and then
say it again," she said. "Be careful not to repeat any letters."

One at a time, she pronounced a word for each student to spell.

Two boys made mistakes right away and had to sit down. With clammy hands, I waited for my turn. After the girl next to me correctly spelled her word, Mrs. Casazza called my name and said, "Your word is 'echo.'"

"Echo," I started. The sound of my own voice startled me. "E."

Then my mind went blank. I couldn't think. Everyone was looking at me, waiting for me to say the next letter. But I couldn't see the word in my head. All I could see were the other kids, and they all had their eyes on me. My face got hot. I swallowed hard. What came next? Was it K? No. It sounded like "k" but it wasn't, was it? It was "c."

"E-C-H-O," I spelled slowly. "Echo."

Oohs and aahs came from the kids beside me. "You repeated the 'E'!" Donna pointed out.

"She's right," Mrs. Casazza said. "You'll have to sit down."

I looked down at the floor and made my way back to my desk. Although I was relieved that I was no longer in the spotlight, I felt like crying because I knew how to spell the word.

Afterward, Mrs. Casazza said, "The spelling bee worked so well, and we all had so much fun, that I've decided to have a spelling bee every Thursday."

It worked so well? We all had so much fun? Every Thursday?

I didn't want another spelling bee! I was afraid that I'd mess up again. And sure enough, when the next Thursday came, I did. I started spelling my first word, and then I suddenly became conscious of everyone in the room staring at me. I stood silent a long time, unable to finish the word. The room was quiet while Mrs. Casazza waited. Finally, she sent me back to my seat.

I dreaded the spelling bee so much that I didn't want to go to school the following Thursday.

"What's wrong?" my mother asked. "Are you sick?"

I told her about the spelling bees, and how each time I messed up my first word and had to sit down.

"But you're a good speller!" she said. "You do so well on your tests!"

"I can't spell when they're all looking at me!" I said.

"Oh, so that's the problem," she said. "You've got stage fright. I heard of an easy way to get rid of that. Just imagine everyone's wearing nothing but their underwear."

I laughed. "Their underwear?"

"Try it," she said. "It will remind you that they're no different from you."

Mom seemed sure that her trick would help me, so I went to school believing it would.

During the spelling bee, my first word was "piece."

"Piece," I started. "P." The feeling that everyone was staring at me began to creep up again, but I remembered what Mom had said. I pretended my classmates were dressed only in their underwear. I must have smiled a little. My head cleared and I concentrated. Now did the word start with P-I or P-E? I knew this. We'd learned that there is a "pie" in "piece."

"I-E-C-E," I said. "Piece."

"Very good," Mrs. Casazza said.

Hooray! I did it once, so I knew I could do it again. And I did, again and again. Throughout the year, I even won a few spelling bees. That was just the beginning. My mother's trick helped me with every speech and book report I had to give. I stopped thinking that I couldn't get up in the front of the class. Of course, I could! With a little imagination, anyone can!

~Mary Elizabeth Laufer

90

Independence Day

Freedom is the oxygen of the soul.
~Moshe Dayan

I can still hear those defiant words blaring from the radio in my mother's Volkswagen sedan. Sitting alongside my mother as we scurried about the streets of our little town, running our usual errands, she sang along without missing a beat. She raised her left arm — the other firmly on the wheel — as if to accentuate the melody, and sang with the passion of someone who could relate to the woman described in the song, with the passion of someone with newfound freedom and independence.

From the frequent screaming and fighting, the abusive language, and the love/hate drama that had unfolded between my parents before my eyes, I knew that "Independence Day," written by Gretchen Peters, was more than just a popular song that summer. For my mother, it was the music of courage and self-confidence. For me, at the formative age of fourteen, it was the music that turned my world upside down.

The song's lyrics told of a woman's response to domestic abuse, seen from the point of view of her eight-year-old daughter. On Independence Day, while her daughter attends the local parade, the woman starts a fire in the house, and she and her abusive, alcoholic husband both perish in it.

The song has double meaning in that the woman was finally gaining her freedom from her abusive husband — thus, it was her Independence Day — and the events occurred on the Fourth of July.

Its message suggests that what the woman did was neither right nor wrong. Instead, it was the only way she could ultimately gain her freedom and, at the same time, protect her daughter from the violent home where her little girl had seen bruises on her mother's face far too many times.

"Let freedom ring, let the white dove sing... Let the weak be strong, let the right be wrong."

Those were some of the lyrics that my mother sang with the deepest passion.

My mother left my father that summer and never went back. A teenager at the time, I was initially angry about it all. The last thing I wanted to do was spend time with the woman who didn't seem to understand me and with the woman whose decision forced me to live in another house, to ride another school bus, to memorize another phone number, and, worst of all, to endure the financial limitations of a single-parent home.

As we continued about our errands that afternoon, I glanced over to the driver's seat at the middle-aged woman my selfish teenage self had begun to resent. With her long red hair, petite figure, sculptured face, and deep brown eyes, my mother truly was a picture of beauty. Although she seemed a bit overbearing and protective at times, she was my strength and I admired her. But she was increasingly down on herself. Inside the radiant beauty that most people saw was an increasingly broken, weary, and sad woman.

She tried to be strong for my younger sister and me, but I'd often see her cry and witnessed how the pain of ending that relationship drove her to a state of depression. I tried to be sympathetic, but there was little that I could say or do to help mend her heart.

Just the night before she had cried herself to sleep and, as we lay beside her, whispered, "I love you girls, more than you will ever know."

As I watched her sing that afternoon, I began to understand why that song was so meaningful for her. And I came to realize how much her freedom, her independence, and her ability to do what made her happy, really meant. I began to gain an appreciation for the sacrifices that my mother made, not only for her own wellbeing, but for my sister's and mine as well. Though we struggled financially, her courage and strength allowed us to live in a home free of fighting and verbal abuse. Her decision allowed us to stop living in fear.

When the song ended and she parked the car, she smiled as big as she could, and said, "I'll be celebrating my Independence Day on July 31st, not July 4th. Bring the fireworks."

It's been ten years since the day I watched my mother harmoniously sing along to "Independence Day" while en route to the grocery store. I'm no longer the teenager in the front seat, dependent on a ride to my destination. I no longer use my Sony Walkman to block out her high-pitched singing. But there's one thing that hasn't changed since that hot summer day in the passenger seat: the significant impact the song's message has on me.

When I hear the words "Independence Day," I don't always think about the fourth day in July, the red, white, and blue, or America the free. Instead, I salute those brave women who, like my mother, had the strength and the courage to make difficult and painful changes in their lives, changes that now face me as well.

Perhaps it's true that history repeats itself. Not long ago, when I left my alcoholic husband, I knew the same kind of pain my mother experienced nearly a decade earlier. Perhaps I should have paid more attention to the lessons of my mother, the lessons of my upbringing, and the frequent anguish of my childhood. But perhaps I was destined to follow in her footsteps, to make her mistakes, to feel her pain, and to develop her courage, strength, and independence.

I know she never wanted me to, but now I know. Now I understand. And as soon as I was able to roll the stone away, I had my Independence Day.

Coincidentally, I left my husband on July 31, 2010 — exactly eight years to the day my mother left my father. "Hard to believe," she said when she reminded me of our shared date. "Only now do you understand why it was so important for me to leave… for me, for you, and for your little sister."

Not long after our phone conversation, I came across that song, which I hadn't heard in years, on one of my late-night drives. Like

Mom always had, I turned up the radio and sang along with passion. And for once that day — probably even that week — it didn't feel so bad to be alone.

Let freedom ring.

~Ellarry Prentice

91

Grandma's Trade Secret

If nothing is going well, call your grandmother.
~Italian Proverb

*I*n the African-American community, there is an old, albeit incorrect, notion that hair is like cholesterol — there are good and bad versions. Fortunately, as the granddaughter of the late Edna Tucker, I never paid much consideration to said labels, because when Grandma Tucker did your hair the only possible way it could come out was good.

I didn't know how she did it; I only knew that when divine intervention (my grandma's hands) touched charcoal-colored wool (my hair), the end result would be one that defied logic. And, much to my delight, I also knew that I could depend on this. It was a constant. Like stars in the sky, cartoons on Saturday mornings, and first-day-of-school jitters.

It was a particularly hot and steamy evening in late August of 1989, and I was very, very concerned. As I snapped the new fluorescent-colored folders into my Trapper Keeper and then splayed my brand new outfit across the chair in my room, I mindfully kept one eye on what was going on outside. The clouds were dark and ominous, and the air was thick and heavy with humidity. On an ordinary day, this wouldn't have bothered me, but this was no ordinary day. I was, in fact, preparing for what I then considered to be a life-altering occurrence: junior high. And the prospect of facing this momentous experience with unruly hair that resembled — in my own words — "cotton candy poofs," was unthinkable. My mother, bless her heart, knew what was at stake here. "You'd better call Grandma," she said.

My mother was spot-on because no one could do hair like Grandma. Grandma's prowess in the hair beautification department was like the eighth wonder of the world. No, Grandma wasn't a card-carrying hairdresser, but as the mother of four daughters, she had certainly learned a trick or two.

"Grandma," I pleaded into the phone. "Can you come over and do my hair?"

She waited a beat, sighed, and then replied with a giggle, "Sure, sugar. I'm on my way."

I am not exaggerating when I say that my pulse returned to its normal rate as soon as I saw Grandma ambling up the walkway with her big black canvas tote bag filled with her arsenal of tools.

The enemy? Frizz. And it didn't stand a chance.

Having just washed and blown dry my hair, I sat patiently at the kitchen table as Grandma drew items from the bag and laid them before me on a pink cotton towel: A jar of pomade with a well-worn label; a black plastic comb; a few sheets of paper towel; a portable stove; and, last but certainly not least, a pressing comb. Anticipation welled up inside me as I watched my grandmother plug the tiny metal stove into a nearby outlet and place the pressing comb inside the stove's opening. As she waited for the pressing comb to heat up, she began to divide my hair into four sections and carefully apply the pomade. The sheer thought that, within an hour's time, my hair would become bone straight, silky, and shiny had my stomach turning over like a rotisserie chicken.

Finally, Grandma would run a piece of paper towel along the back of the comb and an ever-so-faint caramel line would appear: The comb was ready. She then proceeded to gently work the comb through various parts of my hair while I remained as still as a block of ice. I did manage to hold up a mirror from time to time in hopes of catching a glimpse of Grandma's trade secret, that indiscernible thing she did that made all her tools work that much better, but I was left scratching my head every time (no pun intended). Afterward, I helped

Grandma pack up her things and we'd sit and chat about what I had considered to be items of utter importance: running track, algebra, and my crush on a boy named Billy. When the time came, I kissed her goodbye, most appreciative that my dark mane now danced about my shoulders — and that someone had tolerated my rambling about a boy whose name I am surprised I still remember.

It rained like the dickens on the first day of seventh grade, but my hair remained intact. I still have no idea how Grandma did it. My grandma passed away in 1991 — a few years after that memorable humid evening, and a few years before I began to straighten my own hair. My mother and her sisters still maintain that the secret was in Grandma's wrist: "It was the way she turned the comb," my mother says, flicking her wrist with a closed fist.

I tend to agree. Sure, Grandma's wrist played a part. But her heart was in it, too.

~Courtney Conover

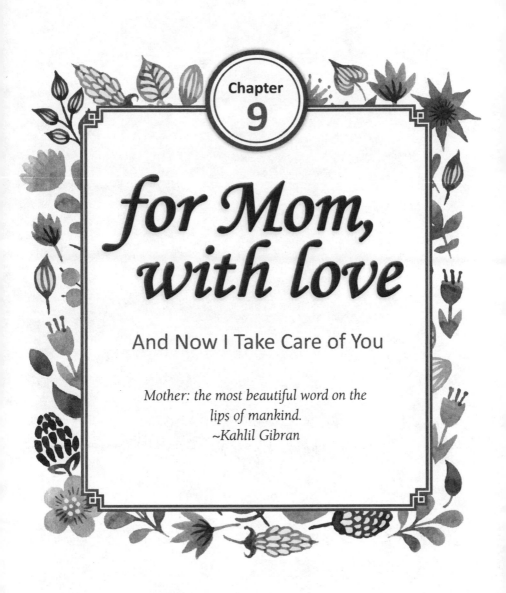

for Mom, with love

And Now I Take Care of You

*Mother: the most beautiful word on the
lips of mankind.
~Kahlil Gibran*

92

Clothed in Love

Turn your wounds into wisdom.
~Oprah Winfrey

I recall sitting in my bedroom, praying for the wisdom I needed to proceed with what I had to do. I had been faced with many challenges in my seventy years, but this could prove to be the greatest. It had become clear that my mother needed more help than I was able to provide for her in her home. There was a fifteen-mile drive separating us — not a huge stretch, but adding that to my responsibilities with a sick husband was more than I could handle. She would have to come to live with us.

Until now, my mother had rejected the idea vociferously. The mere mention of it would result in a huge argument, leaving us at odds for days. Finally, I just crashed and said that we would no longer discuss the issue. Instead, I resolved to spend more time with my husband and visit my mother every few days instead of every day. Always in control, my mother continued to be firm in her resolve, so I was forced to be firm in mine.

There was another issue that I had to come to terms with. It was something that I hated to acknowledge, but if I expected this to work, I would have to take a look at a deeper, more serious issue. It had to do with the resentment I continued to feel toward the mother who had never shown me affirmation or praise, never a warm hug, never acknowledgment of my talents. How would I be able to welcome her, take care of her, cook for her, see to her social life, and pretend that everything between us was fine?

Finally, my mother capitulated and moved in, making it clear that she would do it her way. "I will stay in my room!" she insisted. "You can deliver my meals there, and I will come out to the living room only if I have visitors."

"But, Mom," I cried. "I have a beautiful sun room and deck! You can watch the snow fall and sit by the fire. You'll love it!"

"I think I know what I love," she responded, not budging from her position.

So the months went on until my husband succumbed to his illness. I was wracked with grief and at the same time angry that he, my best friend, left me alone with my mother. I was over seventy now, and my body was rebelling. More than the physical pain, the emotional pain was dragging me down to a level that I understood to be trouble. I made an appointment with a psychologist.

Dr. Janice and I spent months trying to unravel the reasons for my mother's negative behavior.

"Your mother is stuck in the past," Dr. Janice said. "She's never had a life outside of her own environment. She won't change. You have to change. Put aside your hurt and move along."

"But how…" I began. I didn't have a chance to go on.

"Come on," she said, "you're smart enough to figure it out. Reasoning capacity diminishes in old age, so don't expect your mother to suddenly understand, even if you tell her straight out how you feel."

"So, tell me what to do!"

"Find some common ground," she replied. "Something where you can both come together. If you really want to do this, you'll find a way."

I thought about her suggestion for weeks until I finally came up with an idea. Dr. Jan had said that Mom was stuck in the past. Instead of fighting her, why not join her?

I went to the attic, collected her old photo albums, and placed one on her lap. I pulled up a chair beside her. As we began, the tone of her voice became soft and mellow, full of emotion. There were tears as she spoke of her parents, her siblings, cousins, old friends, all gone now. But there was a good deal of laughter too, as she recalled the events surrounding the faded pictures.

"Did you know that my father made moonshine?" she laughed. "The cops were always at our door, but it wasn't to arrest him!" She turned the page. "Oh, here's my brother, Tony. He earned a Purple Heart in the war, you know. And my sisters…"

"Tell me about them, Mom," I said, sincerely interested, taking notes on everything she was relating to me.

Finally, we uncovered a large envelope filled with pictures of me as a child. I had never before seen this treasure. They were not casual pictures, but posed and deliberate. Each picture looked like it could have been in a magazine. The outfits — dresses, coats, hats, sweaters — were beautiful. Plain, simple lines were resplendent with inverted pleats, hand-smocking, crocheted collars, and soft gathers. I was totally shocked!

"Mom," I said, "you always talk about how poor you and Daddy were during the Depression. How in the world could you have afforded to dress me in these clothes?"

"Well, you were my little girl. I loved you so much, and I didn't want you to look shabby just because we had no money. At night, after you were asleep, I made clothes for you. Sometimes, I'd take apart one of my sweaters or skirts. I'd save the thread and the buttons to make dresses for you, and cut the sleeves off sweaters to make leggings. I would crochet around collars and embroider little designs. The lovely white wool coat is from the dress I wore on my honeymoon. It took a long time because I had no sewing machine and no pattern."

"But this outfit is fur," I said, pointing to a beautiful little jacket with matching hat.

"Oh, yes, I remember!" she said. "Before I was married, I had seen a fur coat in a store window. I loved it, so my father bought it for me as an engagement present."

I was spellbound. Listening to those stories made me want to hear more. I went to her room daily and began noticing that her demeanor was changing. She was no longer the demanding, angry mother she had once been. She was softer now, happier.

For the eight years my mother was with me, we continued to

discuss stories of her past. Sharing the trials of her life and her secret desires, I came to understand that, in her time, outward affection was a sign of weakness. She never understood that there could be a different way.

I think of my mother every day now and of how those old photos gave us a chance to be together before she died. The pictures of a little girl in long curls, dressed in high fashion, are a poignant reminder that my mother, in her own way, truly loved me.

She had given everything to me — literally the clothes off her back.

~Pam Giordano

93

In Her Hands

Every problem has a gift for you in its hands.
~Richard Bach

Many of the common struggles of aging can be accelerated by Parkinson's disease. In a much shorter time than normal, a loved one can decline drastically in physical and mental capacities, so drastically that it's hard for family members to keep up with the practical and psychological adjustments demanded by the progression.

For my mother, it seemed that she was healthy and active one day and, in no time at all, debilitated to the point of needing someone with her at all times. The disease left her vulnerable to falls, and the trauma and injuries from two serious falls compounded the challenges of her overall weakened condition. This was a major change for a woman who grew up on a farm, worked most of her adult life in an automobile factory, maintained an immaculate home, and counted her sick days on one hand. It was a major change as well for my father, my siblings, and me because we only knew her as the strong hub of our family. More than anything else, I remember resisting the role reversal that was imposed on me. I would have done anything to help my mother, but it was as if I was hardwired to be the child and allow her to be the parent. After all, that's who we had been to each other all of my life. When I helped her get dressed, monitored her use of the bathroom, and checked that her food was cut into small enough bites, these were precious opportunities to help meet her needs. At the same time, they were such foreign tasks, running totally contrary to our relationship.

I wasn't the only one who struggled with the role reversal; my mother seemed to resist it as well. Sometimes she looked at me with heart-wrenching regret and whispered, "I'm sorry." It was hard enough for her to be incapable of performing basic daily activities, but it must have been harder still to need help from someone she was accustomed to helping. We made the best of the situation, teasing and joking whenever possible, but both of us felt how unwelcome the circumstances were.

Even though I tried to be the epitome of a pleasant, positive presence in my parents' home each weekend when I visited, in my heart I wanted everything to go back to "normal." I wanted to reverse time, only a few months, back to the point that my mother was only slowing down rather than overtaken by a disease. With every phase of her decline, I had to muster more and more willingness to watch her be redefined by Parkinson's.

Then, one Saturday morning, there was a turning point. I had driven from Missouri to Kansas after I got off work the night before, in order to spend the weekend with my parents as had become my custom. My mother had just finished eating breakfast, and I was settling her into a favorite chair in the family room for a morning of visiting. I couldn't keep from doing what I did every weekend — notice, as if for the first time, the many ways that the disease had changed her. She was just a fraction of her previous size and strength, her face was drawn, and her whole body trembled. I looked at her hair, which still needed to be combed, and the cotton robe that was the only attire my father could manage. That's when I saw my mother's hands.

What caught my attention was that I had overlooked a small spill of oatmeal on one of them. I would have to return to the kitchen for a washcloth. But suddenly I was overwhelmed with the recognition of those hands. They hadn't changed, not really, not from age or from disease. Sure, there were some wrinkles and tremors, but they were so clearly the same hands that had cared for me my entire life.

I saw in those hands the person who had scooped out my meal portions, the person who had tucked me into bed, the person who had checked my temperature and bandaged my cuts and scrapes, the

| *And Now I Take Care of You*

person who had examined how my clothes and shoes fit, the person who had studied my homework and admired my report cards, the person who had handed me birthday presents, and the person who had asked to see the first ring that a boy gave me. I realized that it was still my mother inside that aged, diseased body, because those were her hands.

So many things had changed, but the important things were unchangeable. In my mother's hands, I recognized the person who had cared for me more than anyone else in the whole world. That was the person I wanted to care for in return, not some redefined or lessened identity, but my mother, the mother I saw in those hands. That's who she was, still, regardless of frailties or needs.

From that moment until my caregiving ended with my mother's passing, neither she nor I felt any more awkwardness over role reversals or unwelcome tasks. I can honestly say that there wasn't even the slightest sense of drudgery either, not ever. Somehow, in her hands, I caught a change in focus, from the challenging time that would be her last years to the whole that made up her entire life. For other caregivers, it might be a look in the eye, an expression in the face, or a tone in the voice that conveys so clearly, if only for an instant, the person we recognize. Yes, he or she is still there, and that's who we honor with our care.

~Judy Brown

94

The Missing Stocking

A mother's happiness is like a beacon, lighting up the
future but reflected also on the past in the guise of
fond memories.
~Honoré de Balzac

S uddenly I felt my cheeks turn red with embarrassment. How could I have never noticed? Every Christmas my mother enjoyed creating special memories and traditions for her family. Mom loved Christmas — the shopping, baking, decorating, music, gifts — even the hustle and bustle the season brings. Her enthusiasm was contagious and that encouraged my brother, sister, and me to experience the joy and wonder of Christmas. Although Santa came to our home, we were taught that the real reason for the season was to celebrate the birth of our Messiah — Jesus Christ.

Many years have passed since I was a child. Yet I can still smell the aroma of Mom's sugar cookies baking as she prepared a special treat for her family and for Santa. These delicacies were a sure sign that Christmas Day was near.

On Christmas Eve my mother laid all our stockings under the beautifully decorated pine tree my father had picked out and cut down in the forest. Later, in the middle of the night, Santa filled the stockings.

The next morning we excitedly opened our gifts, leaving our Christmas stockings for last. Santa always stuffed our stockings full of tiny toys, trinkets, nuts, oranges, apples, and colorful hard candies in various shapes, sizes, and flavors.

In my twenties, I went Christmas shopping with a friend. She began looking for a small gift to place in her mother's stocking.

"You fix a Christmas stocking for your mother?" I asked.

"Yes," she replied. "Every year I fill a stocking with little goodies and have it waiting for her on Christmas morning. I couldn't bear for my mother to not have a Christmas stocking, especially since she prepares one for everyone else."

That's when I felt my cheeks flush with embarrassment. I realized my mother had not had a Christmas stocking for as long as I remembered. And, even worse, no one had noticed her stocking was missing.

My sister and I determined to start a tradition of our own that year. Excited, we bought jewelry, candy, socks, and an orange. We placed them in a small, red stocking. Christmas morning we snuck it under the tree while Mom was busy preparing breakfast.

Eagerly we waited to see Mom's reaction. She passed out everyone's stockings; then noticed an extra one. She picked up the stocking and read the tag: "To Betty Ann — Love, Santa."

Amazement crossed her face. "Is this stocking really for me?"

We smiled and nodded.

Tears glistened in Mom's eyes. "It's been so long… since I've had a Christmas stocking," she said. "Thank you."

Though I don't remember the gifts I received that year, I have never forgotten how thrilled my mother was to receive a simple, red stocking. Seeing her reaction was the most precious gift of all. And once again, she taught me about the joy and wonder of Christmas… that it is indeed more blessed to give than to receive.

~Teresa Ann Maxwell

95

Talking Potato

Common sense and a sense of humor are the same
thing, moving at different speeds. A sense of humor is
just common sense, dancing.
~William James

eing creative while taking care of my mom during her last year was not only helpful, but an absolute necessity. As the dementia progressed, she didn't say much and mostly stayed on the couch watching TV.

Eventually, getting her to eat became a challenge. Usually the only thing she wanted was a baked potato with butter and cheese.

One day, after fixing her potato, I headed into the living room, only to hear, "I don't want it."

"I have your potato fixed with butter and cheese. It looks delicious, Mom."

"I don't want it!"

"You are going to love it. It will taste good."

"I don't want it! I don't want anything!"

Mom weighed less than 100 pounds and needed to eat.

"Mr. Potato," I said, "Mom says she doesn't want you."

In another voice I replied, "Tell her I taste good and I want her to eat me."

Mom again, "I don't want him."

"But I'm all covered with butter and cheese and just the right temperature."

Mom's head came up a little, but she kept her eyes closed.

"Tell Betty I will cry if she doesn't eat me!"

Mom's body started jiggling with laughter. She cracked a smile and opened her eyes, looked at me, and said, "Tell him I'll eat him!"

And she did!

As I approached the kitchen to fetch my talking potato, I was thrilled she was going to eat and that I had made her laugh, amazed at what I heard come out of my mouth, and so sad about my mom and her condition — all at the same time.

Later that night my thoughts returned to years earlier when I went to the hospital to visit Mom. As I walked through the door of her room, she said, "I prayed all day that you'd come and see me because I knew if you did, you would make me laugh."

Those words changed my life. I knew I was supposed to use my quick wit and sense of humor to help others and I became a Christian humor writer. Now all these years later I was using humor to help my elderly mother.

Even with dementia she knew there was something funny about a talking potato.

~Linda Rose Etter

96

A Turkey of a Thanksgiving

Enjoy the little things, for one day you may look back
and realize they were the big things.
~Robert Brault, www.robertbrault.com

I grew up with the crazy notion that cancer is 100 percent survivable. My mother's first bout with cancer came only a few weeks before my fifth birthday. She was diagnosed with thyroid cancer, and the surgery meant my mother missed my first day of kindergarten. My cousin Charlotte was the one who put me on the bus that morning. I don't really remember the day. My cousin's picture of me standing in my blue dress in front of the house is the only proof I have that my mother wasn't present. And the scar along the crease in my mother's neck is the only proof she'd had a tumor.

Mom survived the thyroid cancer, but as the years passed, the doctors kept finding skin cancer on her face and back. She'd have minor surgery to remove the malignant moles, and life would go on. Cancer didn't seem like such a dirty word to me. Just a nuisance that left my mother with another scar.

And then came my freshman year of college. I was home one weekend when my mother sat on the edge of my bed to tell me she had breast cancer. In hindsight, I should have been terrified, but my fear was tampered by Mom's track record for kicking cancer to the curb. Mom had survived thyroid cancer once and skin cancer more times than I could count. Surely, breast cancer would be just another bump in the road.

The impact of my mom's diagnosis didn't hit me until my dad called my four brothers and me together to discuss Thanksgiving. "Your mother's surgery is just a few days before Thanksgiving. She won't be able to lift anything heavy for a while."

I scratched my head. Why was he telling us this? And why would a mastectomy make it hard for her to lift things? Oh, yes, I was that blissfully ignorant. It wasn't until years later when a tumor was removed from my own breast that I understood how much even a small incision could impact arm movement.

"So…" Dad continued, "there won't be a Thanksgiving dinner this year."

"Wait. What?" My jaw hit the floor. Mom had cancer — again — and Thanksgiving was cancelled?

"What are we going to do instead?" my oldest brother asked.

Dad shrugged. "We'll go out to eat."

I had visions of the family in *A Christmas Story* eating Christmas dinner at a Chinese restaurant. My family would be doing the same for Thanksgiving? Inconceivable!

Apparently, my four brothers felt the same way. I don't remember which of them came up with the idea first, but one of them said, "We'll do it. The five of us kids will make Thanksgiving dinner."

Did I mention I was the only girl in this family with four boys? And none of us had any real cooking experience at this point?

It didn't matter. We quickly jumped on the bandwagon.

"Yeah. We'll each make a part of the meal."

"Mom can just sit in a corner of the kitchen and direct us."

"And tell us where she keeps things. Anyone know where the big roasting pan is?"

"Mom won't have to lift a thing."

"We'll do it all."

I saw the concern in my father's eyes. Could four young men and an eighteen-year-old girl make Thanksgiving dinner on their own? My two oldest brothers were just starting their careers in computer-related fields. My third oldest brother was in his first year of medical school, and my younger brother was a sophomore in high school. Although I'd done a bit of baking, none of us really knew anything about cooking, much less a Thanksgiving feast for seven.

But we were determined we'd have a traditional Thanksgiving dinner with all the fixings. Being techy nerds, my oldest brothers decided to make a Gantt chart for the meal. For the less nerdy, a Gantt chart is a type of bar graph that illustrates the development of a project. The project is broken into smaller elements, and the start and end times of each element are displayed on the chart.

Thus, the Thanksgiving feast was broken into parts and tasks were divvied up. I would make the pumpkin pie. Mike would make the apple pie. Dave was in charge of cranberry sauce and bread. Steve would make twice-baked potatoes. The youngest, Tom, would make the stuffing, and with Dad's help, get it and the bird into the oven.

Then each of the cooks was assigned a time to work in the kitchen. It was absolutely imperative that each cook finish his or her task on time, so the next cook could step in. Mom was deemed Executive Chef, but her tasks were purely supervisory.

Working backwards, with an expected dinnertime of 5:00 p.m., my brothers filled in the Gantt chart.

On Thanksgiving morning, I made two piecrusts. I filled one of these with pumpkin pie filling and got it in the oven. The other I left for my brother's apple pie. He began work on his as soon as I'd finished the piecrusts. After clearing off my end of the kitchen table, Tom stepped in to prepare the stuffing.

By the time my pumpkin pie came out of the oven, Mike's apple pie was ready to go in. By the time his pie came out, the turkey was ready to go in. And so the day continued, each of us taking our turn in the kitchen.

At four o'clock, we set the dining room table with Mom's good china, wine glasses, water goblets, and silverware. At 4:30, the turkey came out of the oven. It was the most beautiful golden brown bird I've ever seen. At five o'clock on the dot, exactly the time prescribed on the Gantt chart, all the food was displayed on the table, and the

| *And Now I Take Care of You*

candles were lit. It could have been a scene from a Norman Rockwell painting. We took pictures so we'd never forget.

We sat down to that Thanksgiving table thankful for so many things. Mom's surgery had gone well. She'd still have chemotherapy and radiation treatment, but she'd survive. Yes, we were also thankful that we'd saved Thanksgiving dinner, but that was part of Mom's doing, too. She had taught us not to fear trying new things. She had instilled in us the importance of family. She had raised us to work together to solve our problems.

Over twenty years have passed since that Thanksgiving. Mom has battled breast cancer two more times. She's had numerous more incidents of skin cancer. She is the very definition of a cancer survivor.

And to honor our mother, my brothers and I still aid in the making of Thanksgiving dinner. Sometimes Mom makes the green bean casserole and helps with the turkey if her health is good. My brothers and I stick with our traditional roles. What had once seemed like it would be a turkey of a holiday has become our standard for the perfect Thanksgiving dinner.

~A.J. Cattapan

97

A Little Child Shall Lead Them

Heavy hearts, like heavy clouds in the sky, are best
relieved by the letting of a little water.
~Antoine Rivarol

My friend Eileen's husband died suddenly after a short illness that took everyone by surprise. Dan was only fifty-six, in good health — or so everyone thought — so how could he be gone?

After the funeral, family and friends gathered to share memories and offer comfort to the newly bereaved widow. Eileen was doing her best to be strong and stoic. She had always been the rock of her family, the kind of woman who could handle any situation and cope with whatever life handed her with grace and aplomb. She moved through the crowd of mourners graciously, accepting condolences, thanking people for coming, pausing to smile at the stories people told her about something sweet or funny or thoughtful Dan had done.

She hid it well but I — and everyone else — could see how shaky and emotionally fragile she was, and we were all tip-toeing around her as if she were a time bomb, being very careful not to say or do anything that might shatter her hard-won control.

Suddenly, in the middle of a funny story one of the mourners was telling about Dan, the one thing everyone was afraid would happen, happened. Eileen stopped smiling and her eyes filled with tears. She looked down into her lap, her hands fisted tightly on her thighs, her chin trembling visibly as she struggled not to break down in front of everyone. But it was no use. Tears coursed silently down her cheeks as she lost the struggle with her terrible, overwhelming grief. Her shoulders started to shake.

Everyone froze. What was the proper thing to do? Should we go on talking, pretend we didn't notice, and give her a chance to compose herself? Should we say something? Should we hug her? Get her a tissue? Offer her something to drink? Should we leave her alone to grieve privately?

While the adults were hesitating, afraid of doing the wrong thing and making things worse, Eileen's eight-year-old granddaughter Lauren sat down beside her and took one of her grandmother's hands in both of hers. "It's okay, Grandma," she said. "You can cry. I'll just sit here and hold your hand while you do."

It was such a simple thing and, yet, so exactly the right thing. While the supposedly wiser adults hesitated, embarrassed and unsure in the face of such raw emotion, eight-year-old Lauren simply and honestly acknowledged Eileen's pain and grief, and offered her the comfort she needed at the moment.

Her innocent, unselfconscious action offered potent proof that simple acceptance and understanding is so often the best response to another's pain.

~Candace Schuler

98

Accidental Destiny

Children are the anchors that hold a
mother to life.
~Sophocles

As a restaurant manager, my days off were few and far between. But tonight I had a rare evening off and I couldn't get out the door fast enough. Just as I was leaving work I heard my assistant call out, "Phone for you, Cecile."

As tempted as I was to pretend I was not there and have them take a message, I took the call. My assistant handed me the phone and he knew right away something was wrong. "Hello, Cecile speaking," I said, forcing cheer into my voice.

The voice on the other end of the line was familiar, but my father's tone was an unfamiliar mix of panic and worry. "Hello, Cecile. Papa here. I'm so glad I caught you. I can't seem to get through on your cell phone." Suddenly, my throat tightened; something was wrong. Mom did the calling in our house, not Papa. He would come on the phone after Mom and I chatted, usually at the end of the conversation so he could say, "So good to hear your voice, Sunshine. I love you!"

"What's wrong, Papa?" I demanded, knowing he tries to sugarcoat things for his little girl.

"I have some news. Are you sitting down?" he said with a choke in his voice. At that instant, I knew that something horrible had happened. Our family unit of three was a solid triangle. We were a team, and little did I know that team was going to become very important and much stronger.

He barely choked out the words, "It's your mother. There was an accident. They don't really know what the damage is, but she hasn't woken up yet."

The room started spinning. My mind was struggling to piece it together. My knees felt weak. My assistant immediately recognized that this was not just a work phone call and something had gone terribly wrong. I felt so helpless and far away.

I began driving as the sun rose. Thirteen hours to the Kingston hospital and I think I made it in eleven. There was nowhere else I wanted to be. I didn't tell my father I was driving, because I knew that would worry him. I just kept calling him and asking for updates.

Finally, I raced through the emergency room doors. "My mom is here; she was hit by a car," I gasped. There was no hesitation from the young girl at the desk as she instantly jumped to her feet. "You must be Wendy's daughter," she said, and led me into a small room where my mother lay hooked to tubes and machines. My father was sitting beside the bed, his head buried in his hands.

The moment I entered, my mom stirred. "Cecile?" Then her voice trailed off and went silent.

My father's head jolted up with the sound of her voice; he had been waiting for her to speak since the accident the day before. He stood up and looked at me; tears streamed down his face as he squeezed me. "God bless you. I knew you would come. I knew you would come."

I tried to share his optimism. I expected bad, but this was worse. Most of her ribs were fractured; she had a broken leg and a back injury. It was the brain injury that changed my mom; it transformed and challenged our family in ways I had never dreamed it could. Getting her out of the hospital was only the beginning. Her rehabilitation included speech therapy, dozens of tests and multiple therapist appointments.

The change in her personality and mental stability was the hardest to grasp. I felt that I had lost my best friend. Our parent/child roles were reversed. My mom had spent her life as an entrepreneur who also volunteered teaching disadvantaged children theatre arts and drama. She still had a strong fighting spirit inside her, and even on those days when her mind was clouded with pain and confusion, determination was there.

For the first two years, I traveled back and forth and I pored over the latest research on brain injury. At first, it was like a foreign language to me. Gradually, I began to not only decipher the information, but I became fascinated by this amazing organ that is the brain. I began devouring medical journals and studying case reports of traumatic brain injuries. The more I researched, the more amazed I became. One day, like a cloudburst, it came to me. This is what I wanted to devote my life to.

Suddenly, college was making a lot of sense. I applied to university, was accepted, and I am now in my third year and in the top ten percent of my class. I continue to manage my mom's ongoing care, and rarely does a day go by that she doesn't exercise her brain with some brain games that research shows improve cognitive function and memory.

Support from the community is so important. In fact, when I discovered there was no brain injury support group in my part of the country, I made some inquiries. One step led to another, and I am now helping to launch a support group in my city and becoming the area's contact for the Brain Injury Association of Canada.

It has been just over five years and I am very content with the life I have chosen. My family is closer than ever and my mom is still my best friend.

~Cecile Proctor

99

Like Mother, Like Daughter

*And mothers are their daughters' role model, their
biological and emotional road map, the arbiter of all
their relationships.*
~Victoria Secunda

I can still remember the day my mother came home from the
hospital after her first operation. It was a sun-filled day, the
weather at odds with the atmosphere in the house, which was
morbid and tense. I had just left college to become my mother's
full-time caregiver — a decision I was already beginning to question
as I surveyed the volume of medical supplies that had accompanied
my mother's return. It was daunting to be faced with the prospect of
looking after someone who had looked after me all my life.

With one operation down and three more to go, my mother was
already unrecognisable to me. The warm, plump woman who had
raised me had been replaced by a pale waif-like creature. The pain
and stress had dulled the brightness in her eyes, and her trademark
dimples had disappeared in her sunken face. Fragile had never been
a word to describe my mother, but now it defined her. For the first
time, the enormity of what I had taken on struck me.

The first few weeks were the most difficult. Like a newborn, she
required constant care and attention. Her wound had to be dressed
every day. She couldn't feed herself, clean herself or even get out of

the bed.

I wasn't sure how to cope with this role reversal. I was so used to my mother being the caregiver, the provider, that I couldn't bear to see her so weak and helpless. I really didn't know how I was going to cope. However, nothing tests character like necessity. It turned out the thoughts of being responsible for my mother's health were far more challenging than the reality. Over the next few months, my mother slowly began to improve. Under my care, she began to live again. I watched the twinkle come back into her eyes as she regained the strength to do small things for herself. We celebrated the little things that we had previously taken for granted — simple things like when she finally had the strength to lift a teacup to drink by herself or when she could sleep through the night without waking from the pain.

One of the happiest days was a sunny day in July. It was a couple of weeks after her final operation, and her recovery had been slow and complicated. When I brought the breakfast tray down to her that morning, she turned to me and said, "It's a pity to be stuck inside on such a nice day." I bundled her up in a scarf and coat and brought her outside.

I will never forget the look of pure joy on her face as she looked up at the blue sky. It was the first time in a year that she had been able to go outside and enjoy something as simple as the heat of the sun on her face. She looked at me, put her hand over mine, and smiled — a smile that said much more than words could express. In that moment, I realised how much I had gained from becoming a full-time caregiver for my mother. I had become more mature and responsible, and I had discovered strengths that I never knew I had. Our relationship had evolved from the traditional one of mother and daughter. I gained a newfound respect for my mother. Through caring for her, I learned to appreciate how wonderful she really is. Her remarkable inner strength, her uncomplaining nature, and above all her ability to smile through the pain are qualities that I can only hope of inheriting.

Caring for my mother has been a turbulent journey full of both tears and laughter. Although we both felt like giving up at times, ultimately, it has brought us closer together and allowed me to count every day we have together as a blessing.

~Anna Fitzgerald

100

Daffodil Month

The flowers of late winter and early spring occupy
places in our hearts well out of proportion to their size.
~Gertrude S. Wister

Mother opened her eyes and stared, unblinking, at the vase of daffodils on the table beside her hospital bed. "Who sent these beautiful flowers?" she asked in a barely audible voice.

"No one sent them, Mother." I squeezed her hand. "I picked them from your yard. It's March — Daffodil Month."

She gave me a weak smile. "Promise me something?"

I nodded. I'd promised a lot since we'd come to accept that the cancer in Mother's pancreas would soon take her life.

"Promise that before you sell my house, you'll dig up my daffodil bulbs to plant in your yard."

I tried without success to hold back my tears. "I'll do that, Mother. I promise." She smiled and closed her eyes, lapsing again into the twilight fog that characterized the last days of her life.

Before Daffodil Month ended, Mother was gone. And in the weeks that followed, weeks so grief-filled that my siblings and I resembled nothing so much as walking zombies, we emptied her house, painted, washed windows, cleaned carpets, and listed the home we'd grown up in with a real estate agency. We hired a neighborhood boy to take care of the yard.

And I gave the daffodils, which had long since quit blooming, not a single thought until a day in late autumn when the house was finally to be sold. My brother and sister and I were to meet the buyers to sign papers early on a morning that I knew would be filled with conflicting emotions. On the one hand, it was good to be out from under the burden of owning an empty house. On the other, we would soon be turning over the keys to our family home to strangers.

Strangers who, I was certain, could never love it as much as we did.

Would this new family cook Fourth-of-July hamburgers on the brick patio grill my dad had built so many summers ago? Would their children spend fall afternoons raking the leaves under the giant maple tree into a mile-high pile to jump in? Would they figure out that one corner of the family room was the perfect spot for a Christmas tree? And would they be amazed at what pushed its way out of the ground in Mother's yard every spring?

Crocuses. Flowering onions. Hyacinths. And hundreds and hundreds of daffodils.

Daffodils! Eight months later, I suddenly remembered the promise I had made my mother as she lay dying. I tossed a shovel and a cardboard box into the trunk of my car and headed for the house and yard that would, in just a couple of hours, belong to someone not related to me.

There was no sign of daffodils anywhere, of course. They had long since been mowed down and were now covered with leaves. But I knew exactly where they were. Ignoring the fact that I was overdressed for gardening, I plunged the shovel's point into the dirt, lifted out a clump of bulbs, and tossed them into the box. Working my way down the fence line, I harvested dozens of daffodil bulbs.

But I left more than I took, certain that the family who'd bought my mother's house would take delight in her lovely harbingers of spring.

As do I. It's been more than five years now since my mother passed away. But every March, I gather armloads of the bright yellow blooms from my own yard and put them into vases. Some I use to decorate my house. Others I take to the cancer wing at a nearby hospital.

"Who sent these beautiful flowers?" a dying patient might ask.

And I will squeeze his or her hand and look into eyes clouded by that all-too-familiar twilight fog and speak words that I believe with all my heart to be true. "My mother sent them, especially for you," I'll reply. "It's Daffodil Month, you know."

~Jennie Ivey

Rewind

A daughter is a gift of love.
~Author Unknown

When I was young, a long time ago
You walked with me nice and slow
You held my hand to keep me safe
And made your steps small to suit my pace

Now it's my turn to do that for you
I hold your hand, it's the least I can do
I walk with you up and down the hall
To keep you from stumbling and taking a fall

You squeeze my hand and smile at me
I squeeze yours back just as gently
You don't know my name, but that's okay
Little by little your memory's slipping away

We're on a journey we didn't choose
I realize each day how much we have to lose
You're slowly traveling back in time
I'm watching your life slowly rewind

Your memories are fading, but I'm still here
Though I know shortly, too, I'll disappear
I'll be erased, no matter how tight I hang on
Your grip will grow weak, but I'll remain strong

I'll hold your hand, I'll keep you safe
I'll keep my steps small to suit your pace
No matter what happens we'll walk side by side
We'll travel together this long goodbye.

~Kala Cota

for Mom, with love

Meet Our Contributors

Meet Amy Newmark

Thank You

About Chicken Soup for the Soul

Meet Our Contributors

Maizura Abas was trained as an English as a Second Language teacher in the United Kingdom. She now resides in Malaysia. Maizura devotes her life to her two children. She is indebted to her husband for proofreading her creative writing pieces and loving her despite her inability to roast the perfect beef and all her innumerable quirks. E-mail her at maizura@yahoo.com.

Monica A. Andermann lives and writes on Long Island where she shares her home with her husband Bill and their little tabby, Samson. Her writing has been included in such publications as *Woman's World*, *Guideposts* and many titles in the *Chicken Soup for the Soul* series.

Ronda Armstrong writes from Iowa about family, faith, and fortitude. Her stories appear in varied anthologies, in addition to Chicken Soup for the Soul books. She rotates with other writers at thebridgemeditations.wordpress.com. Ronda and her husband are ballroom dancers. E-mail her at ronda.armstrong@gmail.com.

William Mark Baldwin is earning his Ph.D in Earth and Atmospheric Science at Mississippi State University. Mark is from Crossville, TN, and is a graduate of Tennessee Technological University (B.S.) and Western Kentucky University (M.S.). Mark enjoys running, storm chasing, and traveling. E-mail him at wmb3@msstate.edu.

Toni Becker received her Bachelor of Arts degree from Lakeland College, Sheboygan, WI. She works for Sheboygan County Health and Human Services, managing two senior centers and doing home outreach to the elderly. In her spare time, she enjoys freelance writing for local and regional publications. E-mail her at lynn-be@hotmail.com.

Carole A. Bell, a licensed professional counselor, writes, speaks, and consults about parenting issues. She writes a weekly Christian parenting column and has stories published in other *Chicken Soup for the Soul* books and *More Christmas Moments*. Her book, *From Birth to Seven: Building a Strong Foundation* will be out February 2016.

Susan Blakeney is a writer of fiction for children and young adults with several projects well underway. These include two historical novels and one work of speculative fiction—the story that awoke her passion for writing several years ago. E-mail her at susan@susanblakeney.com.

Donna Brothers received her B.S. degree in Communications from California Polytechnic University. She worked at CBS Television and then received her teaching credentials in Language Arts and Special Education. She is currently a special education teacher in Yorba Linda, CA. In addition to the *Chicken Soup for the Soul* series she published a short story in *Women's World* magazine. She enjoys photography, baking and hiking.

Judy Brown lives in Holland, MI. She has worked for Evergreen Commons, a senior community center, and the Holland Rescue Mission. She enjoys writing, both academic and inspirational, and plans to continue this endeavor.

Having successfully launched four children into their own lives and completed a B.S. degree, **Rhonda Brunea** is reinventing herself in Orkney, Scotland, where she is rediscovering her love of writing and the healing magic of stories.

Leigh Ann Bryant, author of *In My Defense*, is a survivor of battered women's syndrome. Her passions include God, family, nursing, traveling, educating others about domestic violence, and prison ministry. Learn more about her and her book, a nonfiction memoir about killing her abusive husband in self-defense, at www.leighannbryant.com.

Jill Burns lives in the mountains of West Virginia with her wonderful family. She's a retired piano teacher and performer. She enjoys writing, music, gardening, nature, and spending time with her grandchildren.

Barbara Burris lives with her husband Bruce in a log home set in the middle of three acres of informal cottage and woodland gardens. These gardens serve as inspiration for Barbara's photographs and watercolor paintings. Her future plans include a series of stories about summers at her grandmother's cottage.

A.J. Cattapan is an award-winning author, speaker, and middle school English teacher from the Chicago area. Her bestselling YA novel *Angelhood* has won multiple awards, and her middle grade mystery *Seven Riddles to Nowhere* releases in August 2016. Follow A.J.'s writing and travel adventures at www.ajcattapan.com.

J.D. Chaney is a retired teacher, having received his B.A. degree from San Jose State University and M.A. degree from Cal State, Dominguez Hills. He currently lives in the Bay Area with his therapist wife. J.D.'s daughter attends Oregon State University. His hobbies include traveling and running.

A.B. Chesler is a writer and blogger living in sunny Southern California. She enjoys spending time with her family and friends, as well as finding the lighter side of life. Please feel free to visit her blog at thishouseoflove. net or e-mail her at achesler24@gmail.com.

Courtney Conover is a writer, certified yoga instructor, and curly hair enthusiast. Her first book will debut in 2016. A graduate of the University of Michigan, she resides in Michigan with her husband and two children. Stop in and say hello to her at www.courtneyconover.com.

After thirty-five years in various trades, **Patrick Coomer** has returned to writing. His love of words was inherited from his mother, featured in this book and in *Chicken Soup for the Soul: Think Possible*. Currently a bus operator in Portland, OR, Patrick's stories amuse and inspire his growing audience at patcoomer.wordpress.com.

D'ette Corona is the Assistant Publisher of Chicken Soup for the Soul Publishing, LLC. She received her Bachelor of Science degree in business management. D'ette has been happily married for twenty-three years and has a nineteen-year-old son whom she adores.

Kala Cota lives in a small logging community in Oregon. She teaches preschool and enjoys spending time with her husband, two grown children and granddaughter. Since her mother's diagnosis, she is incredibly grateful for the support and encouragement from family and friends. E-mail her at kccota@frontier.com.

Nancy Bravo Creager was born and raised in Chile. She now lives in Washington State. She is a wife, mother, and grandmother. Nancy enjoys reading the classics; her favorite poet is Neruda, and her favorite writer is Steinbeck. She experiments with writing inspirational prose and poetry.

Tracy Crump enjoys storytelling (the good kind) and has published numerous stories in the *Chicken Soup for the Soul* series. She encourages others through her Write Life Workshops and webinars and edits a popular writers' newsletter, *The Write Life*. But her most important job is Grandma to little Nellie. Visit her at WriteLifeWorkshops.com.

Cindy D'Ambroso-Argiento is originally from New York. She now lives in North Carolina with her family. Cindy is a freelance writer and receives a wealth of material from her family. To read more of Cindy's work check out her website at www.cindyargiento.com. Please e-mail her at cargiento@aol.com.

Angel Dionne is a first year Ph.D student at the University of New Brunswick in Fredericton. She serves as the founder for *Peculiar Mormyrid* magazine and enjoys writing, traveling, and reading. She hopes to continue writing and eventually secure a tenure track teaching position at a university. E-mail her at paper_lantern4@hotmail.com.

Lucille Engro DiPaolo resides in Plymouth Meeting, PA. She has been published in the *Chicken Soup for the Soul* series several times. Lucille loves traveling and has completed many adventures on her "bucket list" including parasailing, ballooning, ziplining, and most exhilarating, dog sledding on Mendenhall Glacier.

Tricia Downing is a professional speaker and athlete. In 2000 she was hit by a car while riding her bicycle and was paralyzed. Tricia credits the examples her mother set regarding faith, resilience and resolve for getting her through the difficult experience. Learn more at www.trishdowning.com or e-mail her at ladyterp_td@hotmail.com.

Logan Eliasen graduated from Wheaton College in 2014 with a B.A. degree in biblical and theological studies. He is currently a law student at the University of Iowa. Logan enjoys reading classic novels and collecting vinyl records.

Shawnelle Eliasen is an inspirational writer. She's contributed numerous stories to *Chicken Soup for the Soul* books. She and her husband live in an old Victorian near the Illinois banks of the Mississippi River with their five sons and a yellow Labrador named Rugby. Follow their adventures at shawnellewrites.blogspot.com.

Linda Rose Etter is a retired teacher with a Master of Arts in Biblical Studies. Her devotional books, *Listen To HIS Heartbeat #2* was published in 2015 and #1 in 2011. Both contain humorous analogies and include scripture so they make great gifts and teaching tools. More information about her books can be found at www.etterlinda.com.

Gail Eynon received her B.A. in psychology from the University of Hawaii at Hilo, her master's degree in Marriage and Family Therapy at Capella University, and her Ph.D from Capella University. Gail spent this last year battling late stage breast cancer and enjoys life to the fullest.

Melissa Face lives in Virginia with her husband and two children. She teaches English part-time at the Appomattox Regional Governor's School and has published more than sixty essays in various magazines and anthologies. E-mail her at writermsface@yahoo.com.

Elizabeth Reardon Farella is a graduate of Molloy College where she received her teaching degree. She went on to earn her master's degree in Literacy. Elizabeth teaches first grade at St. Edward the Confessor School in Syosset, NY. She enjoys reading, writing, and traveling with her family. E-mail Elizabeth at Jeeec@aol.com.

Victoria Fedden is a writer and a mom from Fort Lauderdale, Fl. Her memoir *This is Not My Beautiful Life* will be published in June 2016 by Picador USA. She blogs on her website at www.victoriafedden.com. Visit her Facebook page at www.facebook.com/victoriacfedden.

Anna Fitzgerald received her Bachelor of Arts degree, with honors, and Master of Arts degree from the National University of Ireland, Maynooth. Anna enjoys reading, writing, and traveling. She is currently attending law school. E-mail her at pearl4@eircom.net.

Judith Fitzsimmons is a freelance writer and business consultant who lives in middle Tennessee. Her hobbies are aromatherapy, yoga, and fitness, but her passion is being a mom.

The mother of three adult daughters, Sally Friedman regards them as her most important work. Now mothers themselves, they have provided much of the material for the essays she has been writing for four decades. A graduate of the University of Pennsylvania, she resides in Moorestown, NJ. E-mail her at pinegander@aol.com.

Pam Giordano received her Bachelor of Science degree at Georgian Court University. She is a retired elementary school teacher whose hobbies include writing and painting. Pam is a member of several choral groups. E-mail her at pam.giordano@gmail.com.

Patricia Gordon is a retired elementary school teacher, mother and grandmother. She holds teaching degrees from Illinois State University and Western Michigan University. She now teaches music education at Grand Valley State University and loves to write about her family. She also writes fiction as Patricia Kiyono.

Robin Rylee Harderson enjoys reading, writing, painting and her beautiful granddaughter. She has been married for twenty-eight years to her husband, Marty. Robin has been previously published in *Women's World* and *Sewing Memories*.

Jennifer Harrington recently retired from a career in the computer technology field and enjoys playing music, computer games, and movie night with her husband and four children. She cared for her mother through her journey with Alzheimer's disease and is now a volunteer for the Alzheimer's Association Northern California Chapter.

Isabel Harris lives and teaches in New York City. She plans on writing a memoir about living with major depression and is excited for this opportunity to share part of her story. She has never stopped loving horses and still considers herself to be an urban cowgirl.

Sonja Herbert is the author of an award-winning novel about her mother surviving the Holocaust in a circus, and of many other true stories. Sonja presently lives in Germany, where she is getting re-acquainted with her mother and siblings. E-mail her at germanwriter.com.

Julie Hornok's stories have appeared in several publications and websites, and this is her fourth appearance in the *Chicken Soup for the Soul* series. When she is not busy driving her three kids all around the DFW

Metroplex, she loves to support families living with autism. Contract her through her website at www.juliehornok.com.

Lisa Hutchison is a #1 international bestselling author and holistic educator. She understands the challenges of maintaining a connection within and to the Divine in an overwhelming world. As a licensed psychotherapist, she helps her empathic clients express their authentic voices, protect their energy and trust their instincts. Learn more at www.lisahutchison.net.

Jennie Ivey lives in Cookeville, TN. She is a newspaper columnist and the author of numerous works of fiction and nonfiction, including stories in several *Chicken Soup for the Soul* collections.

Kara Johnson lives in Eagle, ID with her husband Jim, son Weston, and daughter Kyah. She enjoys traveling, scuba diving, camping, rafting, hiking, writing, and trying to keep up with her toddlers. She feels blessed and incredibly indebted for the love Joan has shown her. E-mail her at karagym777@hotmail.com.

Sheridan Kee received her associate's degree in 2014. She is continuing her education in social work at Union University and plans to work with those in need. She enjoys riding horses, baking, spending time with friends and family, and church activities. "Let us not love with words or speech but with actions and in truth." (1 John 3:18)

Jennifer Knickerbocker is a mother of four boys. In her spare time, she runs a non-profit educational organization in Spokane, WA. Jennifer is passionate about her family and her children, but that doesn't mean it is easy. "Motherhood is the best hard work."

April Knight has just completed a romance novel: *Sweet Dreams, 65 Bedtime Stories for Big Girls*. She writes a column called "Crying Wind" for the *Indian Life* newspaper. She is a professional artist and her paintings can be viewed on www.cryingwind.com.

Mimi Greenwood Knight is a mama of four living in South Louisiana. She's blessed to have over 1,000 essays and articles in magazines and essays in thirty anthologies. A newcomer to the sustainable living movement, Mimi is fumbling her way through learning to knit, garden, and keep bees, worms, and chickens.

Nancy Julien Kopp, a Chicago native, has lived in Kansas for many years. Her stories are in seventeen *Chicken Soup for the Soul* books, fifteen other anthologies, magazines and newspapers. A former teacher, she now teaches through the written word. Visit her blog for tips and encouragement at www.writergrannysworld.blogspot.com.

Ann Kronwald is a freelance writer who enjoys writing about and celebrating ordinary life. She never refuses a good hike, as long as it is followed by dark chocolate. Ann is the mother of four grown children, and "Nana" to nine rug-rats, which give her plenty of writing ammunition.

Karen Kullgren is the author of *Grace in the Gray Areas: Thriving in Life's Paradoxes* (available at amazon.com and bn.com). She is a freelance writer/editor with a particular interest in exploring women's lives, spiritual journeys, diverse cultures, and the universality of human experience. E-mail her at graceinthegrayareas@gmail.com or visit www.graceinthegrayareas.com.

Terri Lacher is a freelance writer and speaker, living in Texas with her husband Bob and golden Lab Samson. Her offbeat humor is sprinkled throughout her inspirational short stories, poetry and bi-monthly newspaper columns. E-mail her at btlacher@sbcglobal.net.

Victoria LaFave is a writer and marketing coordinator for nine Catholic schools in Michigan's Upper Peninsula. She has been published in several *Chicken Soup for the Soul* books, along with *My Teacher Is My Hero*. Her stories have also appeared in *Parents, FamilyFun* and *Woman's Day* magazines. E-mail her at vrlafave@sbcglobal.net.

Mary Ellen Langbein has been writing short stories and poetry ever since her grade school days. It is one of her favorite hobbies. She also keeps busy playing golf, paddle tennis, decorating and traveling with her husband. She resides in New Jersey, is married, and Mom to Lauren and Logan.

Mary Elizabeth Laufer has a degree in English Education from SUNY Albany. She recently left teaching to devote more time to writing. One of her stories received honorable mention in *The Saturday Evening Post* 2016 Great American Fiction Contest and will be published in an anthology with other finalists.

Ali Lauro is a fifteen-year-old high school student. She has enjoyed writing and reading from an early age and aspires to work someday in this field. She lives with her parents, twin sister, brother, and two dogs.

Barbara LoMonaco has worked for Chicken Soup for the Soul as an editor since 1998. She has co-authored two *Chicken Soup for the Soul* book titles and has had stories published in numerous other titles. Barbara is a graduate of the University of Southern California and has a teaching credential.

Aimee Cirucci Lorge is a freelance writer and personal essayist with a focus on family, career, and the unique intersection of both in the military spouse experience. A graduate of Wake Forest University and Temple University, she lives overseas and works as a college-level communication instructor. Learn more at www.aimeelorge.com.

A graduate of Queen's University, **Gail MacMillan** has had her work published throughout North American and Western Europe. She is the award-winning author of two books and several short stories and has thirty-five traditionally published books. Gail lives in New Brunswick, Canada with her husband and two dogs.

Teresa Ann Maxwell lives in Washington with her favorite fisherman and husband, Richard. She has many fond memories of snowy, white Christmases spent with family in her home state of Idaho. The family still celebrates Christmas with their stockings — Mom included.

Debra Mayhew is a pastor's wife, mom to seven (usually) wonderful children, and a writer. She loves small town living, long walks, good books and family time. Learn more at www.debramayhew.com.

Annette McDermott is a freelance writer and children's author whose work has been published in both adult and children's magazines and online. She enjoys writing about a wide variety of subjects but specializes in holistic living topics. When she's not busy writing and raising her family, Annette enjoys singing, gardening, and reading. E-mail her at annette@annettemcdermott.net.

Michelle McKague-Radic lives in Ontario with her husband and children. She has bachelor's degrees in English and History and is currently working as a freelance writer as she stays home with her children. E-mail her at misha_beth@yahoo.com.

Chris Mikalson is a retired bookkeeper, who is now enjoying camping with her husband, as well as pursuing the creative "loves of her life" — writing and painting. Chris is a Reiki Master and finds great joy in helping others heal with the aid of this beautiful energy. E-mail her at chris_mikalson@yahoo.ca.

Carrie Monroe lives and writes in Minneapolis, MN. She works in theater and has had stories published in children's magazines. She enjoys writing, biking, swimming and running. Check out her blog at carriemonroewrites.wordpress.com.

Donia Moore is a freelance writer in Southern California. As a "rusty pilot" who hasn't flown in a while, she loves aviation and writes articles for several general aviation publications on a regular basis. Favorite weekend breaks are spent kayaking with her dog in summer and snowshoeing in winter.

Beth Morrissey is a freelance writer based in Dublin, Ireland. She loves to make new friends, so please visit her online at www.bethiswriting.com.

When **Lava Mueller** told her mother that "Cotton Balls" had been accepted for publication, her mother said, "That's great, Sweetheart. I'm glad I could help you get rich. I just ate a bug." Lava's Young Adult novel, *Don't Tell*, can be found on Amazon.com. E-mail her at lavamueller@yahoo.com.

Lee Ann Sontheimer Murphy grew up in St. Joseph, MO, in the shadow of the short-lived Pony Express, but now lives in the Missouri Ozarks. She is a full-time writer, member of both Missouri Writers Guild and the Ozark Writers League. Her short fiction has been widely published and her novel, *Kinfolk*, from Champagne Books was released in 2011.

Hank Musolf was born in Wisconsin and now lives in Minnesota with his family. He plays the cello in his high school orchestra and is also on the Speech Team.

Ava Pennington is a writer, speaker, and Bible teacher. She has published numerous articles in nationally-circulated magazines and contributed to twenty-eight anthologies, including twenty-one *Chicken Soup for the Soul* books. She also authored *Daily Reflections on the Names of God: A Devotional*, endorsed by Kay Arthur. Learn more at www.AvaWrites.com.

A journalist in rural Minnesota, **Ellarry Prentice** studied travel and tourism. In addition to her work as a reporter for her hometown newspaper, she is a freelance writer and photographer, and an advocate for mental health and alcoholism awareness. She enjoys reading, volunteering, and traveling with her husband, Greg.

Cecile Proctor is a full-time student at the University of New Brunswick and the provincial contact for the Brain Injury Association of Canada. She is working towards an honors degree in psychology with a minor in cognitive neuroscience. She plans to continue her education to join the field of neuropsychology.

Winter Desiree Prosapio is an award-winning novelist and humor columnist. Her *Blue Sage Mystery* series features strong mothers and daughters persevering in unique and challenging circumstances with courage, humor, and wisdom. Read more at wdprosapio.com.

Susan R. Ray writes a weekly newspaper column entitled "Where We Are" available at susanrray.com. A retired teacher, she volunteers in a second grade classroom, and she writes, reads, and takes field trips with her eight grandchildren. Susan likes to travel, bake bread, and quilt.

Denise Reich is an Italian-born, New York City-raised freelance writer, dancer and photographer. She's happy to be a repeat contributor to the *Chicken Soup for the Soul* series. Denise currently writes for the Canadian magazine *Shameless*. Her Broadway memoir, *Front of House,* was released in 2015.

Dr. Kelle Z. Riley, author, scientist and safety/martial arts expert, has been featured in forums from local newspapers to national television. Her debut novel, *Dangerous Affairs*, was praised for accurately highlighting women's issues in an easily accessible, entertaining format. Learn more at www.kellezriley.net.

Kimberly Ross holds a Master of Divinity degree from Saint Paul School of Theology. In her former work as a chaplain and pastor, she served in a homeless shelter, VA hospital, hospice, retreat center, and churches. She is a writer, Reiki master, proud mother of three wonderful young adults and an adoring grandma of one.

Jessie Santala is a personal assistant and part-time writer and photographer who resides with her husband in Denver, Co. She has her master's degree in Creative Writing from the University of Denver.

Donna Savage is a pastor's wife who loves encouraging women. When she isn't writing or teaching, she's trying to simplify her life, see more joy, and conquer her addiction to chocolate. Her phone contains over 100 photos of her grandchildren. Connect with Donna at donnasavagelv @cox.net.

John Scanlan is a 1983 graduate of the U.S. Naval Academy and a retired Lieutenant Colonel from the U.S. Marine Corps. He is currently pursuing a second career as a writer and can be reached using ping1@ hargray.com.

Lisa J. Schlitt lives in Kitchener, Ontario. She has been married to Patrick for sixteen years. Together they have four children and are in the process of adopting number five. Lisa hopes to have "The Race" illustrated and published for the children's literature market.

In addition to authoring twenty-six published romance novels, **Candace Schuler** also writes case studies, white papers, grant proposals, press releases, marketing collateral, and more. She shares her life with her husband of thirty-seven years and two seventy-pound Dobermans who think they are lap dogs. Learn more at www.CandaceSchuler.com.

Natalie Scott is a mother of three: Eleanora (who is in heaven), Pierce and Everett. She is married to Nicholas Scott. She is a writer for Easter Seals. She graduated from the University of Delaware in 2005 with a Bachelor of Arts degree in English with a concentration in Journalism.

Multiple award-winning author, **Jacqueline Seewald**, taught writing at Rutgers University, and worked as an academic librarian and educational media specialist. Fifteen of her fiction books for adults, teens and children are published. Her short stories, poems, essays, reviews and articles appear in hundreds of diverse publications and anthologies. Learn more at jacquelineseewald.blogspot.com.

Penny Smith, a seminary graduate, has taught at conferences and retreats at home and abroad. Her writings cover a variety of genres, appearing in numerous Christian periodicals. She authored *Gateways To Growth and Maturity Through the Life of Esther*. E-mail her at psmithgtg@gmail. com or learn more at www.pennyesmith.blogspot.com.

Writer, performer, speaker **Kim Stokely** lives in Nebraska with her husband and three neurotic dogs. Her novels: *Woman of Flames*, *Winter Trees*, and *Spring Rains* are available through Amazon and Barnes & Noble. Visit www.kimstokely.com or Facebook.com/kimstokelyauthor for information on her performances and work.

Daryl Wendy Strauss's story "Mom's Christmas Stocking" brought many donations to her giving project and 2015 was the most successful Mom's Christmas Stocking event thus far. She is a Certified Angel Card Reader, Reiki practitioner, trained actress, and heart lover. E-mail her at darylwendy@msn.com and learn more at www. momschristmasstocking.com.

Janet Taylor is a registered nurse living in Franklin, TN with Robert, her biggest supporter. Her Mississippi family provides inspiration and is often the topic of her stories. E-mail Janet at janet@4door.com.

Michelle Vanderwist is currently a student at Georgetown University. She loves to draw, paint, play the guitar, work with animals, and stay active. Michelle is a terrible cook but has a hidden talent for hula hooping. E-mail her at mav49@georgetown.edu.

Kristin Viola is a Los Angeles-based writer who has contributed to the *Los Angeles Times*, *Zagat*, *Angeleno* and other publications. Aside from running, she loves traveling, reading and a good glass of wine. E-mail her at kjviola@gmail.com.

Holly Wilkinson, her children, and her mother all live in the beautiful Pacific Northwest. She likes coffee, music, and rain, and writes short stories, blurbs and poetry on her *Woman at the Well* blog at womanatthewell-womanatthewell.blogspot.com. She continues to be inspired by the amazing strength of the woman who raised her.

Katrina Anne Willis is a wife and a mother of four. An author and essayist, Katrina was named a BlogHer 2015 Voice of the Year. Her first novel, *Parting Gifts*, will be published by She Writes Press in April 2016. E-mail her at katrina_willis@me.com.

Beth M. Wood lives in St. Louis with her three beautiful kids. She is a twenty-year veteran of the marketing industry, a writer by choice, a devout reader and semi-fanatic editor. She shares her thoughts at blog. bethmwood.com and tweets @a1972bmw.

Lisa Wright-Dixon received her Bachelor of Arts degree in Sociology from Syracuse University. She currently resides in South Carolina with her husband Gregory and their six cats. Lisa is currently working on other short stories and plans to write a book of childhood memoirs.

Meet Amy Newmark

Amy Newmark was a writer, speaker, Wall Street analyst and business executive in the worlds of finance and telecommunications for thirty years. Today she is author, editor-in-chief and publisher of the *Chicken Soup for the Soul* book series. By curating and editing inspirational true stories from ordinary people who have had extraordinary experiences, Amy has kept the twenty-three-year-old Chicken Soup for the Soul brand fresh and relevant, and still part of the social zeitgeist.

Amy graduated *magna cum laude* from Harvard University where she majored in Portuguese and minored in French. She wrote her thesis about popular, spoken-word poetry in Brazil, which involved traveling throughout Brazil and meeting with poets and writers to collect their stories. She is delighted to have come full circle in her writing career — from collecting poetry "from the people" in Brazil as a twenty-year-old to, decades later, collecting stories and poems "from the people" for Chicken Soup for the Soul.

Amy is a frequent radio and TV guest, passing along the real-life lessons and useful tips she has picked up from reading and editing thousands of Chicken Soup for the Soul stories.

She and her husband are the proud parents of four grown children and in her limited spare time, Amy enjoys visiting them, hiking, and reading books that she did not have to edit.

Follow her on Twitter @amynewmark and @chickensoupsoul.

About the Boys & Girls Clubs of America

For more than a century, the Boys & Girls Clubs of America have helped put young people on the path to great futures. Boys & Girls Clubs annually serve nearly 4 million young people, through membership and community outreach, in over 4,100 Club facilities throughout the country and BGCA-affiliated Youth Centers on U.S. military installations worldwide.

The BGCA prides itself on being able to provide its young people with a safe place to learn and grow. Here, young people develop ongoing relationships with caring, adult professionals who introduce the members to life-enhancing  programs and character development experiences. These programs are the cornerstone of the BGCA experience, and their breadth and scope are as dynamic and diverse as its members.

BGCA's CHARACTER & LEADERSHIP programs help youth become responsible, caring citizens and acquire skills for participating in the democratic process. Their EDUCATION & CAREER programs aim to ensure that all Club members graduate from high school on time, ready for a post-secondary education and a 21st-century career

In its HEALTH & LIFE SKILLS programs, BGCA initiatives develop young people's capacity to engage in positive behaviors that nurture their own well-being, set personal goals and live successfully as self-sufficient adults. In addition to teaching core life skills, BGCA promotes the study and appreciation of the Arts. Its programs promote the importance of teamwork and provide an educational, engaging and fun experience. Among the more popular programs offered by BGCA are its Sports, Fitness and Recreation programs. These Club programs help develop fitness, a positive use of leisure time, reduction of stress, appreciation for the environment and social and interpersonal skills.

The Boys & Girls Clubs of America is proud to offer these programs to America's youth. In the end, we hope that through these programs we enable all young people, especially those who need us most, to reach their full potential as productive, caring, responsible citizens. For more information, visit www.bgca.org.

Chicken Soup for the Soul

Thank You

We owe huge thanks to all of our contributors who have written about their moms in our past books. We read their stories and chose from an abundance of possibilities to make this special fundraising edition of *Chicken Soup for the Soul* that will inspire and entertain moms, showing them how appreciated they are, and also help support the good work of the Boys and Girls Clubs of America.

We owe special thanks to Assistant Publisher D'ette Corona and Senior Editor Barbara LoMonaco, who combed through our vast library to choose these stories and shape the manuscript that became this book.

The whole publishing team deserves a hand, including our Senior Director of Production, Victor Cataldo, and our graphic designer, Daniel Zaccari, who turned our manuscript into this beautiful book.

Chicken Soup for the Soul

Sharing Happiness, Inspiration, and Wellness

*R*eal people sharing real stories, every day, all over the world. In 2007, *USA Today* named *Chicken Soup for the Soul* one of the five most memorable books in the last quarter-century. With over 100 million books sold to date in the U.S. and Canada alone, more than 200 titles in print, and translations into more than forty languages, "chicken soup for the soul" is one of the world's best-known phrases.

Today, twenty-three years after we first began sharing happiness, inspiration and wellness through our books, we continue to delight our readers with new titles, but have also evolved beyond the bookstore, with super premium pet food, a line of high quality soups, and a variety of licensed products and digital offerings, all inspired by stories. Chicken Soup for the Soul has recently expanded into visual storytelling through movies and television. Chicken Soup for the Soul is "changing the world one story at a time®." Thanks for reading!

Chicken Soup for the Soul

Share with Us

W e all have had Chicken Soup for the Soul moments in our lives. If you would like to share your story or poem with millions of people around the world, go to chickensoup.com and click on "Submit Your Story." You may be able to help another reader and become a published author at the same time. Some of our past contributors have launched writing and speaking careers from the publication of their stories in our books!

We only accept story submissions via our website. They are no longer accepted via mail or fax.

To contact us regarding other matters, please send us an e-mail through webmaster@chickensoupforthesoul.com, or fax or write us at:

Chicken Soup for the Soul
P.O. Box 700
Cos Cob, CT 06807-0700
Fax: 203-861-7194

One more note from your friends at Chicken Soup for the Soul: Occasionally, we receive an unsolicited book manuscript from one of our readers, and we would like to respectfully inform you that we do not accept unsolicited manuscripts and we must discard the ones that appear.

Chicken Soup for the Soul®

Thanks to My Mom

101 Stories of Gratitude, Love, and Lessons

Amy Newmark
and Jo Dee Messina

A mother's job is never done, but in Chicken Soup for the Soul: Thanks to My Mom, she gets the praise she deserves! Children of all ages share their words of thanks in these 101 stories of love, learning, and gratitude to the woman they couldn't have done without!

978-1-61159-945-9

More Love and Laughter

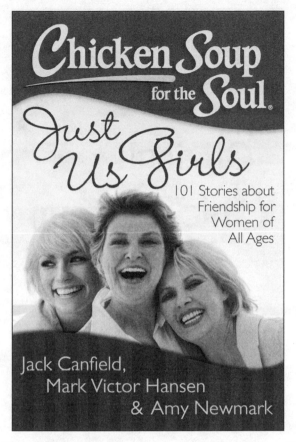

A woman's friends are the family she picks herself. This collection of 101 touching and amusing stories celebrates all that is special about the bonds that women share with their friends — the unique spirit of female friendship.

978-1-61159-928-2

for Moms and Grandmothers

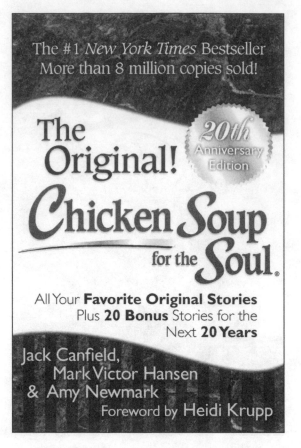

The #1 *New York Times* Bestseller
More than 8 million copies sold!

The
Original!

20th
Anniversary
Edition

Chicken Soup
for the Soul.

All Your **Favorite Original Stories**
Plus **20 Bonus** Stories for the
Next **20 Years**

Jack Canfield,
Mark Victor Hansen
& Amy Newmark
Foreword by Heidi Krupp

The twentieth anniversary edition of the original Chicken Soup for the Soul is brimming with even more hope and inspiration — the stories you've always loved, plus twenty bonus stories!

978-1-61159-913-8

Classic Inspiration

This special anniversary collection has a double-dose of inspiration — personal stories of how Chicken Soup for the Soul changed lives, and the life-changing stories themselves!

978-1-61159-912-1

from our 23 -Year History

Chicken Soup for the Soul: Think Possible will inspire readers to follow their hearts and dreams, with stories of optimism, faith, and strength. In bad times and good, readers will find encouragement to keep a positive attitude.

978-1-61159-952-7

More Bestsellers to

Chicken Soup for the Soul

for the **Soul**.

Hope & Miracles

101 Inspirational Stories of Faith, Answered Prayers & Divine Intervention

Amy Newmark
and Natasha Stoynoff
Foreword by John Edward

Good things do happen to good people! These 101 true stories of wondrous connections, divine intervention and answered prayers show miracles and good happen every day, giving hope whenever you need it most. You will be amazed and uplifted as you read these inspiring stories. Great for everyone — religious and not — who seeks enlightenment and inspiration through a good story.

978-1-61159-944-2

Brighten Your Day

Chicken Soup for the Soul

Changing your life one story at a time ®
www.chickensoup.com

We donate a portion of all proceeds from our books
to the Humpty Dumpty Institute (www.thehdi.org)